Informing the Inklings

George MacDonald and the Victorian Roots of Modern Fantasy

Edited By

Michael Partridge and Kirstin Jeffrey Johnson

Informing the Inklings
George MacDonald
and the Victorian Roots
of Modern Fantasy

Winged Lion Press
Hamden, CT

WINGED LION PRESS

ISBN 13   978-1-935688-42-6

In memory of
Richard Lines (1942-2017)
and
Christopher Mitchell (1951-2014)

About the Cover

The illustration of the king in the rose fire comes from *The Princess and Curdie* (Blackie, 1912). The artist, Helen Stratton (1867-1961), was a follower of Art Nouveau in the style of the Glasgow School of Art. The face of the king appears to be based on George MacDonald.

The rose design framing the inner illustration was adapted from a cover of *At the Back of the North Wind*. (Blackie, 1915)

William Morris (1834-1896) created the fonts used for the title (Morris Troy) and sub-title (p22 Morris Golden). A key figure in the Arts and Crafts Movement and a contemporary of MacDonald (he purchased MacDonald's Hammersmith home and named it Kelmscott House), Morris's fantasy writings also influenced Lewis and Tolkien.

The background color is Oxford Blue in recognition of the "Informing the Inklings" conference being held at Oxford University.

Acknowledgements

With many thanks to Stephen Prickett for his co-selection of these contributions, and general encouragement and facilitation of this project; to the authors for their patience through the long trek to get here; to Annie M. Fergusson for her hours of diligent and cheerful and volunteered assistance from the conference itself, right through to the gritty parts of the manuscript; to our spouses, Liz and Greg, for carrying us and the work of the MacDonald Society in innumerable and oft invisible ways; and finally to Robert Trexler – much more than our publisher: an unassuming scholar, a laboring cohort, and a MacDonaldesque friend.

Table of Contents

Preface

Stephen Prickett

In the middle years of the twentieth century it was not uncommon to find fantasy being treated as in some sense a hangover from earlier literary genres: folk tales, fairy stories, fables, children's stories, classical epics, etc. Even then that was obviously absurd. A category that included Spenser's *Faerie Queene*, Shakespeare's last plays, Milton's *Paradise Lost*, or works by Swift and Fielding was clearly not an obsolete, disappearing or atavistic form. But a world that was shortly to be assailed by Mervyn Peake's *Gormenghast*, Tolkien's *Lord of the Rings*, magical realism from South America, not to mention Philip Pullman, J.K. Rowling, and countless others of the 'dungeons and dragons' variety, clearly had to come to terms with the fact that 'realism' encompassed only a fraction of the human literary imagination, and that 'fantasy' in all its myriad forms was now a major art-form—not to mention big business.

Any academic re-discovery of fantasy as a serious art form, however, has to take into account its upsurge in Victorian times as a quite new medium with the circle of Lewis Carroll, Charles Kingsley, and George MacDonald. It was to MacDonald that Charles Dodgson, the shy Christ Church mathematics don (not yet 'Lewis Carroll'), sent his manuscript of *Alice* to ask whether it was publishable. MacDonald read it aloud to his children, who vehemently approved. Kingsley was a frequent visitor to Alice's parents, Dean Liddell and his household at Christ Church, and shared the manuscript of *The Water-Babies* with Dodgson. Following in their wake was the Pre-Raphaelite William Morris, author of such works as *The Well at the World's End* and *News from Nowhere*. In addition to writing fantasies, Morris was an early socialist, and poet, painter, and textile designer, with many links to the MacDonald circle. His residence, Kelmscott House, on the Thames, was later sold to MacDonald. It was to these groups that Lewis, Tolkien, and the other members of their Oxford literary circle, the 'Inklings', paid both implicit and explicit tribute when they embarked on their own fictional forms: not merely the Narnia stories in Lewis's case, but also *The Great Divorce*, his Dantean fantasy in which MacDonald plays the part of Virgil, and *The Hobbit* and *The Lord of the Rings* from Tolkien. Rarely has a literary tradition been so clearly way-marked. In the preface to his 1946 anthology of MacDonald's writings Lewis is explicit:

I have never concealed the fact that I regarded him
[MacDonald] as my master; indeed I fancy I have never
written a book in which I did not quote from him. But it has
not seemed to me that those who have received my books
kindly take even now sufficient notice of the affiliation.
Honesty drives me to emphasise it.[1]

But, of course, though MacDonald is justly remembered as the
author of the *Princess* books, he was not just a writer of fantasies for
children. *Phantastes* and *Lilith*, his so-called 'adult fairy stories', were
virtually a new genre in themselves, and Lewis drew heavily on them,
also, for his own adult fantasies. Nor, of course, must we forget that
MacDonald was also the author of numerous prose works. It has even
been suggested, not least by Lewis himself, that MacDonald was
essentially a fantasy writer living in an age of prose fiction, who was
forced for financial reasons into a realist literary straightjacket that
never really suited his more expansive symbolic talents. Yet that, too,
fails to account for some of his best writing. Perhaps Lewis himself
was closer to the mark when he described MacDonald as not so much
a fantasy writer, nor a realistic novelist, nor even a poet, but primarily
a *myth-maker*—a story-teller whose narratives somehow carry a much
greater freight than their words seem to suggest on the surface.[2] If, as
I believe, we are looking at nothing less than an 'apostolic succession'
of mythopoesis in the nineteenth and twentieth centuries, this passing
of ideas from the MacDonald circle to the Inklings is surely at the
heart of it.

When a group of us from the George MacDonald Society met for
a conference at Magdalen, C.S. Lewis's old college, in Oxford, in the
summer of 2014, we were particularly conscious of this tradition, and
the many ways in which the Inklings, myth-makers themselves, had
drawn on their literary predecessors. We were, nevertheless, surprised
by both the variety and originality of the papers submitted—a
selection of which are reproduced in this volume—not to mention the
quality of the some of the debates that ensued. As our title suggests,
we have chosen to focus on those papers which relate most closely
to our main theme of that relationship between MacDonald and his
Inkling successors, and how, sometimes in the most literal sense, he
formed and, indeed, 'in-formed' their own creativity in ways that we

---

1   C.S. Lewis, *George MacDonald: An Anthology* (London: Geoffrey Bles,
1946), p.20.

2   Ibid. pp. 15-17.

are only now beginning to understand. If these essays assist in a wider appreciation of both MacDonald and his Oxford successors, then we will have at least begun our task.

Stephen Prickett, Charing

Informing the Inklings:
C. S. Lewis's Debt to George MacDonald

Stephen Prickett

There is, I expect, nobody in this room who is not aware of the Inkling's debt to their Victorian predecessors—to writers like Lewis Carroll, Charles Kingsley, William Morris, and, perhaps above all, to George MacDonald. That is why you are here. In the case of C.S. Lewis, we know about this debt because he told us about it in some detail. Yet ever since March 4th 1916 when the 18 year-old Clive Staples Lewis picked up a copy of *Phantastes: A Faerie Romance for Men and Women* on Leatherhead railway station bookstall, biographers of both writers have been slightly puzzled by what was exactly being acknowledged. At first reading, his account of the event seems utterly lucid in its exact recall.

> Turning to the bookstall, I picked out an Everyman in a dirty jacket, *Phantastes, a Faerie Romance*, George MacDonald. Then the train came in. I can still remember the voice of the porter calling out the village names Saxon and sweet as a nut—'Bookham, Effingham, Horsley train.' That evening I began to read my new book.[1]

Some ten years before, in his preface to *George MacDonald: An Anthology*, published in 1946, Lewis tells us a little more—in particular that he had looked at 'that volume on that bookstall and rejected it on a dozen previous occasions'.[2] Even then, though Lewis apparently bought it as train reading, by his own account he didn't in fact begin to read it until he reached his destination—though the names of the stations he passed through afterwards apparently came to radiate in the afterglow from that delayed subsequent reading. The effect of the encounter with MacDonald is described in terms no less lucid and articulate.

> The woodland journeyings in that story, the ghostly enemies, the ladies both good and evil, were close enough to my habitual imagery to lure me on without the perception of a change. It is as if I were carried sleeping across the frontier, or as if I had died in the old country and could never remember how I

---

1   C. S. Lewis, *Surprised by Joy* (London: Collins, 2012), p. 207.

2   C.S. Lewis, *George MacDonald: An Anthology* (London: Geoffrey Bles, 1946), p. 20.

came alive in the new. I did not yet know (and I was long in learning) the name of the new quality, the bright shadow, that rested on the travels of Anodos. I do now. It was Holiness. [...] There was no temptation to confuse the scenes of the tale with the light that rested upon them, or to suppose that they were put forward as realities, or even to dream that if they had been realities and I could reach the woods where Anodos journeyed I should thereby come a step nearer to my desire. [...] Thus, when the great moments came I did not break away from the woods and cottages that I read of to seek some bodiless light, shining beyond them, [...] For I now perceived that while the air of the new region made all my erotic and magical perversions of Joy look like sordid trumpery, it had no such disenchanting power over the bread upon the table or the coals in the grate. That was the marvel. Up till now each visitation of Joy had left the common world momentarily a desert [...] Even when real clouds or trees had been the material of the vision, they had been so only by reminding me of another world; and I did not like the return to ours. But now I saw the bright shadow coming out of the book into the real world and resting there, transforming all common things and yet itself unchanged.[3]

This deliberately Wordsworthian account is so articulate, so poetic, that it is easy to miss just how odd this statement actually is. To begin with, the future Oxford don was already familiar and comfortable with the incidental paraphernalia of 'Fairyland'—ghosts, giants, goblins, etc.—in a way that perhaps few of us would be. Moreover, what he seems to be trying to describe in this passage, retrospective or not, is very far from the normal use of the word 'holiness'. The 'holy', we recall, describes something separate, special, set apart from the mundane (or what would later come to be described as the 'secular'). It is therefore all the stranger that Lewis, who—no one better—by 1930 knew the derivation and implications of the word, seems here determined to blur the very boundaries between the sacred and the secular that the word 'holy' has traditionally defended.

But we must remember, of course, what he records here took place just after he had declared himself an atheist at the age of 15. This whole event took place some sixteen years before his acknowledged re-conversion to Christianity in 1929-31, so that what he is describing is an entirely *retrospective* vision. As he freely admits in that passage I have just quoted, the sixteen year-old Lewis, the recently declared

---

3   Lewis, *Surprised by Joy*, pp. 207-9.

atheist, would *never* have used words like 'Holiness' to describe that 'bright shadow' that transformed his mundane world. Indeed, the whole idea that Lewis was in some way 'converted' by reading *Phantastes* simply cannot be correct as it stands. Only in retrospect did MacDonald's novel acquire that aura of sanctity with which he later endowed it—the account I have quoted is from *Surprised by Joy*, published in 1955, almost 40 years after the event itself, by which time it had acquired for Lewis a totally new meaning. Any account of Lewis and *Phantastes* must, therefore, be in terms of a historical re-interpretation over much of Lewis's life—a re-interpretation, one should add, that he himself was only too willing to create.

Hints of this on-going process of re-writing his past are to be found scattered throughout Lewis's writings, from his earliest major work of fiction, *Pilgrim's Regress*, published in 1933 when he was in his mid-thirties to the sermon, *The Weight of Glory*, delivered in Oxford ten years later. As he makes clear, this is not so much nostalgia as existential theory. What he came to see as central to his religious experience is a kind of longing—a desire for something not quite tangible, but, simultaneously, infinitely more real than the things which arouse that longing. As a professor of literature, one might expect that this was a kind of 'literary' experience, and so it seems to have been for the rebellious teenager, but Lewis was later careful to insist that it was not so. 'In reading great literature,' he wrote,

> I become a thousand men and yet I remain myself. Like the night sky in the Greek poem, I see with a myriad eyes, but it is still I who see. Here as in worship, in love, in moral action, and in knowing, I transcend myself; and am never more myself than when I do.[4]

But literature is only a half-way house. Powerful as such an aesthetic response is, what Lewis is reaching for is something more, and it is a fundamental category mistake to confuse one for the other. The university study of English literature, he once wrote,

> directs to the study of literature a great many talented, ingenious, and diligent people whose real interests are not specifically literary at all. Forced to talk about books, what can they do but try to make books into the sort of things they can talk about? Hence literature becomes for them a religion, a philosophy, a school of ethics, a psychotherapy, a sociology—

---

4   Ibid. p. 141.

anything other than a collection of works of art.[5]

It is precisely because he does value works of art that he insists that they should not be read in terms of other kinds of values. As with Thomas Traherne, whom I suspect Lewis may be echoing here, aesthetics is a surrogate; a metonymy. Even in seeking to frame his experience of *Phantastes* in terms of an aesthetic description, he is already moving beyond that. Indeed, he is clearly—and quite consciously—using aesthetics to describe something that is not really aesthetic at all. When, again, he writes of

> that unnameable something, desire for which pierces us like a rapier at the smell of bonfire, the sound of wild ducks flying overhead, the title of *The Well at the World's End*, the opening lines of 'Kubla Kahn', the morning cobwebs in late summer, or the noise of falling waves

he is using aesthetic experiences quite explicitly to point elsewhere.

Nevertheless, what this tells us unmistakably is that for Lewis the experience of great art, or great literature, is, if not a religious experience (and, as I have said, he makes it very clear that to identify the two was a fundamental category mistake)[6], it was an experience that ultimately takes its meaning from the essentially religious experience of 'longing' that it itself is emphatically *not*—in exactly the way that moonlight, while not being sunlight, is impossible without the existence of the sun. Virgil, the good pagan, though he cannot come into the presence of Beatrice in the Earthly Paradise, is, nevertheless Dante's guide to reach that point—or, to put this more precisely in Lewis's own terms, it is an ineffable pull of something just outside the range of his own experience that draws the pilgrim of *Pilgrim's Regress* forward on his journey. There may be other ways to that experience, but this was the nearest for him.

In 1946, Lewis had published *The Great Divorce*, a Dantean novella of Hell, Purgatory, and Heaven. It is true that the characterization is often perfunctory and even stereotyped, but, then, what would you expect of those in Hell? For Lewis, the wages of selfishness were, literally, a diminished self. But his vision of the

---

5　*An Experiment in Criticism* (Cambridge: Cambridge University Press, 1962), p. 86.

6　This is the subject of perhaps his worst critical essay, 'Christianity and Literature' (1939) but it is a point he repeatedly touched on in his writings elsewhere.

place—the city of dreadful night where the only punishment is other people—is extraordinarily powerful and haunting. Heaven—reached by a daily bus, free for any to go, and even stay if they wish—is much more so. The only qualification for Heaven is the desire to be there— and, of course, the majority of the day-trippers discover that they hate the place even more than they hated Hell. Though not true Heaven, which would be (is?) unimaginable, this is more Dante's Earthly Paradise—with a beauty both strange and yet still recognizable as earthly beauty. But there is a shock in store for any visitor from Hell. For the denizens of Hell, who have become thin and wraith-like in the searing light of Paradise, the plants and even the water drops of the plains of Heaven, so far from being soft and beautiful, are so 'real' that they are hard and unyielding as diamond. Even to walk on the grass is like treading on knives. If they can only forget themselves they will, in time, grow stronger and more solid and real—and one tripper, one of the least likely, does indeed accept that challenge and choose to stay—but for the rest the only thing they cannot give up is themselves, and they choose freely to return, making their own Hell from what would otherwise be Purgatory. Indeed, as with Dante, *choice* is the key to this whole system. God allows free will—complete and utter unfettered freedom. But since we are outside time, as we know it, choice acts retrospectively—backwards as well as forwards— so that events in the past become good or bad, pleasurable or painful, according to the choices they lead to.

In place of Dante's Virgil, Lewis's guide to this strangely beautiful and disturbingly un-homely place is none other than George MacDonald himself. When Lewis attempts to express his appreciation of MacDonald's writing his attempts at praise are abruptly, if kindly, dismissed. Now that he has seen the reality, the fiction which brought him there is unimportant—and, of course, since what we are reading is itself a fiction, we can draw the parallel conclusion. Just as the letters which make up words disappear as we get into a narrative, so the narrative—and the aesthetic delight we may take in it—disappears as it, in turn, points beyond itself. Elsewhere Lewis has a term for this: 'transposition'[7]—the process by which the richer system is represented by the poorer, just as the inhabitants of E.A. Abbott's *Flatland* cannot conceive of a sphere except in terms of a circle (which unnervingly, for them who can only inhabit two dimensions, varies arbitrarily in size).

In 'The Weight of Glory', the sermon given in Oxford in 1942,

---

7   'Transposition', A Sermon at Mansfield College, Oxford. In *They Asked for a Paper*, London: Geoffrey Bles, 1962.

Informing the Inklings

Lewis is quite explicit about this transposition:

If a transtemporal, transfinite good is our real destiny, then any other good on which our desire fixes must be in some degree fallacious, must bear at best only a symbolical relation to what will truly satisfy.

> In speaking of this desire for our own far-off country, which we find in ourselves even now, I feel a certain shyness. I am almost committing an indecency. I am trying to rip open the inconsolable secret in each one of you—the secret which hurts so much that you take your revenge on it by calling it names like Nostalgia and Romanticism and Adolescence; the secret also which pierces with such sweetness that when, in very intimate conversation, the mention of it becomes imminent, we grow awkward and affect to laugh at ourselves [...] We cannot tell it because it is a desire for something that has never actually appeared in our experience. We cannot hide it because our experience is constantly suggesting it [...] Our commonest expedient is to call it beauty and behave as if that settled the matter. Wordsworth's expedient was to identify it with certain moments in his own past. But all this is a cheat. If Wordsworth had gone back to those moments in the past, he would not have found the thing itself, but only the reminder of it; what he remembered would turn out itself to be a remembering. The books or the music in which we thought beauty was located will betray us if we trust to them; it was not in them, it only came through them, and what came through them was longing. These things—the beauty, the memory of our own past—are good images of our own past; but if they are mistaken for the thing itself they turn into dumb idols, breaking the hearts of their worshippers. For they are not the thing itself; they are only the scent of a flower we have not found, the echo of a tune we have not heard, news from a country we have never yet visited...[8]

I apologize for the length of that quotation, but you can see why. There are those who will respond to this description; and there are also those who will hate it—either because they have never shared it, or, sometimes, because they have. T. S. Eliot certainly began by despising Lewis's theology, though he later came to respect if not to agree with all of it. Yet it is not difficult to pick out phrases from Eliot's later Christian poetry that seem to be very close to Lewis in feeling, if not in language. But like it or hate it, this is not merely why Lewis in the end accepted Christianity, but also why he became a literary critic. It

---

8   'The Weight of Glory', in *They Asked for a Paper*, p. 200.

didn't begin in that order, but then, as in *The Great Divorce*, knowing where you have arrived is necessary to understanding the past.

In this case, what of *Phantastes*—that unlikely location of retrospective 'holiness', with its sense of a country both achingly familiar, and yet never visited? What was it about MacDonald's first great prose romance that was, if only with hindsight, to change Lewis's life—seemingly breaking down the ancient barriers between the sacred and the secular and charging the most mundane with spiritual value? Why *Phantastes*, and not any other book? Perhaps we should stop and think more closely about *Phantastes* itself for a few moments.

It is, after all, by any measure a very odd novel. In its episodic structure it is more like an eighteenth-century picaresque novel by Fielding or Smollett than a densely plotted Victorian fiction. The episodes themselves are strange and mostly humiliating to Anodos, the first-person narrator. Which episodes, one wonders, particularly inspired Lewis? The threatening and nurturing trees, the Alder and the Ash? The little girl and the magic globe? The discovery of his Shadow? The mocking goblins underground? The search for the white lady? The knights in armour? The idol with the monster within? Anodos's own death? None of these would seem to me to be particularly redolent of holiness in any sense of the word I recognise.

The one thing nearly all of these episodes do have in common is a kind of subsumed—and usually frustrated—sexuality. This is by no means unique in Victorian fiction. William Morris's *News from Nowhere* has a similar feel of sublimated eroticism. But that was published a whole generation later, in 1890, and its purpose, a future of free love under Socialism, is very different from MacDonald's. Anodos, to put it brutally, is a klutz—especially with women. He is all desire and no achievement. Even in the opening episode Anodos makes a misguided pass at the variably-sized fairy-figure who claims to be his own grandmother, and from then on it is downhill nearly all the way. Perhaps not surprisingly, therefore, Robert Lee Wolff has famously given it a crudely Freudian interpretation in *The Golden Key* (1961). Whether or not it should be read as a young man's search for his own sexuality, desire for his mother, jealousy of his father, etcetera, what Wolff *does* do, if only by implication, is to call attention to the possibility that there may be more to the structure of the novel than a string of lightly-connected episodes. There is arguably more of a progress, or development, in the unfolding of the plot than might appear at first sight: indeed, Freud or no Freud, what we clearly have here is, in every sense of the word, a *Bildungsroman*.

Let's look in detail for a moment at one of the most famous passages in the book, where Anodos awakes on the morning of his twenty-first birthday to find himself already, in the act of transition from one world to another:

> While these strange events were passing through my mind, I suddenly [...] became aware of the sound of running water near me; and looking out of bed, I saw that a large green marble basin, in which I was wont to wash, and which stood on a low pedestal of the same material in a corner of my room, was overflowing like a spring, and that a stream of clear water was running over the carpet, all the length of the room, finding its outlet I knew not where. And, stranger still, where this carpet, which I had myself designed to imitate a field of grass and daisies, bordered the course of the little stream, the grass blades and daisies seemed to wave in a tiny breeze that followed the water's flow; while under the rivulet they bent and swayed with every motion of the changeful current, as it they were about to dissolve with it, and, forsaking their fixed form, become as fluent as the waters.
>
> My dressing-table was an old fashioned piece of furniture of black oak, with drawers all down the front. These were elaborately carved in foliage, of which ivy formed the chief part. The nearer end of this table remained just as it had been, but on the further end a singular change had commenced. I happened to fix my eye on a little cluster of ivy leaves. The first of these was evidently the work of the carver, the next looked curious, the third was unmistakably ivy; and just beyond it a tendril of clematis had twined itself about the gilt handle of one of the drawers. Hearing a slight motion above me, I looked up, and saw that the branches and leaves designed upon the curtain of my bed were slightly in motion. Not knowing what changes might follow next I thought it high time to get up; and, springing from the bed, my bare feet alighted upon a cool green sward; and although I dressed in all haste, I found myself completing my toilet under the bough of a great tree.[9]

This is, of course, one of the great set-pieces of the novel. A *tour de force* in itself, it also encapsulates and anticipates much that is to

---

9   George MacDonald, *Phantastes & Lilith*, Introduction by C.S. Lewis (Grand Rapids: Eerdmans, 1964), pp. 19-20.

follow. The flowering of the man-made decorations of the bedroom: the carpet and the carved dressing-table immediately suggests that this other word—what MacDonald rather unfortunately calls 'Fairyland'—is to be in some sense more real than the one that is being taken from him. What with us is artifice, there is natural. The stream of water overflowing from the basin is literally a river of life, bringing to life everything it touches. Imitation becomes what it imitates.

But there is something odd even here about the world he is leaving. Remember that carpet—which Anodos himself tells us he himself had 'designed'? The words scarcely call attention to themselves amidst the much greater wonders that are taking place all around. But—wait a minute—how many twenty year olds get to design their own carpets? The pampered son of a millionaire with artistic ambitions might conceivably have done so, but though he has just inherited a large estate, there is little suggestion that this young man is otherwise anything but ordinary. We need some explanation—another sentence would do it—but, significantly, none is forthcoming. Not even Ruskin or Oscar Wilde, as far as I recall, went around designing their own carpets before going up to Oxford. If this is 'realism', it is has curious improbabilities lurking in subordinate clauses. That piece of information is entirely unnecessary in any normal reading of the plot. Which may suggest that we need a more abnormal reading before making any sense of it.

So far as I know, we do not have a detailed analysis of the plot from Lewis in the way we have for *Lilith*. But in a letter to Arthur Greeves of 1933 Lewis stresses the need to interpret both *Phantastes* and *Lilith* as primarily symbolic and *inner* narratives.

> "I have just re-read Lilith," he writes and am much clearer about the meaning. The first thing to get out of the way is all Greville MacDonald's (sic) nonsense about "dimensions" and "elements" [...] That is just the sort of mechanical "mysticism" which is worlds away from Geo. MacDonald. [...] The story runs like this. The human soul exploring its own house (the Mind) finds itself on the verge of unexpected worlds...[10]

As Lewis wrote to Greeves elsewhere, he believed MacDonald's only real artistic form is the symbolic fantasy 'like *Phantastes* or *Lilith*'—the rest of his fiction was a more or less unsuccessful attempt to constrain his imagination to the straightjacket of Victorian realism. *Lilith*, he argues is to be read throughout like *Phantastes*: in other

10 *They Stand Together: the letters of C. S. Lewis to Arthur Greeves (1914–1963)*, ed. Walter Hooper (London: Collins, 1979), p. 459.

words as a psychodrama, in which every external event is to be read as internal. The symbolic importance of that carpet may now be a little clearer: what Anodos has caused to be made as imitation is now real—and presumably (as the final chapter of the book suggests) this is also true of Anodos himself. This transition is some kind of 'transposition' (in Lewis's sense of the word) to a greater reality. What is breaking down—if you like, what is being physically washed away—is Anodos's own self-constructions. He has surrounded himself, literally, with a carpet of imitation flowers. Now, to his complete bemusement, they have become real. But if this is so, there is another layer of irony that emerges.

As his old bedroom vanishes before Anodos's astonished eyes we are suddenly enabled to see it—that is, his symbolic self-constructed environment—with a new intensity of detail. The unexpected metamorphosis of the room from 'art' to 'life' shows us the clichéd luxuriance of flower and vegetation patterns dear to mid-Victorian boudoirs with the shock of seeing the familiar for the first time. The juxtaposition with the 'other' world shows us our own for perhaps the first time. And that, of course, is the purpose of MacDonald's whole technique. The deliberate aesthetic inversion, from artificial to real, provides an ironic second layer of meaning: in the story we are suddenly brought from art to life; in reality, of course, since the story we are reading is a work of fiction, we are moving not so much from art to life as from life to art, or even from art to more art, or from one level of artifice to the next. This 'new reality' experienced by Anodos is being created by MacDonald, as author, in order to reveal what is latent but not explicit in the old familiar reality. The relationship between the two worlds, the two levels of reality, is not so much one of simple displacement as of irony. Every assumption of the young naïve Anodos is, in turn, disconfirmed—his attempt to help the little girl is a disaster; the lady of the quest will never be his; the shadow emerges from a door he should not have peered through. Fairyland—in MacDonald's somewhat peculiar sense—is not just implicit in mundane reality, but is the provider of a continual ironic commentary on it.

And this is where things may become a bit more familiar—even to those not as habitually conversant with the paraphernalia of Fairyland as Lewis. Who was it, after all, that said, 'He who would save his life, must lose it…'; 'love your enemies'; or 'the Sabbath was made for man, not man for the Sabbath'? Jesus's teachings are nothing if not an ironic and destabilizing commentary on the clichés of ordinary life.

Was it this, perhaps, that gave Lewis his unexpected and retrospective vision of 'holiness'? Not so much the existence of another world—a 'Fairyland' in the normal sense—as an ironic revaluation of this one. But this is not merely a revaluation of the mundane world, it is also a revaluation of our normal literature. Anodos's naïve expectations—constantly and bafflingly deflated in this other parallel universe—are based usually on other literature. His great expectations, as were Pip's in Dickens's novel of that name, are based on totally false premises.

So, too, I believe, with Lewis's first reading of *Phantastes* as an atheist. MacDonald had lured him into certain novelistic expectations, and, like the good critic he already was, Lewis was delighted to have those expectations promptly disconfirmed. If we look for sources to this, we need to look not so much to English fairy-stories, nor even, initially, to German ones, but to what one of the greatest German writers had done with that genre. I have written elsewhere on MacDonald's use of his German sources—the Schlegel brothers, Novalis, and Goethe—and there is not time to rehash it here, but it is worth quoting again Thomas Carlyle's Introduction to the first edition of his English translation of Goethe's *Wilhelm Meister*:

> To judge of this book,—new and peculiar as it is, and only to be understood and learned from itself, by our common notion of the novel, a notion pieced together and produced out of custom and belief, out of accidental and arbitrary requisitions,—is as if a child should grasp at the moon and stars, and insist on packing them into his toy-box.[11]

My evidence for this argument is, I admit, circumstantial. In the absence of further evidence, we cannot be certain *what* it was peculiar to *Phantastes* that, retrospectively, gave Lewis that sensation of 'holiness' and, we are told, began the transformation of Lewis's life even as he believed it was going in the opposite direction. But Lewis was a literary critic of some subtlety—he was also my old Cambridge professor. This is not to say I understand the way in which his mind worked—we can rarely make that claim about another human being— but at least I think I know where he was coming from. And that, of course, is what this conference is all about.

---

11 Johan Wolfgang von Goethe, *Wilhelm Meister's Apprenticeship and Travels*, trans Thomas Carlyle, 2 vols.(New York: J.D. Williams, 1882), 1:7.

BIBLIOGRAPHY

Goethe, Johan Wolfgang von, *Wilhelm Meister's Apprenticeship and Travels*, trans Thomas Carlyle, 2 vols., New York: J.D. Williams, 1882. Print.

Hooper, Walter, ed., *They Stand Together: the letters of C.S. Lewis to Arthur Greeves (1914-1963)*, London: Collins, 1979. Print.

Lewis, C.S., *An Experiment in Criticism*, Cambridge: Cambridge University Press, 1962. Print.

Lewis, C.S., 'Christianity and Literature', *Rehabilitations*, London: Geoffrey Bles, 1939. Print.

Lewis, C.S., *George MacDonald: An Anthology*, London: Geoffrey Bles, 1946. Print.

Lewis, C.S., *Surprised by Joy*, London: Collins, 2012. Print.

Lewis, C.S., 'The Weight of Glory', *They Asked for a Paper*, London: Geoffrey Bles, 1962. Print.

Lewis, C.S., 'Transposition, A Sermon at Mansfield College, Oxford'. *They Asked for a Paper*, London: Geoffrey Bles, 1962. Print.

MacDonald, George, *Phantastes & Lilith*, Introduction by C.S. Lewis, Grand Rapids: Eerdmans, 1964. Print

"Needles of Eternal Light"
How Coleridge Roused MacDonald and Lewis

Malcolm Guite

This conference is concerned with the Victorian roots of modern fantasy, and particularly with the existing literary and philosophical traditions upon which the Inklings drew from for form, sustenance and inspiration. In this paper, I would like, if I may, to dig into the roots a little deeper and peep past our eminent Victorian fantasists, MacDonald, Kingsley et al, to the roots on which they drew, the roots of the Romantic movement itself, and particularly to the vital figure of S.T. Coleridge.

In particular I want to ask how C.S. Lewis understood that Romantic tradition, or stream, as he preferred to call it, and to ask how the thought and influence of Coleridge, one of the prime sources of that stream, flowed down to him, both directly and also, how it flowed to him through the channels of George MacDonald and Owen Barfield, enriched with their own emphasis and interpretation.

Now I am very conscious that there are people in this room who know far more than I do about just how extensive and fruitful was the influence of Coleridge in the nineteenth century and beyond. Stephen Prickett did so much to lay out the ground for all of us in *Romanticism and Religion* (reprinted 2008), and he is especially helpful on the way in the Church of England apparently diverse groupings, both 'the Broad and the high', if I can use that term in Oxford, drew on the very same passages in Coleridge for inspiration. I am also aware that we have scholars here who have made a detailed study of the way MacDonald both learned from but also refined and developed Coleridge's teaching about the imagination. In particular I have found Kerry Dearborn's *Baptized Imagination* (2006) and Gisela Kreglinger's *Storied Revelations* (2013) very helpful.

So, much of the terrain has been mapped for us and it's good to have some of those cartographers here. What I would like to do is follow one of these channels of inspiration upstream, with a few diversions on the way, and see where it leads us.

Lewis's first Christian book *The Pilgrim's Regress*, was originally subtitled: *'An Allegorical Apology for Christianity, Reason, and Romanticism'*. Many have written books on his understanding of Christianity and of Reason, but it is also worth asking, especially in the context of this conference, 'what did he mean by *Romanticism*'?

Fortunately, we have a poem addressed to fellow poet Roy Campbell and almost totally overlooked by Lewis scholars in which he sets out exactly what tradition he stands in and it is the tradition of philosophical romanticism in which Coleridge plays a central role.

> For though your verse outsoars with eagle pride
> Their spineless tunes (of which the old cow died).
> Yet your bloodthirsty politics and theirs
> Are two peas in a single pod, who cares
> Which kind of shirt the murdering Party wears?
> Oh Roy, repent: some feet of sacred ground
> A target to both gangs, may yet be found,
> Sacred because, though now 'tis No-man's-land,
> There stood your father's house: there you should stand.

So here is what Lewis says to Campbell appealing to him to stand on that 'sacred ground' the 'No-man's-land' to be gained by a Romanticism come of age (to borrow Barfield's phrase):

> In England the romantic stream flows ...
> ...from Scott; from Coleridge too.
> A bore? A sponge? A laudanum-addict? True;
> Yet Newman in that ruinous master saw
> One who restored our faculty for awe,
> Who re-discovered the soul's depth and height
> Who pricked with needles of the eternal light
> An England at that time half numbed to death
> With Paley's, Bentham's, Malthus' wintry breath.[12]

There are a number of very remarkable things going on in these few lines. I want to turn shortly to the particular virtues and vocation in Coleridge that Lewis singles out in this passage, but first I want to reflect on the fact that he praises Coleridge to Campbell through Newman! Now one might say that he chooses to do it this way because Campbell is a Roman Catholic and if Lewis wants to win a fair hearing for the Coleridgean ideas he regarded as so essential, then it is helpful

---

12 C.S. Lewis, *The Collected Poems of C. S. Lewis* (London: HarperCollins, 1964/1994), p. 80. By citing Scott, and then Coleridge as read by Newman, Lewis is appealing to a particular understanding of imagination within a religious frame. For a fuller account of this tradition see John Coulson, *Religion and Imagination*, Oxford 1981 and Paul Avis, *God and the Creative Imagination: Metaphor, Symbol and Myth in Religion and Theology*, London 1999. For my own discussion of the importance of this tradition see *Faith, Hope and Poetry*, Surrey 2010, pp. 4-9.

to have Newman's imprimatur! I'm sure that is partly true, but it is nevertheless worth reflecting on the fact that Lewis had himself been reading and internalizing Newman and that Newman, in his turn, had been reading and internalizing Coleridge! We put people into boxes and categories. We think of Coleridge inspiring Maurice and MacDonald and a liberal broad church understanding, but we don't think of Newman in the same category. Likewise Lewis has found so many evangelical supporters that we can forget how catholic in every sense his mind and reading habits were. Still it is surprising. Lewis read Newman consistently and deeply. He was quoting the *Apologia Pro Vita Sua* in letters to his father at the age of 16 when he was just becoming a teenage atheist, and enjoying the *Dream of Gerontius* well into his last years.

And what of Newman's perhaps surprising debt to Coleridge? At first, and whilst Coleridge was still alive, Newman could only see Coleridge's, 'obvious personal failings', as John Beer points out in his introduction to *Aids to Reflection*. But having been influenced already through Pusey and Thomas Dyke Acland's absorption of Coleridge's ideas Newman finally came to Coleridge's work directly in 1835, just after his death. Once that happened then all kinds of ideas in Newman, all kinds of arousings and wakenings that had been implicit began to take shape and cohere.

What was it in particular the Coleridge had to offer Newman and others?

Stephen Prickett is here very helpful on what Coleridge had to contribute as much to Newman, as, more famously to F.D. Maurice: 'English theology of the eighteenth century [...] with the exception of the Coleridgean and Liberal Anglican tradition,' up until the mid-nineteenth century that was 'obsessed with the clash between empiricism and the belief in the literal inspiration of the Bible [and in which] miracles must either be explained away, or shown [...] as not inconsistent with a scientific world-picture'. [13]

Coleridge found a way out of this dilemma by showing that both the reductive atomizing, mechanistic view of nature, which seemed to clash with the bible, and the equally reductive and mono-linear literalist reading of the Bible, were in fact inadequate. That the two great books of God's revelation, Nature and the Bible were rich, symbolic, indeed, in a key word for the Oxford movement 'poetic' and that both nature and the bible need to call forth and inspire the

---

13 Stephen Prickett, *Romanticism and Religion* (Cambridge: Cambridge University Press, 2008), p. 132.

shaping spirit of the imagination if they are to be understood, and when that happens, there is not a flat contradiction but a rich and mutually informative conversation. So Coleridge brings a profound understanding of poetic language to bear on religious language in a way that inspires both Newman, and later, Lewis.

Coleridge analysed this problem of literalism, both religious and scientific, in *The Statesman's Manual*:

> A hunger-bitten and idea-less philosophy naturally produces a starveling and comfortless religion. It is among the miseries of the present age that it recognises no medium, between Literal and Metaphorical. Faith is either to be buried in the dead letter, or its name and honours usurped by a counterfeit product...[14]

It is from the numbing effects of the 'dead letter' of trenchant biblical literalism on the one hand, and the 'counterfeit product' of mechanistic scientific materialism on the other, that Coleridge was rousing England as much through his influence on Newman, as on Maurice, MacDonald and later Lewis, Barfield and Tolkien as through his own voice.

Let's return now to the passage in Lewis's poem.

Through Newman's praise Lewis suggests that Coleridge has given us three vital gifts: a restoration, a rediscovery, and a rousing or awakening. First that he restored the faculty for awe, then rediscovered the soul's depth and height (language in which Lewis is deliberately echoing Ephesians 'that you may comprehend the depth and height') and finally that he is arousing and awakening a whole nation which has been benumbed, and as it were bewitched by the wintry breath of a materialist and utilitarian philosophy represented by the triad of Paley, Bentham and Malthus.

He is not only doing this for the England of his day, through his rousing effect on three such disparate men as Maurice, MacDonald and Newman, but he does it independently and through them for Lewis and the other Inklings. For Lewis himself I think this threefold restoration, rediscovery and arousing is an unfinished task, a task to which Lewis, post-conversion, addressed all of his powers. Indeed, Lewis may be remembering and developing that image of one who could arouse and awaken those who had been benumbed and imprisoned by 'wintry breath' in the beautiful episode in *The Lion the*

---

14   S.T. Coleridge, 'The Statesman's Manual' in *Lay Sermons* edited by R.J. White (Princeton: Princeton University Press, 1972), p.30.

Witch and the Wardrobe where Aslan wakes up the imprisoned statues in the White Witch's castle.

So how did these threefold Coleridgean gifts come down to Lewis?

Directly, of course, for he always goes to primary sources, and these are I think, chiefly the poetry and the *Biographia Literaria*, and indirectly especially, but in very different ways, through MacDonald, and Barfield.

Let me deal first with the direct influence of the vision of poetry itself, and by extension 'mytho-poeia' set out by Coleridge in the *Biographia*. Though Lewis would have read Coleridge's *Biographia Literaria* as a matter of course, he was fortunate in having as a close friend and 'wisest and best of my unofficial teachers,'[15] Owen Barfield for whom Coleridge's understanding of imagination was essential for a complete renewal of the way we see the world. But perhaps the most helpful mapping of the terrain Lewis was to body forth and explore, in books like the Ransom trilogy, *The Chronicles of Narnia* and *Till We Have Faces*, is to be found in the program Wordsworth and Coleridge set themselves at the beginning of the Romantic movement, as it was later recalled by Coleridge in *Biographia Literaria*:

> In this idea originated the plan of the lyrical ballads in which it was agreed that my endeavours should be directed to persons and character supernatural, or at least romantic; yet so as to transfer from our inward nature a human interest and a semblance of truth sufficient to procure for these shadows of imagination that willing suspension of disbelief for the moment, which constitutes poetic faith. Mr. Wordsworth, on the other hand, was to propose to himself as his object, to give the charm of novelty to things of every day, and to excite a feeling analogous to the supernatural by awakening the mind's attention from the lethargy of custom, and directing it to the loveliness and the wonders of the world before us; an inexhaustible treasure, but for which in consequence of the film of familiarity and selfish solicitude we have eyes, yet see not, ears that hear not, and hearts that neither feel nor understand.[16]

We can see both these 'endeavours', as Coleridge calls them, at

---

15 See dedication of C.S. Lewis, *The Allegory of Love: A Study in Medieval Tradition* (Oxford: Oxford University Press, 1936).

16 S.T. Coleridge, *Biographia Literaria* Vol. 2 (Princeton: Princeton University Press, 1984), pp. 6 -7.

work in Lewis's best writing. Certainly he procures for his 'characters supernatural, or at least romantic' just that transference and bodying forth of our 'inward nature' that Coleridge was aiming for: whether the icy White Witch or the golden goodness of Aslan, whether the numinous Eldils of the Ransom trilogy or the beautifully embodied figures of Psyche and Orual in *Till We Have Faces*. But in some ways it is the Wordsworthian, as well as the Coleridgean side of his achievement that makes Lewis such an effective imaginative apologist. The power to 'excite a feeling analogous to the supernatural' by 'awakening the mind's attention' and 'directing it to the loveliness and the wonders of the world before us'.

It has often been remarked that it is easier to portray evil than to portray goodness, but many people have noted that Lewis is an exception: the sheer goodness of his 'good' characters, the sense of 'solid joys and lasting treasure' which he evokes in *The Weight of Glory*[17] and sustains so beautifully throughout *The Great Divorce*. Michael Ward has drawn attention[18] to the extraordinary imaginative skill and intertextual layering with which Lewis built up what he (Lewis) called the 'kappa element' in his evocation of the 'Donegality' or unique quiddity, of rich particularity and 'inexhaustible wonder' of each of the seven *Chronicles*.

This power of re-enchantment, of removing the 'film of familiarity' and 'awakening the mind's attention' is something Lewis was striving for in his writing. He makes this clear in his important essay *On Three Ways of Writing for Children*. In this essay Lewis makes a distinction between the kind of 'fantasy' writing that is mere ego pleasing and this-worldly wish fulfillment of which he says: 'Its fulfillment on the level of imagination is in very truth compensatory: we run to it from the disappointments and humiliations of the real world: it sends us back to the real world undivinely discontented. For it is all flattery to the ego.' [19]

And, by contrast, the kind of imaginative writing, 'imaginative' in the Coleridgean sense, which he is aiming for. Of this he says:

It would be much truer to say that fairy land arouses a longing

---

17   See L. Walmsley, (ed.), *C. S. Lewis Essay Collection: Faith, Christianity and the Church* (London: HarperCollins, 2002), pp.96-106.

18   In Michael Ward, *Planet Narnia: The Seven Heavens in the Imagination of C. S. Lewis* (Oxford: Oxford University Press, 2008).

19   Walmsley, L (ed.), *C. S. Lewis Essay Collection. Literature, Philosophy and Short Stories* (London: HarperCollins, 2002), p.102.

for he know not what. It stirs and troubles him (to his life-long enrichment) with the dim sense of something beyond his reach and, far from dulling or emptying the actual world, gives it a new dimension of depth. He does not despise real woods because he had read of enchanted woods: this reading makes all real woods a little enchanted.[20]

At its best, this is what Lewis's writing continually achieves, this re-enchantment upon return. We return from the Narnian woods to find all our real woods 'a little enchanted'.

Now let us turn to the indirect, or mediated influences. This renewing and awakening Coleridgean stream is also flowing to him through George MacDonald and in a very different way, through Owen Barfield, and picking up new and in some ways complementary nuances and emphasis by their passage through those writers.

Kreglinger has given a detailed and careful account of the ways in which MacDonald drew on Coleridge, concluding, I think rightly that Coleridge allowed MacDonald to see the imagination as absolutely central to all our perceptions and our very nature as created beings, as she says,

> according to both men [the imagination] is at work in all spheres of life both on a conscious and subconscious level. MacDonald's sees the imagination at work in human cognition; in creative, artistic expression of which the poet is the prime example; and in humanity's reception of God's redemptive work (101).

Now she goes on to suggest that MacDonald rejects what she thinks of as 'Coleridge's strong tendency towards idealism' and suggests that MacDonald 'establishes the imagination within a more carefully developed Christian framework'. I differ from her a little in that, whilst I agree with everything she says about MacDonald, I don't think Coleridge is quite as unorthodox as she fears. Everything turns of course on how you interpret the famous 13th chapter of the *Biographia*. And in particular the sentence which describes the Primary Imagination as 'a repetition in the finite mind of the eternal act of Creation in the infinite I Am'.

If you take the phrase 'the infinite I Am' as reaching primarily back into Schelling and transcendental idealism then you might have cause for concern that Coleridge is not distinguishing sufficiently between Creator and Creature, and '*repetition*' will also therefore seem

---

20 Ibid., p. 103.

a stronger word. But if you also root '*I Am*' in God's self-disclosure to Moses at the burning bush then the imagination becomes part of the *imago dei* in us and not a pretence to transcend our creatureliness.

But whatever the case was with Coleridge, Kreglinger is absolutely right to highlight how MacDonald emphasizes the distinction between our contingent creativity and God's absolute creation *ex nihilo*. So she quotes a passage from *A Dish of Orts*, which Lewis would have applauded to the rafters:

> the poet can present us with new thought-forms—new, that is, as revelations of thought. It has created none of the material that goes to make his forms. But it takes forms already existing, and gathers them about a thought so much higher than they, that it can group and subordinate and harmonise them into a whole which shall represent, unveil that thought (96).

Though one wants to set beside this passage that very Coleridgean insight, also in a *Dish of Orts,* that the imagination is nevertheless, within its limits, an exercise in creation, that in some senses God's image in us is imagination: 'Imagination is, therefore, that faculty in man, which is likest to the prime operation of the power of God, and has, therefore, been called the creative faculty and in its exercise creation. Poet means maker.'

If MacDonald offers to Lewis a Coleridge who exalts the human imagination as a truth-bearing and shaping faculty whilst clearly preserving the transcendence of the divine (one half of the complementary polarity of transcendence/immanence and object/subject with which Coleridge was so concerned, for as he pithily said, 'All knowledge rests on the coincidence of an object with a subject'),[21] then Owen Barfield offered Lewis the other immanent side of Coleridge, sometimes disturbing to Lewis himself, the side that discerns a God who is also within.

But by doing so, Barfield paradoxically delivered Lewis from what he himself called 'the poison of subjectivity'.

As Barfield put it in *Romanticism Come of Age*:

> [from] the fallacy that mind is exclusively subjective, or, to put it more crudely, that the mind is something which is shut up in a sort of box called the brain, the fallacy that the mind of man is a passive onlooker at the processes and phenomena of nature, in the creation of which it neither takes nor has taken any part, the fallacy that there are many separate minds, but

---

21 S.T. Coleridge, *Biographia Literaria* Vol. 7 (Princeton: Princeton University Press, 1984), p. 252.

no such thing as Mind.[22]

The place where the Barfieldian Coleridge comes alive in Lewis is in his own poetry and particularly in 'The Adam at Night'.

Something that both MacDonald and Barfield emphasize in their reading of Coleridge, is that whilst the imagination, when it is given over to and informed by God, can disclose truth, and even become the arena of divine encounter, we must also be aware of false imaginations, not the 'organic whole' of Primary, or true Secondary Imagination but the arbitrary and mechanistic constructions of the 'fancy' which as Coleridge says has 'nothing but fixities and definites to work with'.

Barfield explored the destructive power of these false 'figurations' as he called them in *Saving The Appearances: A Study in Idolatry*. Only a true, and truly participative imagination can deliver us, he believed, from the falsely mechanistic and atomized picture of the world we have constructed to suit ourselves and exclude God, the idol we have constructed for ourselves and to which our modern age is still, to some degree in bondage.

MacDonald is aware of exactly the same problem and explores it largely in both *Lilith* and *Phantastes: A Faerie Romance For Men and Women*, though he is perhaps ultimately more optimistic than Barfield. In a crucial passage from *Orts*, cited by Kreglinger, MacDonald brings the human imagination right back to its source in the light of the divine making and gives us grounds for hope:

> But God sits in that chamber of our being in which the candle of our consciousness goes out in darkness, and sends forth from hence wonderful gifts into the light of that understanding which is His candle. Our hope lies in no most perfect mechanism, even of the Spirit, but in the wisdom wherein we live and move and have our being. Thence we hope for endless forms of beauty informed by truth [...] If the dark portion of our own being were the origin of our imaginations, we might well fear the apparition of such monsters as would be generated in the sickness of decay which could never feel only—declare—a slow return towards primaeval chaos. But the Maker is our light (25).

The light of which MacDonald speaks here is the source of just those needles of eternal light with which Coleridge continues to prick us to our true awakening.

---

22 Owen Barfield, *Romanticism Comes of Age* (Middletown: Rudolph Steiner Press, 1966), p.148.

CONCLUSION

I want to conclude these remarks by sharing with you a specific example of the way in which Lewis has taken up and made something new with specifically Coleridgean insights brought to him through MacDonald, the way an image that starts almost as an aside from Coleridge, is wonderfully opened up by MacDonald and is then taken up in turn and given further life and insight by Lewis. And I choose this particular example because in all three writers it is the imaginative embodiment of what we have just been discussing, that is to say the danger of making a false intellectual construction of the world, a shrunken and diminished model, rather than an imaginatively apprehended whole, the danger that arises when a destructive and suspicious intellectual skepticism is not balanced by the more holistic and intuitive apprehensions of the imagination.

Coleridge, you remember, interrupts his own chapter on imagination in *Biographia Literaria* with the insertion of a 'very judicious letter' from a friend saying that what he has to say about imagination is so important it should be reserved for his (never-to-be written!) book on the Logos. The letter was of course written by Coleridge himself and in it, to convey how completely he has overturned the materialist and empiricist intellectual assumptions of his day, and restored the neglected poets and mystics to their proper place, he uses this image:

> Those whom I had been taught to venerate as almost super-
> human in magnitude of intellect, I found perched in little
> fretwork niches, as grotesque dwarfs; whilst the grotesques, in
> my hitherto belief, stood guarding the high altar with all the
> characters of Apotheosis (301).

Now in *A Dish of Orts* MacDonald takes up this suggestive image, of the supposedly giant intellect which has become a dwarf because it has lost the childlike capacity for awe and imaginative apprehension, and develops it a little further:

> We spoil countless precious things by intellectual greed. He
> who will be a man, and will not be a child, must—he cannot
> help himself—become a little man, that is, a dwarf. He will,
> however, need no consolation, for he is sure to think himself a
> very large creature indeed (322).

Lewis immediately saw the dramatic and ironic possibilities in this image of the dwarf who thinks he's a giant and deployed it to wonderful effect in *The Great Divorce* in a scene which he has

MacDonald himself witness, for it was from MacDonald's riff on Coleridge that he drew the image. Though Lewis is now using the image to embody another aspect of our self-deception, and so he shows us:

> A great tall Ghost, horribly thin and shaky, who seemed to be leading on a chain another ghost no bigger than an organ grinder's monkey [...] I noticed that the little Ghost was not being led by the big one. It was the dwarfish figure that held the chain in its hand and the theatrical figure that wore the collar around its neck. In second place, I noticed that the Lady was looking solely at the dwarf Ghost. She seemed to think it was the Dwarf who had addressed her [...] Love shone not from her face only, but from all her limbs, as it were some liquid in which she had just been bathing. Then, to my dismay, she came nearer. She stooped down and kissed the Dwarf (116).

The first act of the redemptive love on the lady's part is to see through the grand illusions of the theatrical figure and find the 'dwarf' who is really speaking, so that he can indeed lose his self-important delusions and grow into a man.

In *The Last Battle* Lewis again returns to the Coleridgean image of the deluded dwarf, and this time focusing it on the very issue for which Coleridge deployed it. The so-called intellectual giants who turn out in the Coleridgean view to be dwarfs, are precisely those empiricist and mechanistic, and systematically skeptic, philosophers from Descartes through Locke and Hume to Hartley whose reductive system and failure of imagination has constructed the eidolon, the whole 'Watch-making scheme of things' as Coleridge called it, from which he is trying to set us free.

Lewis avails himself of both the Coleridgean insight and the Coleridgean image in the wonderful chapter in the last Battle entitled 'How the Dwarves refused to be taken in'.

That indeed was the situation of England when Coleridge began to realize that the so-called enlightenment had indeed constructed *a prison of the mind* and that the imagination, as an agent both of perception of renewal might at last unlock it—a golden key. He began in his day to spring us from the prison and thankfully he handed that key on to MacDonald and others, they in their turn to the Inklings, and the Inklings to us. There is more to do of course, but like MacDonald, Lewis also had Hope. For the last words of that remarkable chapter are 'The door flew open'!

BIBLIOGRAPHY

Barfield, Owen, *Romanticism Comes of Age*, Middletown: Rudolph Steiner, 1966. Print.

Coleridge, Samuel Taylor, *Biographia Literaria*, eds. Kathleen Coburn, James Engell, and W. Jackson Bate, Vol. 2, Princeton: Princeton University Press, 1984. Print.

Coleridge, Samuel Taylor, *Biographia Literaria*, eds. Kathleen Coburn, James Engell, and W. Jackson Bate, Vol. 7, Princeton: Princeton University Press, 1984. Print.

Coleridge, Samuel Taylor, *Aids to Reflection*, ed. John Beer, *Collected Coleridge*, Vol. 7, Princeton: Princeton University Press, 1993. Print.

Coleridge, Samuel Taylor, 'The Statesman's Manual' in *Lay Sermons*, ed. RJ White, *Collected Coleridge*, Vol. 6, Princeton: Princeton University Press, 1972. Print.

Dearborn, Kerry, *Baptized Imagination*, Surrey: Ashgate, 2006. Print.

Kreglinger, Gisela, *Storied Revelations*, Eugene: Pickwick, 2013. Print.

Lewis, C.S., *The Allegory of Love: A Study in Medieval Tradition*, Oxford: Oxford University Press, 1936.

Lewis, C.S., *The Pilgrim's Regress: An Allegorical Apology for Christianity, Reason, and Romanticism*, London: Geoffrey Bles, 1943. Print.

Lewis, C.S., *The Collected Poems of C.S. Lewis ed Walter Hooper*, London: HarperCollins 1964/1994. Print.

MacDonald, George, *A Dish of Orts: Chiefly Papers on the Imagination, and on Shakespeare*, London: Samson, Low, Marston, 1882. Print.

MacDonald, George, *Lilith: A Romance*. London: Chatto and Windus, 1895. Print.

MacDonald, George, *Phantastes: A Faerie Romance for Men and Women*, London: Alexander Strahan, 1884. Print.

Prickett, Stephen, *Romanticism and Religion: The Tradition of Coleridge and Wordsworth in the Victorian Church*,

Cambridge: Cambridge University Press, 2008. Print.

Walmsley, L (ed.), *C.S. Lewis Essay Collection. Literature, Philosophy and Short Stories*, London: HarperCollins, 2000. Print.

Walmsley, L. (ed.), *C.S. Lewis Essay Collection. Faith, Christianity and the Church*, London: HarperCollins, 2000. Print.

Ward, Michael, *Planet Narnia: The Seven Heavens in the Imagination*, Oxford: Oxford University Press, 2008. Print.

Rooted Deep:
Relational Inkings of the
Mythopoeic Maker, George MacDonald[1]

Kirstin Jeffrey Johnson

Deviating a little from the usual conference pattern, this morning I am going to describe a journey—a progress, if you will—along a part of my own adventurous path of discovery with George MacDonald. The passage is far from over: I am still a pilgrim. Like MacDonald's characters, I have taken a lot of pauses in libraries filled with other books, stopped in houses hosted by grandmotherly women, meandered down paths which were perhaps not mine, and even at times lain ineffectually like MacDonald's Adela on a couch, requiring the intervention of friends to be sufficiently fortified before carrying on. When I do pick up the thread again, I can feel overwhelmed by the multifaceted path that spins out before me—yet MacDonald's transcendent tales continue to compel me onward.

ON THE SHELVES

Two decades ago I rediscovered George MacDonald. Needing a break from a paper I was supposed to be writing on John Bunyan, I picked 'The Golden Key' up off a friend's shelf—a book I had not read since my early teens. It was delightful to rediscover Tangle and Mossy, the Green-haired Grandmother, and the Old Men. I was not surprised to recognize hints of *Narnia* here and there in the tale. What I had not expected was to be finding hints of Bunyan as well; and what seemed to be more than hints—perhaps even a response to Bunyan. Suddenly my initial plan for the Bunyan paper was out the window, and I was off to the library to find out more about this man MacDonald, whose stories I had loved as a child but about whom I knew very little.

The library did not have masses of material, but with what it did have I was able to build up a picture. I was excited to discover that not only could I easily establish that MacDonald was a close reader

---

1 The title comes from a phrase used initially by MacDonald, when referencing *England's Antiphon*: 'rooted deep in all its story' (3). The sentiment is reiterated by Tolkien in *The Lord of the Rings* when he writes: 'Deep roots are not reached by the frost' (I 257).

of Bunyan, but that he and his family had gained some renown for their performances of *The Pilgrim's Progress*. I was somewhat thrown by the fact that the only critical writing I could find specifically on 'The Golden Key' assured me that that key was a phallic symbol and that MacDonald's writing was determined by 'frustrated desires' and a life-long angst induced by deprivation of breast-milk as an infant.[2] Not quite the explication I had expected. But I remained nonetheless fascinated by the author that was emerging, and I began to wonder about conducting more than simply a class paper on MacDonald.

Here was—so I read—a rural preacher who, despite a childhood of repressive and dour Calvinism that warned against the evils of such things as fiddle music and fairytales, had somehow risen above his circumstances to become one of the grandfathers of modern fantasy. Having escaped the narrowness of a small backwater town, MacDonald's world was transformed at university, and especially by his accidental discovery of the German Romantics. This serendipity was essentially his salvation, for as a failed preacher kicked out of his church, MacDonald turned to writing fiction in order to feed his ever-growing family. Although *Phantastes* was pretty much universally scorned when it came out, MacDonald's 'realistic novels' were more popular, and through them and the *Pilgrim's Progress* performances he was able to keep things going: a failed preacher turned novelist, and fortunately fantasist as well, as his non-religious—at times even anti-religious—fantasy is the only reason he is still known today.

That is the picture I gleaned from the texts to which I had access twenty-one years ago.[3] And that is pretty much how I presented him to others—with the exception of the non-or-anti-religious fantasy bit. I had not re-read enough of the fantasy to be categorical, but even in the little I had re-read there was enough reiteration of Bible verses and even explicit—and positive—references to God, that that perspective did seem problematic to me. But it added to my curiosity. How did this creative writer appear out of nowhere, crafting these amazing tales? Tales that—so I discovered the more reading I did—had been such an influence on so many other great writers: G.K. Chesterton, C.S. Lewis, J.R.R. Tolkien, James Barrie, E. Nesbit, Madeleine L'Engle, Ursula Le Guin, Maurice Sendak, Frederick Buechner and Jeffrey

---

2   Cf. R.L. Wolff, *The Golden Key: A Study of George MacDonald* (New Haven: Yale University Press, 1961).

3   I must add that as I eventually travelled to other libraries (in those pre-internet days) I discovered a wider range of MacDonald criticism than represented in my initial foray.

Overstreet among others. MacDonald was a storyteller for storytellers, really: a pioneer whose work was to inform not only twentieth-century fantasists, but now twenty-first century fantasists as well.

INDEPENDENT DELVING

I had C.S. Lewis's *Anthology* of George MacDonald quotations sitting—unread—on my shelf, so I pulled it down and perused the introduction. What Lewis wrote certainly countered the claims that MacDonald's fantasy was non-religious, and while he gave mixed reviews on MacDonald's style he clearly adulated MacDonald's ability to craft stories that could change lives—and not just his own. Lewis connected this with MacDonald's gift of what he called the 'mythopoeic'. Lewis also included a bit of biography, but it was limited in detail (and, I later realized, in accuracy as well) and so began a new stage on my journey: a foray into primary material.

Thus, too, began a very protracted reconstruction of my image of who MacDonald was and what he did. The more I read about MacDonald's home and childhood, the more nuanced my understanding of that environment became. The same happened with my perception of his early experiences as a preacher and as a novelist. I soon became addicted to library and university archives, because in these—both in the UK and North America—I was discovering letters and memoirs that were not only filling in missing pieces, but were sometimes directly contradicting 'received truths' that had been passed down—albeit in good faith—through twentieth-century scholarship.[4] I also discovered that some of the published letters had been abbreviated, or had portions of sentences removed without acknowledgement—even to the extent of altering one's interpretation of those sentences. And MacDonald himself was not looking anything like the description I gave above. Nor was he appearing quite the 'miracle child' he had once seemed. Rather, he was emerging as an almost predictable product of his environment... once one was acquainted with the actualities of that environment.[5]

---

4   The older I get, and the more mistakes I myself make, the greater my grace for the mistakes of others. I am deeply grateful for examples such as the Inklings scholar Christopher Mitchell, who was widely acknowledged for his humility. It is not a quality easily cultivated in academia, yet in the long run it elicits much better scholarship.

5   The libraries and archives from which the following information was gleaned are primarily: Beinecke Library, Yale University; Brander Library,

Instead of the survivor of a stereotyped 'Calvinist childhood', I discovered a man whose father clearly articulated his desire for God over denomination, willingly discussed varying doctrines, and openly voiced his desire to continue to change and grow in how he perceived the Divine. With *his* father a Catholic-born, fiddle-playing, Presbyterian elder; his mother an Independent church rebel; his first wife (MacDonald's mother) a sister to the Gaelic-speaking radical who became Moderator of the disrupting Free Church; and his second wife (MacDonald's step-mother, to whom MacDonald was also very close) the daughter of a Celtic Episcopalian minister—merely using the tag 'Calvinist' for his son's theological background began to seem both simplistic and misleading.

The church of MacDonald's childhood is sometimes described as 'Cowie's church', followed by a damning description of Reverend Cowie's fundamentalism. But I quickly discovered that aside from the fact that Cowie's theology is said to have changed fairly dramatically from when he founded the church to when he retired from the post, Cowie actually died a full twenty years before MacDonald was even born—hardly a key influence.[6] And MacDonald himself was no miracle aberration from that congregation—if anything, it was the congregation itself that was an aberration: amongst MacDonald's peers alone there emerged a Celtic scholar, at least three biblical scholars, a doctorate of divinity, three journal editors, two church denomination moderators, several pastors and missionaries, and Britain's first Sinologist—who taught in Oxford and whose work is still studied in China today. That's an admirable collection of youth. Lest these pursuits appear deviant to the community: not only was MacDonald invited back to small rural Huntly to lecture on Tennyson and Milton, but the Sinologist—James Legge—was also invited back to lecture on Confucius. Perhaps this is all a little less surprising when one learns that the ecumenically-minded man who actually *was* MacDonald's minister used his spare time for such ventures as offering classes on Hebrew to Huntly's adults.[7]

Huntly; King's College Archives, Aberdeen; King's College University Library, London; Marion E. Wade Center, Wheaton College; Gladstone's Library, Hawarden, Wales.

6   Cf. Robert Troup, *The Missionar Kirk of Huntly* (Huntly: Joseph Dunbar, 1901), p. 8ff.

7   James Legge, Introduction in *Lectures on Theology, Science, and Revelation* (London: Jackson, Walford, and Hodder, 1863), p. ix.

As I delved, I also learned that not only were fairytales and fiction *not* banned from MacDonald's childhood (as a few sources had assured me they were), he was actually raised in an unusually literate environment. For example, one of MacDonald's maternal uncles was a famed Celtic scholar and editor of the *Gallic Highland Dictionary*, who collected fairytales and Celtic poetry in the midst of his campaign to keep the Gallic language and culture alive; MacDonald's paternal grandfather had supported the publication of an edition of *Ossian*—that controversial Celtic text that some claim kick-started European Romanticism and was certainly key to Goethe's *Young Werther*; MacDonald's step-uncle was a Shakespeare scholar; his paternal cousin another Celtic scholar; and his parents were both readers—his dad with an acknowledged penchant for Burns, Newton, Cowper, Chalmers, Coleridge, and Darwin, to name a few; his mother with a classical education that included multiple languages.[8]

In reflections on his childhood, MacDonald speaks of reading *The Arabian Nights* obsessively; of loving, if not understanding, his father's copy of *The Rime of the Ancient Mariner*; and of initiating his passion for Shakespeare.[9] As a youth he actually delighted in reading *Paradise Lost* whilst flung across the back of his horse.[10] MacDonald's schoolmaster recollected him regaling classmates with legends of the local castle.[11] And MacDonald and his cousins regularly taught Bible stories in Sunday School.[12] MacDonald was no wonder child deprived of literature and story yet miraculously discovering it; his upbringing was unusually rich in a family-sanctioned Western literary tradition. And all this in addition to the remarkable Scottish education system from which he clearly benefitted—even in his primary school this not

---

8   See *Rooted in all its story, more is meant than meets the ear* (Kirstin Jeffrey Johnson, PhD Thesis, St.Andrews University, 2010) for more specific detail.

9   Barbara Amell, *The Art of God: Lectures on the Great Poets by George MacDonald* (Portland: Wingfold Books, 2004), p. 103.

10   Greville MacDonald, *George MacDonald and His Wife* (London: Allen & Unwin, 1924), p. 54.

11   N.a., 'Huntly Correspondent—Obituary: George MacDonald' (*Banffshire Journal*, 1905).

12   This particular Sunday School was initiated by the Legge brothers, one of whom—also briefly a bookseller in Huntly—is said to have been fluent in Shakespeare, Milton, Cowper, Young, Pope, and numerous contemporary poets. Legge's father, an elder of MacDonald's childhood church, is described as one who enjoyed *Gulliver's Travels* and *Robinson Crusoe*. (Legge, xxii)

only included Rhetoric, Mathematics, and French, but also the study of Classics in Latin and Greek.[13]

At some point in this reconstruction of who I understood MacDonald to be, it hit home to me that he did not even grow up in the town of Huntly. Rather, he grew up on a farm outside Huntly. I also learned that that frequent representation of the negative reception of *Phantastes*, referenced above, was suspect: once I started looking at the actual contemporary reviews, I found many more positive ones than negative ones. The 'second-hand symbol shop' review that is so frequently quoted in MacDonald scholarship is colourful and conveniently dramatic—but not at all representative. In fact, three years after *Phantastes: A Faerie Romance For Men and Women* was published, journals actually declared the novel 'a very decided success'.[14]

Yet despite my increasing familiarity with—and reconfiguration of—MacDonald's biography, there was one piece that still had not really shifted for me. I still saw MacDonald as a preacher-turned-author. What finally woke me up to the inaccuracy of this was my return to that word used by C.S. Lewis to describe MacDonald's fiction: 'mythopoeic'. Lewis calls MacDonald 'the greatest genius'—in what 'may even be one of the greatest arts': Mythopoesis.[15] That is a pretty high accolade. I discovered that Tolkien had also ascribed the term to MacDonald; so, too, had their student, W.H. Auden. As all three men were not only successful writers, but also highly respected literature scholars and professors, I decided to ascertain what exactly they meant by the term, to see if this would help me better understand how a (supposedly) failed minister ended up becoming such a great story crafter.

---

13 P.W. Scott, *The History of Strathbogie* (Glasgow: Bell & Bain Ltd, 1997), p. 144; n.a., *The New Statistical Account of Scotland* (Edinburgh: W. Blackwood & Sons, 1845), p. 1043.

14 Mary Ann Gillies, *The Professional Literary Agent in Britain, 1880-1920* (Toronto: University of Toronto Press, 2007), p. 186. An 1861 article reads, '*Phantastes* has proved a success even as regards its circulation, and a very decided success as concerns the influence it has exerted on minds of the highest order'. Ironically it is MacDonald's own humoured quotation of the damning 'symbol shop' review in a now-published letter that led to its frequent reiteration by contemporary critics.

15 C.S. Lewis, *George MacDonald: An Anthology* (London: Geoffrey Bles), p. xviii.

AN INFORMATIVE DIVERSION

So I turned briefly aside from MacDonald and looked at how Tolkien and Lewis used this word, Mythopoesis. As I have detailed my discoveries on this elsewhere, I shall not be exhaustive here, but I do believe that clarity on certain aspects of the term can enable significant insight into MacDonald's import and impact as a 'foundational fantasist'.[16] The written and verbal discussions Tolkien and Lewis held about this 'great art' reintroduced it to the public consciousness—and in the process they identified MacDonald as a prime practitioner. Often today the word 'mythopoeic' is used to mean 'a literary myth', or is even used simply as an adjective describing something reminiscent of Middle Earth or Narnia. At its most broad, it is no more than a synonym for 'fantasy'. But it is important that Literature scholars and, most particularly, those interested in fantasy and/or the Inklings, recognize that this is not how Lewis and Tolkien used the term. Indeed for them the word was not even restricted to the genre of fantasy—although they did argue that that realm lends itself particularly well to it. Understanding 'mythopoeic' as applied by those Oxford Literature professors who became some of the century's greatest fantasy authors can shed light on not only their own literary creations—and those of MacDonald—but also on those who can be considered to be following in the lineage: writers such as Le Guin, L'Engle, Gaiman, Clarke and Overstreet.

Tolkien and Lewis's understanding of Mythopoesis was finessed by their engagement with the ideas of another Inkling, Owen Barfield. Barfield, better known as a philosopher and author of books such as *Poetic Diction* and *History in English Words*, was also a fantasist—having authored *The Silver Trumpet*. Barfield and Lewis had been friends since undergraduate days. They were delighted when they discovered that Tolkien too was a lover of language and of myth, and that he similarly valued Imagination—and soon the three of them were having deep discussions around the subject.

These discussions—perhaps the most important of which occurred as Tolkien and Lewis wandered along Addison's Walk in here in Magdalen—had some pretty significant long-term consequences, but I will just touch on some of the key ones for the purposes of

---

16 For greater detail see 'Tolkien's Mythopoesis' in Hart and Khovacs' *Tree of Tales: Tolkien, Literature, and Theology* (Baylor Press, 2007), and *Rooted in all its story, more is meant than meets the ear* (Kirstin Jeffrey Johnson, PhD Thesis, St. Andrews University, 2010)

this discussion. First: they concurred that a myth is 'a story out of which ever varying meanings will grow for different [recipients] in different ages', and that there exists both factual and fictive myths.[17] For instance, they would call the Christian Gospel a myth—not meaning that it did not happen, but rather that, regardless of whether or not it happened, its *story* is one that has persisted across time and cultures, and has repeatedly been considered relevant by at least some part of the population (despite how incredibly different their culture might be from that out of which the story first came). A 'mythopoeic' work such as MacDonald seemed able to craft was one that not only had transcendent potential but one that also, within its space of a 'Secondary World', bore the potential for a transformative experience on the part of the reader. Not that a reader would necessarily be changed in how they saw or engaged with the Primary World once they had set the tale aside, but the possibility was there. For instance, consider Tolkien's King Théoden—and the many readers who have journeyed with him in Rohan, who forever look at trees with new eyes after having met the Ents; or, of Lewis's Lucy—and the many readers who have journeyed with her on *The Dawn Treader*, for whom the phrase 'that is only what a star is made of' is somehow deeply satisfying: the change could be seemingly minor or clearly revolutionary, but something about who one is or how—or what— one sees, is different. Although G.K. Chesterton, preceding Barfield, Tolkien, and Lewis, never used the word 'mythopoeic', his assertions readily concur with Lewis's as to MacDonald's 'mythopoeic gift'. He claims that reading *The Princess and the Goblin*, more than anything he had ever read, changed his way of engaging with and viewing the entire world; it 'made'—to use Chesterton's own phrase—'a difference to my whole existence'.[18] Lewis made a similar claim of *Phantastes*.[19]

Much of what Lewis and Tolkien discussed with Barfield they later wrote about in essays such as 'On Fairy-stories'[20] and 'On Stories'[21]

---

17 This particular phrase is found in C.S. Lewis' letters, 22 September 1956.

18 G.K. Chesterton, Introduction in *George MacDonald and His Wife* (London: George Allen & Unwin, 1924), p. 9.

19 Lewis, *Anthology*, p. xxi.

20 J.R.R. Tolkien, 'On Fairy-stories', *Tree and Leaf* (London: HarperCollins, 2001).

21 C.S. Lewis, 'On Stories', *Of This and Other Worlds* (Glasgow: William Collins & Son Ltd, 1982).

and, as indicated, it was represented in their fantasy—but for anyone who has read MacDonald's essays 'The Imagination: Its Functions and Its Culture' and 'The Fantastic Imagination', it is conspicuous that little these scholars were saying is new.[22] I do not know if Barfield had read MacDonald's essays—it is definitely possible.[23] Regardless, Barfield and MacDonald were certainly drawing on some of the same sources. That Coleridge was a significant influence is well-recognized; not, however, their engagement with Philip Sidney.

In his conversations with Lewis and Tolkien, as well as through his books, *Poetic Diction* and *History in English Words*, Barfield drew their attention to Sidney and specifically to Sidney's discussion of poets and poetry. Sidney, in his *Defense for Poesy*, uses examples such as *Aesop's Fables* and the biblical story of David and Nathan as proof of the educational power of 'poetry'.[24] One could even substitute the term 'creative writing' for 'poetry' because (as Barfield pointed out to Tolkien and Lewis) when discussing the term 'poet' Sidney means, essentially, 'creative writer': a 'maker'—one who makes. Barfield details Sidney's explanation of how a 'maker' studies 'Nature', contemplates the ideas 'behind' Nature, and thus is able to 'deliver forth' new 'makings'.[25] It

22 MacDonald recognized the significance of his essay 'The Imagination'. He described it as 'one of the best things, I think, that I have ever done' (Peel 9). It is the only known lecture—of hundreds, over decades—that MacDonald ever gave from a written text. And he frequently offered it as an option. Before it appeared as the opening essay in *A Dish of Orts*, he published a part of it anonymously in 1867—it appeared in at least three journals: *The British Quarterly Review; Scott's Monthly Magazine*; and *New York's Eclectic Magazine of Foreign Literature*.

23 Barfield gifted Lewis with a copy of *Diary of an Old Soul* in 1929, and Lewis's thanks indicate that both men were already familiar with that MacDonald text. (C.S. Lewis, *Collected Letters: Books, broadcasts and war 1931-1949* [London: HarperCollins 2004, p.172])

24 Philip Sidney, *Defense of Poesy and Poems* (London: Cassell, 1909), p. 61. Following the tradition partaken in by his literary mentor Sidney, MacDonald likewise does not consider the terms 'poetry' and 'story' mutually exclusive. He articulates this clearly in *England's Antiphon* in his discourse on the ballad (235). In his anthology on Sidney he highlights the quotation: 'verse being but an ornament, and no cause to poetry; since there have been many most excellent poets that never versified. [...] It is not riming and versing that maketh a poet [but] that feigning notable images of virtues, vices, or what else, with that delightful teaching...' (*Gems* 149).

25 Owen Barfield, *History in English Words* (London: Faber and Faber, 1926), pp. 188-190.

is because of the act of contemplation, as a result of that contemplation upon that which lies outside the maker, that he or she is able to then make something new. This applies not only to the contemplation of one's physical environment, but also to the contemplation of the makings of other makers—works of literature, music, art.

Barfield explained that the term 'invention' in the Seventeenth Century had different implications than it does today, noting that the verb *invenire* meant 'to find'.[26] MacDonald had also emphasized this in his discussion of the author as *trouver*: 'finder'. One finds, so that one might 'make'.[27] Tolkien coined another term in his response to this discussion: 'sub-creation'—being able to assist 'in the effoliation and multiple enrichment' of God's creation. Rather than an author or artist being a 'mini-creator', he or she is a type of co-creator.[28] Humans do not create *ex nihilo*, from nothing—like the Deity—but in response to, or perhaps even in reaction against, something: something found, something engaged, something related. Such an act can even be—according to these scholars—a type of participation.

Tolkien and Lewis were particularly struck by Barfield's discussion of the ancient semantic unities of language and myth—indeed Tolkien claims his entire outlook was modified by it. Barfield pulled Lewis and Tolkien's attention back to a time when language and myth were so closely entwined that they could not really be separated: not only was, say *spiritus* the word for 'wind' and the word for 'spirit' and the word for 'breath', but each of those things was understood by means of their relation to the other: one understood what 'breath' was because one knew what 'spirit' was because one knew what 'wind' was because one knew what 'breath' was. Barfield believed that though words had once 'embodied' this 'unified perception', consciousness had become increasingly fragmented as conceptual thinking developed.[29] He hoped that some day humans would once again be better able to reconcile the literal and the abstract, with a renewed perception informed by the past, rather than merely reverting to it.[30]

---

26 Ibid., p. 190.

27 George MacDonald, 'The Imagination: Its Function and Its Culture', *A Dish of Orts* (Whitefish: Kessinger, 2004), p. 14.

28 Tolkien, 'On Fairy-stories', p. 73.

29 Qtd in Humphrey Carpenter, *The Inklings* (London: George Allen & Unwin, 1978), p. 42.

30 These Inklings discussions are concurrent with the 'Futurist' movement, which was arguing for liberation from the weight of the past. Marinetti's

Now Lewis and Tolkien concurred that a decision to seek renewed perceptions informed by the past must apply to their creative crafting if it applied their philosophies of life, and they recognized that this necessitated informed and intentional engagement with their literary past. And so as teachers and writers they modeled this: Tolkien drew upon northern European myths, such as *Beowulf* and the Icelandic sagas, and on British sources such as the *Mabinogion* and William Morris. Lewis's work is not only rampant with such predecessors as Lucius Apuleius, Dante, Milton, and Spenser, but also with near-contemporaries such as Mauriac, Haggard, Chesterton, and MacDonald. Both Lewis and Tolkien came to be recognized for this careful attention to and engagement with the stories they were studying and teaching, as well as for manifesting delight in what Lewis called 'source-hunting': rooting around, being *trouvers*, finding the roots of the texts they were reading and studying in those that had come before.[31] Their great skills at doing this *invenire*—finding—resulted eventually in their own rich 'inventions', sub-creations. Tolkien called this carefully intentional apprehension and engagement, which shaped the subsequent creative transmission, an act of Mythopoeia.[32] Their recognition of a literary lineage and the choice to actively engage with it—not just recognize it, not just borrow from it, but to seek it out, try to understand it, and to even 'converse' with it—underscores the relational element that must be considered in order to understand Mythopoesis in the tradition of the Inklings.

MACDONALD RE-ASSESSED

After this deviation in my MacDonald journey, delving into Lewis and Tolkien and Barfield, I set aside some time to consider: did the Inklings' discussion of the mythopoeic lead me to gain a deeper understanding of MacDonald as an author, even as a fantasist? Was this 'apprehension and studied engagement', this shaping of the 'subsequent transmission in new forms', representative of MacDonald's apparently 'mythopoeic writing'? Were his tales—claimed by so many to transcend time, to invite personal transformation—intentionally

---

Manifesto of 1909 summed up the major principles of the movement, which included a loathing scorn of ideas from the past, directed most frequently at political and artistic traditions.

31 Lewis, *Anthology*, p. 20.

32 The experience of receiving such a story; of participating in transformation.

informed by those that had gone before? Was MacDonald more than just referencing, and borrowing symbols 'second hand', but rather actually as interested in multiple literatures of the past as these Oxford Literature professors who sought to craft their fantastical stories with the same sort of literary engagement that they modeled in their classes and in their academic writings? Well, yes.

It did not take me long to discover that a close reading of any of MacDonald's writings will indicate that he is very intentionally rooting himself in the tradition of apprehension, engagement, and transmission. In fact, I suspect this is one of the pedagogies to which Lewis—who had an equivalent encyclopedic mental library—was referring, when he called MacDonald his 'Master'.[33] I decided to count the explicit references to other books and authors within MacDonald's first 'realistic novel', *David Elginbrod*—and discovered over ninety. This number only includes obvious references, and not the myriad of allusions or unmarked quotations that also exist. Many of those references, while implicitly shaping the story, are discussed in detail by the novel's characters, or by the narrator. And every single one of those ninety references, in some way or another, contributes to or engages with the main story line. Not one—should one pick up the thread and follow—is irrelevant. The clearly evident literary influences upon MacDonald's works alone number in the hundreds, and he is careful to draw explicit attention to many of them. This is not a case of simply borrowing ideas—this is something quite other.

A few years into my research on MacDonald, I no longer considered him the wonder-boy aberration—not now that I knew more about the riches of his upbringing, even before he went off to university and discovered yet new literature. But still, to change from Congregationalist preacher to a pretty literarily focused author? It would be one thing if his literary references were mostly just biblical, or even patristic or medieval mystics—and there is no shortage of those. But once I started looking, I realized that MacDonald is a whole compendium of the literature of Western Civilization in and of himself.

And that is where, after years of studying MacDonald, years in wonderfully musty archives, I was finally brought up short. I finally did the math. I did the math—and, I met the mentor. First, the math: MacDonald was a minister at Arundel for twenty-eight *months* in his

---

33 Lewis, *Anthology*, p. xviii.

early 20s.[34] In contrast to those twenty-nine months, MacDonald was a professor of English literature for ten years (in his 30s) and a lecturer on English Literature for forty years. Waking up to this ratio was my biggest paradigm shift as a MacDonald scholar. The man I was studying was not a preacher-author (let alone a failed preacher). He was a teacher-author—and a very successful one. One who was, incidentally, in huge demand to preach for the majority of his life but who refused ever to receive payment for doing so (he turned down highly paid offers to be a minister). He would preach as a gift; his teaching—of Literature—was his paid profession. And it was his profession, his vocation—not just a nice little sideline. MacDonald was passionate about teaching literature. That was obvious even in his novels in which, while there certainly is the contemporary show of preaching therein, is also included—as indicated—a considerable amount of literary exegesis. But something started to strike me as distinctive about MacDonald's lectures: with the exception of Dante, MacDonald only ever lectured on British authors. And then I realized that his published 'non-fictionalized' criticism, little of it that there is, was also only on British writers—starting with a review of Browning in his 20s, and including his anthology of Phillip Sidney, his textual study of *Hamlet*, and of course *England's Antiphon*.

Suddenly I had a new twist in my journey. Why only British literature (plus Dante)? Especially when it is clear that MacDonald loved German Literature—and French Literature, and Classical Literature, even Russian Literature.[35] Why not lecture on these too? Well, that brought me to the mentor.

MacDonald's Mentor

After those twenty-nine months in Arundel, MacDonald

---

34 From October 1850 to May 1853. Just before his intended ordination in Arundel, December 1850 (due to haemorrhage attack, it had to be postponed six months) MacDonald wrote to his brother Charles: 'I don't think I am settled here for life... I hope either to leave this after six or more years, or to write a poem for the good of my generation. Perhaps both' (Raeper 80).

35 While discussion of MacDonald's engagement with German literature is prolific, few critics are aware that MacDonald quotes Tolstoy in his letters, and talks of how it is best to read Russian novels in French—perhaps even fewer know that he and his wife Louisa crafted an English version of Zola's *L'Assommoir* for his family to perform. (Greville 381) MacDonald's complex engagement with Plato—let alone with other Classical writers—is perhaps one of the most surprisingly overlooked areas of his work.

moved to Manchester. And the reason he moved there was to be near his mentor: the man to whose lectures MacDonald had dragged his friends and fellow students—and his fiancée—when he was still in seminary; the man under whom MacDonald had specifically chosen to study, and whom he named his greatest influence other than his father. I knew his name: A.J. Scott. My recollection from biographies was that he had been a pastor. What I did not know, and was amazed to discover, was his true claim to fame: A.J. Scott was the first ever full-time English Literature professor.

We only have time today for some tantalizing tidbits, though truly Scott is worthy of a full book biography. It is not without reason that MacDonald chose him as a mentor: he was an amazing person. Thomas Carlyle, John Ruskin, Fréderic Chopin—they all agree.[36] But what is particularly important to underscore for the purposes of this conference in its broader exploration of the Victorian roots of modern fantasy, is that this mentor Scott was—like MacDonald, Tolkien, and Lewis—a passionate teacher of Literature. Like MacDonald, Tolkien, and Lewis, Scott read widely, in multiple languages, and his taste was by no means restricted to English Literature. He was fluent in Hebrew, Greek and Latin, he was highly proficient in Italian, French and German, and capable in Anglo-Saxon and old German. He studied texts in all of these.[37]

But although Scott himself found it fascinating to spend hours in the British Library, delving into early manuscripts such as those of Bede and Chaucer, he was struck at how few of his 'well-educated' English acquaintances could even adequately converse about the literature of their own country. At Oxford and Cambridge the literature that was studied was Classical Literature: Greek and Roman, and some Continental. It was assumed anything British would be studied in one's leisure time. But the reality was that most people were not studying it in their leisure time. In fact in one lecture Scott opines that while there seemed to be a growing interest in the *Niebelungen*, he could scarcely find a person who cared about *Beowulf*—he claims the prevalent English tone is that of disdain for their own ancient literature, tending to be particularly disparaging (while yet ignorant)

---

36 Cf. references to Scott in archived letters of each.

37 Letters show that MacDonald spent hours reading German Romantic fairytales from Scott's library; Scott not only introduced MacDonald to Italian texts, but even to real-life Italian revolutionaries such as Mazzini and Saffi.

of pre-Reformation Literature.[38]

Scott's concerns however were by no means limited to his 'educated' friends—he, along with his colleague F.D. Maurice and other such 'social reformers' (the 'Robert Falconers' of their day), were involved in setting up multiple institutions that offered university education to those who could not at that time earn a degree from Oxford or Cambridge: a rather long list, including not only working class men, or any class of women, but also anyone not part of the Church of England: Baptists, Methodists, Congregationalists, Catholics, Atheists, Jews, etc. Scott—and Maurice, for that matter—was not just insistent that *all* persons should have the opportunity to receive higher-level education: he believed that it was an important aspect of self-identity, for an individual as well as a community, to know the stories of one's heritage. In fact, Scott believed that his students would be better readers of foreign literature, and better neighbours to other cultures, for understanding who they themselves were and from whence they came.[39]

Scott was particularly concerned about the widespread disintegration of long-term community that had been occurring throughout the Industrial Revolution, and which showed no signs of abating. He firmly believed that an effective way of fighting the unraveling of identity was to proactively re-root people in the stories of their identity. And so Scott, in his lectures, focused increasingly on British literature, history, and philosophy—whether when lecturing to the upper-class folk at various culture institutes or to workers down in London's docklands. With F.D. Maurice and Thomas Carlyle, Scott also worked to establish public lending libraries, so that the gift of literacy was not stymied by a lack of accessible material. Eventually, in 1848, the University College in London appointed Scott as their first full-time English Literature professor, where he taught his students about *Beowulf*, and Chaucer, and Bede, Shakespeare, and Milton, and Sidney. As this was still a revolutionary thing to do, Scott actually had to defend the choice and argue for the importance of studying these British authors in his public lectures.

---

38 A.J. Scott, *Notes of Four Lectures on the Literature and Philosophy of the Middle Ages* (Edinburgh: T. Constable, 1857), p. 14.

39 In particular, see: 'A Lecture on Popular Education' (*Woolwich Gazette*, 10 October 1840); 'On University Education', *Introductory Lectures on the Opening of Owens College, Manchester* (London: T. Sowler, 1852); and *Suggestions on Female Education: Two Introductory Lectures on English Literature & Moral Philosophy* (London; Taylor, Walton & Maberly, 1849).

It should be emphasized: Scott was passionate about literature from all cultures. According to his students, he even could reference texts from the Koran, the Vedas, and sacred Zoroastrian texts 'without notes to hand'.[40] But he believed that for the British to better understand their current story—the one they were living—they needed to know the stories, the literature and the history, that fed into that. Recognizing those roots would enable them to see how other literatures and stories had also contributed to and shaped their own. Knowing one's identity better equipped one for dialogue. And dialogue across the ages and between disparate cultures greatly interested Scott. He believed that despite the changes and differences, from Homer to Plato to Dante to Chaucer to Shakespeare and on up to Elizabeth Gaskell, one could identify a continuum of common threads, common signs, and common truths. And these commonalities, according to Scott, demanded attention.[41]

Scott's one non-English exception as his lectures became more focused on British Literature was the same exception made by MacDonald: Dante. A number of Scott's obituaries actually name Scott as the top Dante scholar of the age—both Ruskin and Carlyle seem to agree.[42] Scott explained his passion for Dante repeatedly in lectures. He detailed how Dante was revolutionary in writing in his own everyday language so that a broader audience of everyday Italians could read his work. Emphasizing the deep reverence Dante had for stories and poetry that had preceded him, Scott relayed Dante's belief that close readings of such work had actually transformed his worldview, and that Dante's desire to both communicate and replicate this transformation, informed and enriched his writing.[43]

While Dante was not one of the British writers Scott believed England needed to rediscover and learn to read well, I believe Scott allotted this particular attention to Dante because Dante so completely

40 J. Patrick Newell, *A.J. Scott and His Circle* (Edinburgh: Edinburgh University, 1981), p. 345.

41 A.J. Scott, *Two Discourses: The Kingdom of the Truth: The Range of Christianity* (London: Macmillan & Co., 1866), p. 277.

42 For instance, see: 'The Late Professor A.J. Scott' (*Scotsman*, 19 January 1866), p. 23; *The Carlyle Letters Online* (20:72-4); and John Ruskin, *The Winnington Letters: John Ruskin's Correspondence with Margaret Alexis Bell and the Children at Winnington Hall*, V.A. Burd, ed. (Yale: Harvard University Press, 1969), p. 109 and 110.

43 In particular, see: *Notes of Four Lectures on the Literature and Philosophy of the Middle Ages* (Edinburgh: T. Constable, 1857).

embodied the message Scott was passionate to convey. Dante modeled that continuum of common threads, common signs, and common truths.[44] His rigorous emphasis on rootedness in story, on communal responsibility to both persons and texts, on the general importance of communication and relationship was Scott's own. The need to recognize and understand one's own identity-forming history, to glean intentionally from the stories that have shaped one's community and oneself, combined with the realization that humanity is called to carry forward the meta-narrative by its response to these communications, were resonances with Dante that became recurrent themes in Scott's lectures. Scott saw Dante as the transition to the new modern age—because he was someone who explicitly drew upon the past so that he might speak into the present, preparing for the future (not unlike Barfield). As such, Scott believed that Dante's epic work continued to offer transformative insight—right up to the Nineteenth Century. Scott urged his students to pay attention to not only the *Comedy*, but to other engagements with the *Comedy* in the centuries that followed.

RELATIONAL READING

That Scott made an exception and spent so much time devoted to this particular reading—in the midst of his emphasis on British literature—sent me forward to a new passage of my own journey, to look a little more closely at MacDonald's own obsession and close, scholarly engagement with Dante.

I wasn't surprised to discover in that process that a mutual intimate friend of both Scott and MacDonald, John Ruskin, was also quite passionate about Dante. Reading their various conversations with and about Dante gave me deeper insight—and much greater delight—in the Dantean aspects, implicit and explicit, of *Lilith*.[45] Threading around those relationships sent me travelling back to some of the discussions about Dante in *Seaboard Parish*, a book in which MacDonald engages

---

44 Scott believed that reading in a manner that enabled one to recognize shared truths, repeated patterns, common symbols could even open the reader to 'the sort of inner revelations' of which Dante spoke (*Middle Ages* 71).

45 Incidentally, although *Lilith* was written at the end of the Nineteenth Century amidst the blossoming of 'penny-novels', it was written with the pre-mid nineteenth-century expectation that a book is to be read and re-read, poured over for deeper and multi-layered meanings—never to be fully grasped at first engagement.

with a number of Ruskin's concepts from *Modern Painters*—the first volume of which had been MacDonald's engagement present to his wife. While re-reading *Seaboard* I was suddenly struck by a passage that sounded very familiar: a discussion about *spirit, breath, wind* and, essentially, their ancient semantic unity. Almost verbatim. Could Barfield have been inspired by *Seaboard*? I knew such a passage was not in Sidney's *Defense of Poesy*. I looked elsewhere in Sidney's writings but could not find it. Then by accident I found it in Ruskin's *Sesame and Lilies*. Of course: not only was MacDonald engaging with this text in *Seaboard*, but half a century later Barfield too had been conversing with and drawing upon Ruskin.[46]

However, whilst searching through Sidney this time I was struck by how many of the shared emphases of both Scott and MacDonald were clearly iterated first by Sidney—emphases reiterated yet again in Barfield, Lewis, and Tolkien. This makes sense, as they are all arguing and modeling the same thing: that nothing comes from nothing; story begets story; poesis evokes poesis; authors transformed by their reading of a text are likely to attempt to communicate some of that engagement in the works that they themselves choose to write. These authors believed, and partook in the belief, that the more relational they were as readers, seeking to find things (*invenire*) in the works of others, the more inventive their own sub-creations would be. The writers I have mentioned—Sidney, Dante, Scott, MacDonald, Tolkien, Lewis—all believed this was even a divine calling: to intentionally delve deep into literature, and then respond in kind. To be *trouvers*: finders, and thence, *makers*. These men were incredible literature scholars: they read closely, engaged with the text, delved deep and imbibed, even chewed upon it—and thus was evoked fantastic new stories. Their imaginations were rich because they had filled their coffers for years.

And they do tell us that they are doing this: Lewis says, 'go to MacDonald'; MacDonald says, 'go to Sidney, to Dante, to Wordsworth, to Shakespeare, to Goethe, to Herbert, to Plato, to Thoreau'—a whole huge library. MacDonald uses the image in *England's Antiphon* of antiphonal choral song: one writer responding to the next, each building upon that which had been 'heard'. 'No man could sing as he has sung, *had not others sung before him*. Deep answereth unto deep...'.[47]

---

46 Appropriately that text of *Sesame and Lilies* had begun as a lecture Ruskin gave in Manchester four years before *Seaboard* was published, to assist A.J. Scott in raising money for public lending libraries and working class schools.

47 George MacDonald, *England's Antiphon* (Whitehorn: Johannesen, 1996), p. 3. [italics mine]

The clearly evident 'voices' to which MacDonald's work responds number in the hundreds—and he is careful to draw explicit attention to many of them. A close reading of any of MacDonald's writings will indicate that he is intentionally placing himself in this tradition of apprehension, engagement, and transmission. MacDonald even goes so far as to describe this as a 'relationship' with writers of the past, saying that engaging this way can at times 'place in your hands a key to their inmost thoughts'.[48] They are not thoughts with which MacDonald always agrees: even with his beloved Dante he champions some ideas, argues with others, and suggests a different angle of approach to yet others. But repeatedly he—a good student of A.J. Scott—draws attention to the continuum of common threads, symbols, insights. MacDonald never engages with only one text in his creations; rather, he is engaging in a conversation of texts, balancing arguments against each other, and seeking those points of convergence.[49] It is little wonder that libraries are the setting for so many important relational engagements in his novels. Look closely at an image or phrase and one will see, for instance, how MacDonald is engaging with Ruskin's engagement with Blake's engagement with Sidney's engagement with Paul's engagement with the Greek myth of *Psyche*.

The writers whom MacDonald references most frequently, repeatedly, are those who also intentionally place themselves in this tradition of literary conversation, a relational tradition that recognizes that its participants cannot stand alone. As to his effectiveness, well, that other encyclopedic brain, Ruskin—who knew all of Britain's literati—writes: 'I am always glad to hear you lecture myself—and if I had a son, I would rather he took his lessons in literary taste under you than under any person I know, for you would make him more than a scholar, [you would make him] a living and thoughtful reader'; and 'of all the literary men I know, I think you most love literature itself; the others love themselves and the expression of themselves; but you enjoy your own art, and the art of others, when it is fine'.[50] MacDonald himself writes that 'the best thing you can do for your fellow, next to

---

48 George MacDonald, *Donal Grant* (London: K. Paul, Trench, & Co., 1886), p. 227.

49 Strikingly, the stories that arise from these conversations are not only cohesive, but have been found by many readers to be transformational.

50 John Ruskin, Letter to George MacDonald, George MacDonald Collection (Beinecke Rare Book & Manuscript Library, Yale University), 1/3/127.

rousing his conscience, is—not to give him things to think about, but to wake things up that are in him; or say, to make him think things for himself'.[51] While it does seem to me that there are times in which MacDonald's own opinions do get in the way of his achieving this, it is clearly a goal of his—and certainly sufficient testimony exists that he has been successful with plenty of readers from the Nineteenth Century through to the Twenty-First. Not only have his stories pointed readers to other pieces of literature, by modeling discussions with them, but in doing so he has successfully invited his readers into that conversation. Others have become *trouvers*: partaken, engaged, concurred, refuted. Related.

Relationships require effort. Literary relationships, as well as personal ones. Some readers are more like Vane in *Lilith* or Stoddart in *Annals of a Quiet Neighbourhood*: better at hiding in books and avoiding the complications and taxations of people.[52] Other readers are more like the Little Ones in Lilith: lovers who haven't really even tried to learn. MacDonald dares to say that if one must judge, to be the latter is better than the former: 'to understand' he writes, 'is not more wonderful than to love'.[53] Still, he is very clear: to love without making an effort to understand is problematic—he details this clearly with the Little Ones. MacDonald—and Tolkien and Lewis after him—believed that in order to be a sub-creator, one must study works of creation: closely, with intention. Nothing comes from nothing. The more rich the foundation, the fount from which one's ink is drawn, the more rich the new creation. The greater the depth of engagement with that which has come before, the greater the dimensionality of the new creations that follow—creations likely, says MacDonald, to carry even more meaning than the authors intend.

In plainspeak: should one wish to write fantasy, these men would argue that the more intentional one is about reading texts that have engaged in that long conversation, and about reading such texts deeply, carefully—actually engaging with them, developing a type of relationship with them, spending time—the better one's fantastical writing will be. One will be less likely to have 'mythopoeic' slapped on by an optimistic publisher, and more likely to go down in the

---

51   Lewis, *Anthology*, p. 29; George MacDonald, 'The Fantastic Imagination', *A Dish of Orts* (Whitefish: Kessinger, 2004), p. 196.

52   'We spoil countless things by intellectual greed' ('Fantastic Imagination,' p. 194).

53   MacDonald, *Lilith*, p. 5.

annals as a truly mythopoeic writer in the tradition of the Inklings and MacDonald: a story crafter because one is a story scholar—and even more importantly, a story lover.

CONCLUSION

So, forget the small-town boy who broke free from his repressive religious background into the forbidden delights of Romanticism. Forget the penniless preacher forced to write fiction to feed his kids. Consider, instead, the farmboy raised in a world rich with story and imagination—of multiple genres—and with a love of science and of creation. Consider the young man encouraged by his father to explore theology and discover mentors worthy of admiration. And consider one of English Literature's early teachers—mentored by its first ever full-time professor. MacDonald was a Celt fluent in German and French literature, who read daily in Hebrew and Greek, who knew Shakespeare inside out,[54] and who wanted everyone to know his 'friends' Dante and Sidney and Herbert. He was a teacher-author passionate to draw others into a potentially transformative conversation of story upon story, agreeing, disagreeing, interweaving through genre and culture; keen to enable others to recognize patterns and convergences from classical and biblical through patristic and Celtic, medieval and renaissance, up through Romantic literature and beyond; determined to urge others to then respond to them—in the deep conviction that such responsive reading would evoke new perceptions.

Beware of pigeon-holing MacDonald into a category—beware even more pigeon-holing his influences. In the wealth of those stories that begat his own lie the roots of twentieth and twenty-first century fantasy, roots that will continue to sustain well into the centuries yet to come. Personally, I have discovered that the more effort I make to become acquainted with the many disparate writers to whom MacDonald proffers introductions, and the more I learn from my colleagues about who and what they have discovered, the further I progress in my own journey of understanding MacDonald as a writer. I have had to let go of many pre-conceptions and misconceptions

---

54 In 1874 MacDonald was a vice-president of the 'New Shakespere Society' [sic], which included a number of royals, academics, artists and bishops, including Ruskin, Dante Rossetti, the Cowper-Temples, Thomas H. Huxley and Max Müller (*Issue Two* 1). Browning was the president. That year, in London, MacDonald gave a six-lecture series on Shakespeare (Kings London 8/5/3).

along the way, and I have no doubt that such letting go will need to continue. But in trying to come to grips with what Lewis and Tolkien meant when they called MacDonald a mythopoeic writer, I think I have also come to a place of better understanding what makes their own fantasy as rich as it is. It is not pastiche; it is not second-hand symbols. Many such 'fantasy' novels do exist, and are currently being written. But there are also fantasy writers—'living and thoughtful readers'—such as Terry Pratchett, Neil Gaiman, Jennifer Trafton, Jeffrey Overstreet, Andrew Peterson—who, like Tolkien and Lewis and MacDonald, have read deeply, widely, well; who value dearly the conversations that have gone before, even those with which they do not agree; and who are now relating their own 'inventions'. Such are authors who love the mythopoeic art.

The authors who pioneered the way for modern fantasy were convinced that writers must be transformed by engagement with others before they could give voice to something new—especially if that work was to invite transformative insights or experiences for the reader. To stand in a tradition of mythopoeic story is both to receive and to be part of 'passing on' that which is infused with myths that have gone before. It is rooting oneself deeply in an inheritance of participation.[55] For me, this discovery was a—not the, a—golden key in my on-going progression of navigating the fantasy of Teacher–Author George MacDonald.

---

55 'When we read rejoicingly the true song-speech of one of our singing brethren, we hold song-worship with him and with all who have thus at any time shared in his feelings, even if he has passed centuries ago into the "high countries" of song' (*England's Antiphon*, p. 2).

BIBLIOGRAPHY

Amell, B., *The Art of God: Lectures on the Great Poets by George MacDonald*, Portland: Wingfold Books, 2004. Print.

Auden, W.H., Afterword, in MacDonald G., *The Golden Key*, London: The Bodley Head (1867), pp. 81-6. Print.

Barfield, Owen, *History in English Words*, London: Faber and Faber, 1926. Print.

Carlyle, Thomas, The Carlyle Letters Online [CLO]. http://carlyleletters.org [accessed September 2007]. (20:72-4)

Carpenter, Humphrey, *The Inklings*, London: Allen and Unwin, 1978. Print.

Chesterton, G.K., Introduction, in MacDonald G., *George MacDonald and His Wife*, London: George Allen & Unwin (1924), pp. 9-15. Print.

Gillies, M.A., *The Professional Literary Agent in Britain*, 1880-1920, Toronto: University of Toronto Press, 2007. Print.

Legge, J., Introduction, in G. Legge, *Lectures on Theology, Science, and Revelation*, London: Jackson, Walford, and Hodder (1863), pp. ix-xcviii. Print.

Lewis, C.S., *Collected Letters: Books, Broadcasts and War 1931-1949*, London: HarperCollins, 2004. Print.

Lewis, C.S., *George MacDonald: An Anthology*, London: Geoffrey Bles, 1946. Print.

Lewis, C.S., 'Myth Become Fact', *God in the Dock*, Glasgow: William Collins & Son Ltd, (1955), pp. 39-45. Print.

Lewis, C.S., *Letters of C. S. Lewis*, W.H. Lewis (ed.), London: Geoffrey Bles, 1966. Print.

Lewis, C.S., 'On Stories', *Of This and Other Worlds*, Glasgow: William Collins & Son Ltd (1982), pp. 25-45. Print.

MacDonald, George, *David Elginbrod*, London: Hurst & Blackett, Ltd, 1863. Print.

MacDonald, George, 'The Imagination: Its Functions and Its Culture', The British Quarterly Review, London: Hodder and Stoughton (1867), pp. 46-70. Print.

MacDonald, George, 'The Imagination: Its Functions and Its Culture', in J.H. Agnew (ed.), *The Eclectic Magazine of Foreign Literature, Science, and Art*, New York: Leavitt, Trow & Co. (1867), pp. 257-72. Print.

MacDonald, George, 'The Imagination: Its Functions and Its Culture', in W.J. Scott (ed.), *Scott's Monthly Magazine*, Atlanta: J.J. Toon (1867), pp. 658-69. Print.

MacDonald, George, *Donal Grant*, London: K. Paul, Trench & Co., 1883. Print.

MacDonald, George, *The Seaboard Parish*, London: K. Paul, Trench, & Co., 1886. Print.

MacDonald, George, *What's Mine's Mine*, Eureka, California: Sunrise Books, 1994. Print.

MacDonald, George, *Lilith*, Whitehorn, California: Johannesen, 1995. Print.

MacDonald, George, *England's Antiphon*, Whitehorn: Johannesen, 1996. Print.

MacDonald, George, 'The Fantastic Imagination', *A Dish of Orts*. Whitefish: Kessinger (2004), pp. 192-8. Print.

MacDonald, George, 'The Imagination: Its Functions and Its Culture', *A Dish of Orts*, Whitefish: Kessinger (2004), pp. 2-28. Print.

MacDonald, George, *Annals of a Quiet Neighbourhood*, London: Kegan Paul, Trench, Trübner, & Co. Ltd, n.d. Print.

MacDonald, George, *The Art of God: Lectures on the Great Poets by George MacDonald*, B. Amell (ed.), Portland: Wingfold Books, 2004. Print.

MacDonald, Greville, *George MacDonald and His Wife*, London: Allen & Unwin, 1924. Print.

MacDonald, Ronald, *From a Northern Window: A Personal Reminiscence of George MacDonald by His Son*, M. Phillips (ed.), Eureka: Sunrise Books, 1989. Print.

Newell, J.P., *A.J. Scott and His Circle*, Edinburgh: Edinburgh University, 1981. Print.

Peel, A., *Letters to a Victorian Editor: Henry Allen, Editor of the British Quarterly Review*, London: Independent Press, 1929. Print.

Raeper, William, *George MacDonald*, Tring: Lion Publishing, 1987. Print.

Ruskin, John, Letter to George MacDonald, 18 August 1865, George MacDonald Collection: Box 1, Folder 3, Document 27, Beinecke Rare Book & Manuscript Library, Yale University. [accessed November 2004].

Ruskin, John, *Modern Painters, Vol. 1-3*, Kent: George Allen, 1888. Print.

Ruskin, John, *Sesame and Lilies: Three Lectures*, New York: J. Wiley & Sons, 1888. Print.

Ruskin, John, *The Winnington Letters: John Ruskin's Correspondence with Margaret Alexis Bell and the Children at Winnington Hall*, V.A. Burd (ed.), Yale: Harvard University Press, 1969. Print.

Scott, A.J., *Two Discourses: The Kingdom of the Truth: The Ranges of Christianity*, London: Macmillan & Co., 1866. Print.

Scott, A.J., 'A Lecture on Popular Education', *Woolwich Gazette*, 10 October 1840. Print.

Scott, A.J., *Suggestions on Female Education: Two Introductory Lectures on English Literature & Moral Philosophy*. Delivered in the Ladies' College, Bedford Square By AJ Scott, Professor of the English Language & Literature in University College, London, London: Taylor, Walton & Maberly, 1849. Print.

Scott, A.J., 'On University Education', *Introductory Lectures on the Opening of Owens College*, Manchester, London: T. Sowler, 1852. Print.

Scott, A.J., *Notes of Four Lectures on the Literature and Philosophy of the Middle Ages*, Edinburgh: T. Constable, 1857. Print.

Scott, Patrick W., *The History of Strathbogie*, Glasgow: Bell & Bain Ltd, 1997. Print.

Sidney, Philip, *A Cabinet of Gems* (1891), G. MacDonald (ed.), London: Elliot Stock, 1893. Print.

Sidney, Philip, *A Defense of Poesie and Poems*, London: Cassell, 1909. Print.

Tolkien, J.R.R., *The Lord of the Rings, Book I*, London: HarperCollins, 1993, p. 257. Print.

Tolkien, J.R.R., 'Mythopoeia', *Tree and Leaf*, London: HarperCollins, 2001, pp. 85-90. Print.

Tolkien, J.R.R., 'On Fairy-stories', *Tree and Leaf*, London: HarperCollins, 2001, pp. 3-81. Print.

Troup, Robert, *The Missionar Kirk of Huntly*, Huntly: Joseph Dunbar, 1901. Print.

Wolff, Robert L., *The Golden Key: A Study of the Fiction of George MacDonald*, New Haven: Yale University Press, 1961. Print.

(no author), *The New Statistical Account of Scotland*, Edinburgh: W. Blackwood & Sons, 1845. Print.

(no author), 'The Late Professor A.J. Scott', *Scotsman*, 19 January 1866, p. 23. Print.

(no author), Issue Two of the New Shakespere Society: Romeo and Juliet, P. Daniel (ed.), London: Trübner, 1874. Print.

(no author), 'Huntly Correspondent–Obituary: George MacDonald', *Banffshire Journal*, 19 September 1905. Print.

Materiality, Metaphor and Mystery
Imagination and Humanity in
George MacDonald's *A Dish of Orts* (1893)

Trevor Hart

The place of imagination in mediating our distinctly human engagements with the world is a topic of vital interest to scholars in all manner of different intellectual fields, so pervasive is the phenomenon itself. This is true notwithstanding the difficulty of providing any very widely agreed account of what 'imagination' or 'the imaginative' actually is, and despite the fact that we naturally associate the relevant vocabulary with so many different sorts of activity and experience. What is likely to be of interest to the scholar concerned with all this, who, let us suppose, stumbles across a dusty copy of MacDonald's *A Dish of Orts*[1] in a secondhand bookshop and flicks through its pages, is the prescience both of the centrality which he afforded to the imaginative in the texture of human experience and of some of the concrete claims and insights concerning its particular function in regions of concern and modes of practice proper to a remarkably wide range of disciplines. MacDonald himself, of course, straddled an impressive range of learning, having benefitted from a Scottish education in which breadth rather than specialism was (and still is) held to be a desideratum in the formative stages. This is duly reflected in his capacity to discourse comfortably across intellectual boundaries which nowadays tend rather to divide learning up into a fragmented series of –isms and –ologies that find it increasingly hard to talk to one another, let alone understand one another. In this little volume of MacDonald's essays, those conversant with accounts of the imaginative and its distinct contributions in their own proper fields—whether philosophers, theologians, poets, cognitive scientists, psychologists, or others—are likely to find interesting suggestions and anticipations of ideas and connections prominent in cutting edge treatments of the subject today, well over a century after MacDonald's pieces were written.

My purpose in this essay is simply to offer an overview of some of the more distinctive claims MacDonald makes about the importance of the imaginative in human life, and to do so under three headings:

---

1   George MacDonald, *A Dish of Orts* (Whitehorn: Johannesen, 1996) [orig. Sampson Low, Marston and Co., 1893].

(1) Imagination is that in us which images God most fully

Theologians and biblical scholars have wrestled since the beginning of Christian history to offer a satisfactory account of just what it means to say that human beings, distinct in this from any other of God's creatures, are made in the image and likeness of God. Plenty of confident suggestions have been made—for instance, that it is in our power of reasoning, or our freedom, or our essentially social and relational nature as persons that we bear some creaturely analogy or likeness to who God is, imaging him forth, as it were, in the midst of the world.[2] No doubt MacDonald was familiar enough with the exegetical complexities, and the resilient density of the biblical text itself, resisting any easy or neat interpretation. But he was confident enough to throw in his own ten dollars worth anyway! Surely, he suggests, it is in our imaginative disposition towards things that we draw closest to God in his own disposition towards us as our Creator?[3]

Imagination, MacDonald argues, is that which gives form to things[4]—in our case, giving meaningful form to thought, beheld first and foremost in our mind's eye, but capable of utterance or issue in the external world through some sensible manifestation. But is this, he enquires, not precisely an analogy of God's own creative activity— first conjuring up an orderly cosmos in his eternal mind's eye, an immanent 'Logos' or meaning through which God then, in his own good time, summons into being an actual external world teeming with form, and with the potential for more form and more meaning to be broken forth from it yet at the hands of creatures endowed, like himself, with the imagination and creative vision to do so. Thus, he suggests, as God's creatures we actually have an ambiguous and wonderful status—for while on the one hand we are quite distinct from God himself, existing alongside him and able to enter into fellowship or dispute with him, viewed from a different perspective we are, like the characters in a novelist's novel or the shapes and colours on a painter's canvas, first and foremost thoughts in the mind of the divine artist. We are, as MacDonald puts it, 'the offspring of

---

2   For a helpful overview as well as distinctive treatment see Philip Edgcumbe Hughes, *The True Image: The Origin and Destiny of Man in Christ* (Grand Rapids: Eerdmans, 1989); J. Richard Middleton, *The Liberating Image: The* Imago Dei *in Genesis 1* (Grand Rapids: Brazos, 2005).

3   MacDonald, *A Dish of Orts*, p. 3.

4   Ibid., p. 2.

(God's) imagination',[5] and in the strictest sense, therefore, all that we in our turn make or are capable of making or that is capable of being made also lives and moves and has its being first and foremost in the *imaginatio Dei*—the imagination of God. Not everything that God imagines, we must suppose, is thereby possessed of actual existence alongside him; but all that exists begins with an act of divine imagining, and not otherwise. And here, of course, we run up quickly and hard against a fundamental difference between God and us, and between the power of God's imagination and ours. For God himself is not the product of anyone else's imagining, whereas we are always the product of his. And whereas, in our own imagining, whatever we imagine must always begin with the world God has placed us in and borrow something from its given forms and possibilities, God's imagining borrows from nothing and no one, being the sole instance of absolute origination.[6]

MacDonald's line of argument here anticipates that developed in the late 1930s by Dorothy L. Sayers, first in her drama *The Zeal of Thy House* (1937), and then subsequently and more fully in her popular monograph *The Mind of the Maker* (1941). The latter was presented (and is generally understood) as a piece of skillful apologetic intended to commend the doctrine of the Trinity to the reading public. Although it certainly does this, its more profound theological point lies in its positing of a strong analogy between the structure of acts of creative imagination as experienced humanly on the one hand and the inner ratio of God's own being and life as Father, Son and Holy Spirit on the other, 'an earthly trinity/to match the heavenly'.[7] MacDonald, though, was much more circumspect in his handling of the theological idea, insisting that the differences between divine and human imagining far outstrip the likenesses, not least as regards the sources of human imagining in God's own, so that *stricto sensu*, no human artist is ever

---

5   Ibid., p. 4.

6   Ibid., p. 4.

7   Dorothy L. Sayers, *The Zeal of Thy House* (London: Victor Gollancz Ltd., 1937), p.110. See further: Dorothy L. Sayers, *The Mind of the Maker* (London: Methuen, 1941), passim; Dorothy L. Sayers, 'Towards a Christian Aesthetic' in V. A. Demant (ed) *Our Culture, Its Christian Roots and Present Crisis* (London: SPCK, 1944), p.50-69. On the more immediate roots of Sayers' idea in the writings of R. G Collingwood, Jacques Maritain and others see Trevor Hart, *Making Good: Creation, Creativity and Artistry* (Waco: Baylor University Press) p. 267-73.

a 'Creator', not even yet a 'poet', but merely a *trouvère*, a 'finder'.[8] C. S. Lewis no doubt learned his own theological resistance to prodigal uses of the language of 'creativity' from MacDonald, and in one of the earliest reviews of *The Mind of the Maker* he takes Sayers to task on this very point.[9]

(2) IMAGINATION, AS THE ORGAN OF MEANING, GRANTS US A WORLD FIT FOR HUMAN HABITATION

The nineteenth century has often been seen as the period in which literary 'realism' came into its own, with the documentary prose of the novels of Eliot, Dickens, Dostoevsky and others all concerned in some sense to show 'reality as it truly is'. Despite his association with the genres of fairytale and fantasy, in his novels MacDonald was not immune from this wider literary trend, yet even here his working definition of 'reality' was calibrated rather differently to some. Mindful of the impact of contemporary science—or, more accurately, the materialistic philosophies which all too often clung to and hijacked the findings of science proper—MacDonald was forever concerned to challenge the positivist suggestion that 'reality' may ever be had at the level of empirical observation alone, even if it may not be had apart from it. So he has little time for an art concentrated on mere empirical mimesis. Instead, his writing conjures up a vision of a world in which a complex order of non-material and spiritual realities is set in glorious counterpoint to the material sphere of 'Nature', and human beings are understood (as indeed, as a Christian, MacDonald himself understood them) to be wonderfully—if at times uncomfortably— situated as conscious participants in both dimensions at once. In us and perhaps in us alone, in other words, the material and the non-material meet and interpenetrate, and it is the predicament of our circumstance to have to hold these together and to mediate the realities of each to and through the realities of the other.

What MacDonald sees is that it is imagination which is at the very heart of our capacity to do this, and which is thus in some sense the vital centre of operations of all that is truly human. Taking his cue from the observation of Novalis that 'The imagination is the stuff of

---

8   MacDonald, *A Dish of Orts*, pp. 2, 20.

9   C. S. Lewis, review of Dorothy L. Sayers, *The Mind of the Maker*, in *Theology* (London: SPCK) Volume XLIII, No. 256, October 1941, pp. 248-9.

the intellect',[10] he offers a shrewd account of the imagination's role in discerning and constructing the fields of 'meaningfulness' which are basic even to our most 'hard-edged' and 'detached' engagements with Nature.[11] Having trained as a chemist, for instance, he entertained (and would tolerate) no romantic illusions about the dispassionate, objective, law-based labours of men and women in white coats and brandishing clipboards. From the levels of observation and experiment upward, he insists, science is from first to last a thoroughly *imaginative* enterprise, and nowhere more so than when it ventures into the territories of the as yet uncharted. Thus, 'The region belonging to the pure intellect is straitened: the imagination labours to extend its territories, to give it room. She sweeps across the borders, searching out new lands into which she may guide her plodding brother'.[12] MacDonald's point, though, is not to perpetuate sharp and unhelpful distinctions between 'faculties' of intellect and imagination, but to suggest their insufficiency to address the complex phenomenology of thought and experience.

Where language (including that forged in the sciences) is concerned, MacDonald illustrates the irreducibility of the imaginative nicely by observing that all the words we use to refer to 'inner' or non-material realities and states are borrowed from a lexicon pertaining in the first instance to the physical realm.[13] So, for example, when we say that we are paying attention (a mental, non-material state of affairs), a bit of careful etymology quickly reveals a bit of inspired poetry buried deep in the apparently straightforward utterance. The Latin word *attentio* originally meant a physical 'stretching towards' something (in the gym, or while cleaning windows), its meaning having at some point itself been stretched by metaphorical transference and given

---

10 MacDonald, *A Dish of Orts*, pp.14

11 MacDonald himself would have been quick to point out the irreducibly metaphorical and ironic nature of such ways of describing the scientific *modus operandi*.

12 MacDonald, *A Dish of Orts*, p. 14. Lewis develops this point in his own way, insisting that the imagination is the organ of 'meaning', and the intellect the organ of 'truth'. *Meaning*, he observes, 'is the antecedent condition both of truth and falsehood, whose antithesis is not error but nonsense'. See 'Bluspels and Falansferes' in C. S. Lewis, *Rehabilitations and Other Essays* (London: Oxford University Press, 1939), p. 157.

13 MacDonald, *A Dish of Orts*, pp. 8-9.

a quite new task to perform.[14] The underlying connection is obvious enough with the benefit of hindsight, but someone once made or traced that connection, and so enlarged and enhanced the range of language, and granted the power of expression to a reality which otherwise remained mute. Plenty of other examples could be supplied, because, MacDonald argues, finally all inner states, all thoughts, all feelings can only be shared, uttered, articulated in meaningful ways by virtue of our capacity to clothe them in concrete form, to associate them with realities with which we have to do in the material world— whether those are words, or bodily gestures, or material objects taken and used or modified in particular ways.

Viewed from the other side, it is imagination which sees *more* than the eye alone presents to us for consideration, grasping material objects and events as something *more* than, considered in and of themselves, they actually are—as charged with meaning and significance, things that the eye *cannot* see and the hand *cannot* touch. The power of symbol or the poetic image, and our capacity to fashion and to grasp these, in other words, far from being some peripheral extra or playful ornament to a human existence more properly focused on hard facts, is absolutely fundamental to our meaningful human intercourse with the world itself and with other people.[15] Indeed, to identify something as a 'fact' at all is already to have behaved imaginatively, endowing some object contained in space and time with 'significance', a judgment situating it in the terms proper to a quite different order of existence, and so placing one foot on the slippery slope that leads to artistry. Indeed, artistry, for MacDonald, is at its best a heuristic device just as powerful in penetrating to the reality of things as any scientific model or hypothesis, its poor 'country cousins', so to speak, in the shared world of the imaginative. The felicitous metaphor, the arresting painting, the heart-rending sonata each prove to be so much more than, considered as assemblages of sensory data alone, they themselves are—opening out onto a world of meaning and feeling otherwise unavailable to us, and every bit as 'real' as the stone we bump into inadvertently on the footpath.

---

14 MacDonald borrows the example from Thomas Carlyle.

15 MacDonald, *A Dish of Orts*, pp. 10-14.

(3) Imagination as the Reflex of Creation Unites Creativity and Discovery, and so Grants Us Hope

How then are we to account for all this? How is it that there exists an entire dimension of meaning and value and shared significance into which imagination keys us humanly just as surely as our bodies extend us into the world of spatial and temporal coordinates? Is it all, as we might say, *just* our imagination? Is the whole cultural, linguistic, artistic order which sheathes the material world and makes it habitable by creatures like ourselves no more than a fleeting epiphenomenon, 'unreal' in the strictest sense, so much spume on the surface, waiting to be blown away by the slightest wind of history, transience or death? MacDonald was well aware that there were plenty of materialist intellectuals out there peddling some such account in his day, just as there are in ours; but it is one which he frankly finds incredible, and genuinely expects the majority of his readers, after only a little serious reflection, to do the same.[16]

Materialism (and its intellectual twin Idealism) leave humanity, after all, in a forbidding and finally hopeless cosmos in which our capacity and desire for 'humanitas' itself (the realization of civilization, culture and the flourishing of the human spirit) appears as cold comfort, being little more than a cruel joke played upon us by 'cold, impassive, material law',[17] the casting of a coloured shadow over the meaningless indifference of mechanical necessity. And such an account inevitably showers accolades on human shoulders for the sheer creative prowess which has conjured such a marvellous world (illusory, but marvellous) into being, credit to which, MacDonald realizes, few of the genuine poets and artists among us would wish to lay claim at all, knowing their own 'creative' relation with the things to be of a much more subtle and complex sort than this, and as much about finding and discovering what is there as it ever is about making or constructing something new.[18]

---

16 His argument against such reductionist visions (which in many ways anticipates those articulated by C. S. Lewis sixty years or so later) is contained chiefly in the essay 'A Sketch of Individual Development' [1880] in MacDonald, *A Dish of Orts*, pp. 43–76.

17 MacDonald, *A Dish of Orts*, pp. 62.

18 Ibid., p. 24. MacDonald addresses directly the then current (and today still common) speculation that would push the relevant creative mechanism into the shadows of the unconscious (individual or corporate). He sees no reason to deny this, but every reason to offer a solidly theological account of

MacDonald's vision, therefore, was of a material cosmos wedded naturally and properly to a non-material order which penetrates it through and through, the links between them being such that the things of the material cosmos may be invested with and bear and express the significances of the immaterial, not by sheer convention and the arbitrary designs of human imagining, but naturally, by virtue of a deeper connectivity forged in the creation of the world itself, that it might be a habitation fit for the flourishing of human beings, those most imaginative of creatures.[19] This is how MacDonald understood it—a world crying out for imaginative response, because already laden with a surplus or excess of symbolic significance. A world, furthermore, teeming with further meaning as yet to be discovered or given birth. For here, again, in the sphere of imaginative response, MacDonald recognised, there is a paradoxical interplay between the heuristic and the creative,[20] even our most daring trespasses beyond what the world already has to offer frequently feeling as though the new creative thought or vision itself is one in some sense already 'out there' placing us under obligation, revealing itself to us, waiting to be uncovered or given voice, rather than sheerly summoned into being by the artistic imagination. And in some sense, of course, it is always thus. No artist or writer or composer ever begins *de novo*, but draws more or less consciously on fragments, samples of experience which he then reconfigures into something new. But MacDonald insists upon a theological and religious rather than a merely sociological or psychological account of the matter. God, he suggests, has hidden things—meanings, imaginative possibilities, works and worlds of art—in the depths of the world that he has made. And even in our most creative ventures, therefore, we are in truth 'following and finding out' what God has already imagined and given to the world as part of its developmental potential,[21] and in poetry as well as in science (albeit often in a different mode) the chief role of imagination

---

the matter: 'From that unknown region we grant they come, but not by its own blind working. ... God sits in that chamber of our being in which the candle of consciousness goes out in darkness, and sends forth from thence wonderful gifts into the light of that understanding which is His candle. Our hope lies in no most perfect mechanism even of the spirit, but in the wisdom wherein we live and move and have our being' (pp. 24-5).

19 Ibid., p. 8.

20 'The man who cannot invent will never discover'. Ibid., p.13.

21 Ibid., pp. 41-2.

is '(t)o inquire into what God has made'.[22]

In one of his own critical essays G. K. Chesterton suggests that the achievement of the great critic is to bring forth from the poem, the novel, the painting or whatever it might be, new depths of meaning which have hitherto remained hidden, possibly even to the artist him or herself. MacDonald has a cognate thought, though he insists that God is the only artist whose work cannot contain more potential for meaning than he himself is aware of. Nonetheless, the plenitude of meaning divinely invested in the world in the beginning takes time to unfold; much of it (perhaps by far the larger part) remains even yet hidden, requiring the work of human imagination and human hands to find it and share in its realization. In this task, MacDonald's account places us—as those created in the image of an imaginative God—in the role of Chesterton's critics, whose own creative labours are always secondary and subordinate to a world of meaning which holds them accountable, but without whom much of that world will remain mute, obscure and so unenjoyed. This is true of each of us, since each of us is called to respond imaginatively and make more (rather than less) of what we have been given; but it is true in a particular way of those in human society who most obviously and deliberately lay hold of some part of the world and, by reconfiguring it, offer it back to us for consideration and delight. For MacDonald, in other words, the poet and the artist provide a fitting paradigm and symbol of all that it means to be human in God's world, and while, as we have seen, he was nervous about applying the term 'creation' to their work (only God truly 'creates' anything he insists),[23] he nonetheless clearly understood that work (and with it our own) as a sharing in God's own continuing creative engagement with the world, a coinherence of imaginative energies and a dynamic sharing in the glory which is properly God's own.

Although I have noted in passing some themes in MacDonald's account of our imaginative disposition towards the world taken up by others associated with the Inklings, I have not attempted to justify my earlier suggestion that his thought anticipates the insights and emphases of cutting edge theorists in other fields today. To do so properly would demand a much longer essay. But readers familiar

---

22   Ibid., p. 2.

23   Thus 'We must not forget … that between creator and poet lies the one unpassable gulf which distinguishes … all that is God's from all that is man's; … It is better (therefore) to keep the word creation for that calling out of nothing which is the imagination of God'. Ibid., pp. 2-3.

with the work of philosophers such as Richard Kearney and Mark Johnson, or treatments of language by George Steiner and Paul Ricoeur, or the remarkable work of Iain McGilchrist on the structure of the human brain and its implications for understanding Western culture will already have identified MacDonald's work as eerily prescient of developments whose 'time' has only come more than a century after MacDonald put pen to paper.[24] His conviction that the imaginative was in some sense the clue to so much in our 'species being' is corroborated and summed up neatly (albeit in less explicitly theological terms) by Kearney's tantalizing suggestion that, for human beings such as ourselves, 'Better to appreciate what it means to imagine [is] better to understand what it is to be'.[25]

---

24   See, e.g., Richard Kearney, *The Wake of Imagination* (London: Routledge, 1988); Richard Kearney, *Poetics of Imagining: Modern to Postmodern*, 2nd edn., (Edinburgh: Edinburgh University Press, 1998); *Mark Johnson, The Meaning of the Body: Aesthetics of Human Understanding* (Chicago: University of Chicago Press, 2007); George Steiner, *After Babel: Aspects of Language and Translation*, 2nd edn. (Oxford: Oxford University Press, 1992); Paul Ricoeur, *The Rule of Metaphor: Multidisciplinary Studies of the Creation of Meaning in Language*, trans. R. Czerny and others (Toronto and Buffalo: Toronto University Press, 1977); Iain McGilchrist, *The Master and His Emissary: The Divided Brain and the Making of the Western World* (New Haven: Yale University Press, 2009).

25   Kearney, *Poetics of Imagining*, p. 1.

BIBLIOGRAPHY

Kearney, Richard, *Poetics of Imagining: Modern to Postmodern*, 2nd edn, Edinburgh: Edinburgh University Press, 1998.

Lewis, C.S., 'Bluspels and Falansferes', *Rehabilitations and Other Essays*, London: Oxford University Press, 1939. p. 157.

Lewis, C.S., 'Review of *The Mind of the Maker*', *Theology*, London: Society for promoting Christian Knowledge, Vol. XLIII, No. 256, Oct 1941, 248-9.

MacDonald, George, 'A Sketch of Individual Development', (1880), *A Dish of Orts*, Whitehorn: Johannesen, 1996. pp. 43-76.

MacDonald, George, 'The Imagination: Its Functions and Its Culture', (1880), *A Dish of Orts*, Whitehorn: Johannesen, 1996. pp. 1-42.

Sayers, Dorothy L., *The Mind of the Maker*, London: Methuen, 1941.

Sayers, Dorothy L., *The Zeal of Thy House*, London: Victor Gollancz, 1937.

Organised Innocence:
MacDonald, Lewis and Literature
'For the Childlike'

Daniel Gabelman

There is a place where contraries are equally true.   William
Blake, *Milton*

The beautiful is that in which the many, still seen as the
many, become one.   S. T. Coleridge, 'On Principles of Genial
Criticism'

In 'The Fantastic Imagination' George MacDonald claims
'not to write [fairytales] for children, but for the childlike, whether
of five, or fifty, or seventy-five'.[1] Similarly, C. S. Lewis says that he
never set out to write fairy tales for children but instead 'everything
began with images' that 'bubbled up' in his mind.[2] Once these
images began sorting themselves out he discovered a 'longing' for the
fairy tale form as the best means of saying what he wanted to say.
Following the lead of J.R.R. Tolkien, Lewis also denies that fairy
tales are intrinsically connected with children: 'the whole association
of fairy tale and fantasy with children is local and accidental'. The
fairy tale 'gravitated to the nursery when it became unfashionable in
literary circles'.[3] Both writers, in other words, deliberately distance
themselves from the 'children's literature' label, refusing to accept the
child/adult dichotomy. One of the obvious reasons for this is because
stories written specifically for children are often seen as aesthetically
second-rate. Since children lack certain faculties of judgment, the
argument goes, it is easy to give them artistically inferior works.
Lewis says that he is 'almost inclined to set it up as a canon that a
children's story which is enjoyed only by children is a bad children's

---

1   George MacDonald, 'The Fantastic Imagination', in *A Dish of Orts*
(Whitehorn: Johannesen, 1996), p. 317.

2   C. S. Lewis, 'Sometimes Fairy Stories May Say Best What's To Be
Said', in *Essay Collection & Other Short Pieces* (London: HarperCollins,
2000), p. 527.

3   C. S. Lewis, 'On Three Ways of Writing for Children', in *Essay
Collection & Other Short Pieces* (London: HarperCollins, 2000), p. 508.

story.[4] Likewise MacDonald speaks of fairy tales as 'genuine works of art,' and he compares them to living things such as butterflies, bees, fireflies and roses.[5] Both writers are thus concerned with defending the aesthetic integrity and vitality of their stories against people who want to reduce them to their meaning or moral. 'The only moral that is of any value,' says Lewis, 'is that which arises inevitably from the whole cast of the author's mind. Indeed everything in the story should arise from the whole cast of the author's mind [...] the story should be a part of the habitual furniture of our minds.'[6] Good stories in some sense reflect the shape, structure and ethos of an author's mind. Lewis's comment here gestures to a philosophical reason why he and MacDonald avoid characterizing their fairy tales as merely 'for children'. When MacDonald says he writes 'for the childlike', he is not—to use Tolkien's phrase in 'On Fairy-stories'—'indulging in waggeries' and 'false sentiment'.[7] Instead, 'the childlike' is integral to MacDonald's 'whole cast of mind'. It is part of his habitual mental furniture, as it is also for Lewis.

The first part of this paper will therefore attempt to place MacDonald's concept of the childlike within the philosophical and theological dialogue about the nature of childhood and the role of stories in education. Echoing Plato's comments in *The Republic* on the role of stories in education, John Milbank says, 'since children first learn through pictures and stories, the selection of the right stories told the right way [is] *the most central concern of philosophy*', and I think MacDonald and Lewis would agree.[8] MacDonald's concept of the childlike is a deep, sustained reflection upon numerous philosophical and theological traditions, striving to get at this 'most central concern of philosophy'. And MacDonald, to my mind, is one of the pre-eminent thinkers on the subject. In the second part, I will consider how this idea of the childlike transformed MacDonald's whole cast of mind to such an extent that not just the content of his fairy tales was affected but the form itself. If Lewis is right about good stories reflecting the mental shape and atmosphere or their authors, then we

---

4   Ibid., p. 507.

5   MacDonald, 'The Fantastic Imagination', p. 317.

6   Lewis, 'On Three Ways of Writing for Children', p. 514.

7   J. R. R. Tolkien, 'On Fairy-stories', in *A Tolkien Miscellany* (New York: Science Fiction Book Club, 2002), p. 115.

8   John Milbank, 'Fictioning Things: Gift and Narrative', *Religion & Literature* 37.3 (2005), p. 9.

should be able to observe the childlike emerging continually in their stories, not just in the characters, themes and images but in the very structure and style.

PART I: INFLAMING THE IMAGINATION

The genre known today as 'children's literature' is sometimes said to have been birthed in the philosophies of John Locke and Jean-Jacques Rousseau.[9] Locke can be linked with the didactic trend in children's literature whereas Rousseau championed the rival view of Romanticism. In a book entitled *Some Thoughts Concerning Education* (1693) Locke argues that in all adults 'nine parts of ten are what they are, good and evil, useful or not, by their education'.[10] In other words, the child's mind is a 'tabula rasa', a blank tablet on which parents and educators inscribe. Thus it is of paramount importance what reading is given to a child; blank slates are also easily marred. Initially, children should be given 'easy pleasant books' which they enjoy so that they 'may learn to read without knowing it' for, Locke says, 'children should not have any thing like work, or serious, laid on them; neither their minds, nor bodies may bear it.'[11] Locke advocates the use of play and games to teach children reading and writing because 'thus children may be cozen'd into knowledge'.[12] Nevertheless educators must make sure not to 'fill his Head with perfectly useless trumpery, or lay principles of Vice and Folly'.[13] To this end, he recommends *Aesop's Fables* because they are able simultaneously 'to delight and entertain a child' and yet 'they may afford useful Reflections to a grown man'.[14]

This may seem fairly sensible and restrained, yet in everything

---

9   According to Jacqueline Rose, 'Literature for children first became an independent commercial venture in England in the mid- to late-eighteenth century, at a time when conceptualization of childhood was dominated by the philosophical writings of Locke and Rousseau.' She further says that 'children's fiction has never completed severed its links' with these philosophies of childhood. Jacqueline Rose, *The Case of Peter Pan: The Impossibility of Children's Fiction* (Philadelphia: University of Pennsylvania Press, 1984), p. 8.

10   John Locke, *Some Thoughts Concerning Education* (London: J. Hatchard and Son, 1836), p. 7.

11   Ibid., pp. 236, 233, 231.

12   Ibid., p. 231.

13   Ibid., p. 236.

14   Ibid., pp. 236-37.

Locke stresses usefulness and instrumentality. One wonders what Locke would have considered 'useless trumpery'—quite possibly he would have judged the fairy tales coming out of the French court in the late 17th century as such. Even Aesop's Fables are not advocated as being good in themselves, but merely because in adult life they might prove *useful*—their clear morality guards them from being an embarrassment to the adult. In England Locke's educational theory was the cardinal work for most of the eighteenth century, and it laid the groundwork for the Enlightenment and Utilitarian ideas about children's literature that dominated until the Romantics and continued to exert a powerful influence on Victorian Britain.

Coupled with Locke's view of the instrumentality of books for children was the Puritan and Evangelical view typified by John Bunyan. In a prefatory poem to his *Book for Boys and Girls* (1686) Bunyan says:

> Nor do I blush, although I think some may
> Call me a Baby, 'cause I with them play
> I do't to shew them how each Fingle-fangle,
> On which they doting are, their Souls entangle,
> As with a Web, a Trap, a Gin, or Snare
> And will destroy them, have they not a Care.
>   [...]
> By their Play-things, I would them entice
> To mount their Thoughts from what are childish Toys
> To Heav'n[15]

Bunyan condescends to childish rhyming only in order to save children's souls from the webs, traps and snares of childish games and toys. The child, for Bunyan, like all humanity is born into sin and is beset by dangers on every side. Children need to learn to fear the wiles and deception of ephemeral amusements lest they are led along the broad and easy path to Vanity Fair. The most important thing for Bunyan, therefore, is the religious message of the books given to children—the poetry is a mere vehicle for transmitting theology in a form deemed suitable to children. Bunyan assumes for himself the role of a wise guide or correcting shepherd who pulls lost lambs back from hidden precipices and ravenous wolves. Caught between this potent mix of enlightened Utilitarianism and Evangelical piety, no wonder the eighteenth century has left little in the way of children's

---

15 John Bunyan, *A Book for Boys and Girls* (London: Elliot Stock, 1889), p. xxxi.

literature that appeals either to children or adults today.

The concatenation of these two didactic trends meant that fantastic literature for children was frowned upon by the educated and fairy tales were forced underground. Writing at the end of the eighteenth century, Maria Edgeworth (whose influence lasted long into the nineteenth century) argued that 'the history of realities' were 'better suited to the purposes of education [...] than improbable fictions'.[16] She particularly recommended natural histories such as 'the histories of the bee, the ant, the caterpillar, the butterfly, and the silk-worm'.[17] In the preface to her own book of *Moral Tales* she claims to 'display examples of virtue, without initiating the young reader into the ways of vice' and that her tales will 'neither dissipate attention, nor inflame the imagination'.[18] What Edgeworth and others like her offer are moral and practical paragons; even the titles of her stories are blatant in their moral aim ('The Good Aunt', 'The Bad Governess' and 'The Good Governess'). Writers for children were supposed to produce ideal exemplar characters of high virtue and moral standing that children could then emulate. Meanwhile, Edgeworth warns against the dangers of 'inflaming the imagination' of children with impossible journeys and creatures because it might cause dissipation and discontent in later life. Here again, great anxiety overshadows literature for children. Above all, children need protection, but they also need moral prodding if they are to develop into useful, well-socialized adults.

Edgeworth's disciples in the nineteenth century included Sarah Trimmer who wrote a book called *Fabulous Histories* in which she teaches children about nature through a variety of talking birds. Anxious not to be seen as 'inflaming the imagination' of children, Trimmer, somewhat too self-consciously, says 'before [my children] began to read these Histories, they were taught to consider them, not as containing the real conversations of birds, (for that is impossible we should ever understand,) but as a series of Fables, intended to convey moral instruction applicable to themselves'.[19] Writers in this tradition

---

16 Maria Edgeworth, *Practical Education* (New York: Harper & Brothers, 1855), p. 250.

17 Ibid., p. 252-3.

18 Maria Edgeworth, *Moral Tales* (New York: W. B. Gilley, 1819), pp. iii, iv.

19 Sarah Trimmer, *Fabulous Histories* (London: J. G. & F. Rivington, 1838), p. 1.

seem to have a genuine fear that children will suddenly fly away to the birds if they are not regularly and solemnly reminded that fantasy is not real. As blank slates and wayward souls, children cannot be trusted to interpret things for themselves—they must be checked and corrected at every step.

Of course, this is only part of the story. Even in the eighteenth century a subterranean host of chapbooks and 'penny dreadfuls' kept the commoners and educational deviants well supplied with fantastic stories—particularly fairy tales such as the *Arabian Nights* and 'Jack the Giant-Killer'. In a letter to Coleridge from October 1802, Charles Lamb laments the influence of Edgeworth and Trimmer on children's literature, calling them 'Blights and Blasts of all that is human in man and child' and wondering 'what you would have been now, if instead of being fed with tales and old wives' fables in childhood, you had been crammed with geography and natural history!'[20] The monolithic, domineering reign of utility and rationality thus led almost inevitably to the revolution of Romanticism.

Jean Jacques Rousseau was obviously crucial in initiating Romanticism and shaping its view of the child. Despite the treatises of Locke and other philosophers, Rousseau claims that 'we do not know childhood'.[21] For Rousseau, the child was not a blank slate, nor an unformed adult, but a pure being existing close to the natural state of things. Reacting against the excesses of rationality and industrialization and drawing on the tradition of 'the noble savage', Rousseau thought the child was born completely in accord with nature. Like the peaceful, honest and kind savages of which Europeans were receiving news and imaginatively constructing as imperialism extended its reach across the globe, children were innately good, loving and beautiful. Above all, the child displayed the attribute of innocence. Rousseau abandoned the Christian doctrine of original sin as an explanation for the corruption within humanity, instead saying that society was the source of the taint. Oppressive institutions like governments, schools, churches and businesses taught the child selfishness, cruelty and perversity. *Emile*, Rousseau's book on the ideal education of a child, begins: 'Everything is good as it comes from the hands of the Author

20 Charles Lamb, *The Best Letters of Charles Lamb*, edited by Edward Gilpin Johnson, Project Gutenberg http://www.gutenberg.org/files/10125/10125-8. txt [accessed 29 November 2014].

21 Jean Jacques Rousseau, *Emile*, translated by William H. Payne (New York and London: D. Appleton and Company, 1918), p. xlii.

of Nature; but everything degenerates in the hands of man'.[22] As a result of human corruption, Rousseau removes his ideal child from culture and rears him in nature. Nature is a better teacher—or rather the child already has the essential teachings within them, they just need to be sheltered in nature's bosom from the depravity of society. Rousseau thus believed that learning knowledge and facts should not begin until thirteen—giving nature sufficient opportunity to nurture and educate the child without human interference. Rousseau also denied books to children—they were too dangerous, for they carried the seeds of innumerable cultural weeds that might at any moment sprout in the child's isolated and carefully guarded Eden. Jacqueline Rose observes how 'there is an obvious paradox that Rousseau should be seen as a founding father of children's fiction in England given his suspicion of writing'.[23] Moreover, in Rousseau's thought the child also becomes a kind of portal or bridge for adults who have lost their innocence. There is not a smooth transition between child and adult; rather the two are cut off by the corrupting taint of commerce, culture and sexuality. The child's world, says fellow Romantic Novalis, is 'terrae incognitae'.[24] In other words, the child is foreign, strange and possessed of mysterious powers—powers the adult can only dimly recall but for which he longs fervently.

This philosophy led to a radical counter-trend in children's literature which slowly gained ground against the moralistic, didactic literature for children, and which emerged relatively victorious by the end of the nineteenth century. Lewis Carroll, Hans Christian Anderson and Edward Lear were amongst many who held this Romantic position. For them, the child exists in a sort of sacred state that is purer than the adult condition, and as a result the desires of children should be paramount. At first blush, this view seems to let the child read whatever she pleases, but of course an essential caveat is that seriousness, morality and usefulness must be denied the child because of the fear that contamination from the adult world might potentially infect the child's natural innocence and inflame their imagination.

---

22 Ibid., p. 1.

23 Jacqueline Rose, *The Case of Peter Pan: The Impossibility of Children's Fiction* (Philadelphia: University of Pennsylvania Press, 1984), p. 47.

24 Quoted in *Bettina Kümmerling-Meibauer*, 'Images of Childhood in Romantic Children's Literature' in *Romantic Prose Fiction*, edited by Gerald Gillespie, Manfred Engel and Bernard Dieterle (Amsterdam: Benjamins, 2008), p. 184.

Aesthetics is thus given priority over utility, though pristine beauty also requires anxious guarding. So, for example, when Lewis Carroll sent George MacDonald's oldest daughter Lilia a somewhat didactic children's book solely for the sake of the decorations he writes: 'the book is intended for you to look at the outside, and then put it away in the bookcase: the *inside* is not meant to be read. The book has got a moral—so I need hardly say it is *not* by Lewis Carroll'.[25] The statement is playful, but clearly it veils certain anxieties about what is and is not appropriate for children. Pretty Pre-Raphaelite designs: yes—earnest adult morality: no. It also suggests that Carroll feared that children might view him as an adult, because adults are outsiders, and potential adulterators of the child's untainted world. Even worse, if the child perceived Carroll as a threat to her innocent idylls she might deny him access to her Eden.

In *Alice in Wonderland* Carroll satirises the moralistic strain in Victorian education particularly in the character of the Duchess who confidently tells Alice: 'tut, tut, child! Everything's got a moral, if only you can find it'.[26] The Duchess is condescending throughout her conversation with Alice, and like the Queen of Hearts who threatens the Duchess with execution, freely employs violence when dealing with subordinates, even her own child. To Carroll morals similarly are a kind of violence to children because morals seem to transgress uninvited from the adult world of power and possessiveness into the child's carefree world of fun, demanding that the child see the world like an adult—for its usefulness. Oscar Wilde articulates this view even more clearly in his story 'The Devoted Friend' in which a linnet tells a story with an unambiguous moral to a water-rat, who represents something of the Wildean persona:

> "I am afraid you don't quite see the moral of the story," remarked the Linnet.
> "The what?" screamed the Water-rat.
> "The moral."
> "Do you mean to say that the story has a moral?"
> "Certainly," said the Linnet.
> "Well, really," said the Water-rat, in a very angry manner, "I think you should have told me that before you began. If you

---

25 Morton N. Cohen, ed., *The Letters of Lewis Carroll*, 2 vols. (London: Macmillan, 1979), I: p. 96.

26 Lewis Carroll, *The Complete Works of Lewis Carroll* (New York: Barnes and Noble, 1994), p. 88.

had done so, I certainly would not have listened to you; in fact, I should have said 'Pooh,' like the critic. However, I can say it now"; so he shouted "Pooh" at the top of his voice, gave a whisk with his tail, and went back into his hole.

The Linnet then encounters a mother duck who asks him what happened, and he responds:

'I am afraid that I have annoyed him, I have told him a story with a moral.'
'Ah! That is always a very dangerous thing to do,' said the Duck.
And I quite agree with her.[27]

The Water-rat takes the moral as a personal affront—as if he had been slapped or directly insulted—because like Carroll he thinks morals are violent intrusions in the world of art, beauty and innocence. But morals are not just aesthetically distasteful; it is 'always a very dangerous thing' to find morals in things. Wilde concludes with his own moral against morals, one that reflects the trend in children's literature begun with Rousseau to wall the child off in their world of innocence and not allow anything 'dangerous' in from the tainted adult world to disturb their play. As Bettina Kümmerling-Meibauer observes of children's writers in this Romantic tradition, 'all things not corresponding to this ideal [of the child as having the virtues of simplicity, purity, proximity to nature and religious awe] such as erotic content, ironic comments, and social criticism, were eliminated or reduced in order not to destroy the image of a light-hearted idyll of childhood'.[28]

So while the moralistic tradition feared 'inflaming the imagination' through works of fantasy, the Romantic, aesthetic tradition feared inflaming adult sophistication in the child. In contrasting ways, therefore, both traditions see childhood as fragile and easily combustible, and both come across as full of anxiety about stories for children. Children with stories are a bit like children with matches—adults don't want to leave the two together unsupervised. C. S. Lewis summarizes both tendencies in his essay 'On Three Ways of Writing for Children,' when he proposes how children should be addressed: 'the child as a reader is neither to be patronized nor

---

27 Oscar Wilde, *The Happy Prince and Other Stories* (London: Penguin, 1994), p. 55.

28 *Kümmerling-Meibauer*, 'Images of Childhood', p. 189.

idolized'.[29] Fearing that children are dimwitted or easily led astray, the moralistic trend patronizes children, speaking down to them and giving them clear, unambiguous meanings. On the other hand, fearing that the sanctity and purity of childhood might at any moment be made unclean, the aesthetic tradition treats children as idols, to be kept ritually separated from the menacing secular world of adults. This protective stance is partially for the sake of the child but also for the sake of the child-worshipper, who desires to retain access to the otherwise inaccessible mystery and magic of childhood.

PART II – THE 'FREE FEARLESS SOUL' OF THE CHILDLIKE

MacDonald is often seen as a Victorian Romantic, so we should expect his idea of the childlike to come largely from the Romantics. Roderick McGillis argues that MacDonald 're-Christianizes Romanticism' but that he 'offers little that is new in the movement of ideas'.[30] Whether or not this is generally true, I want to suggest that MacDonald's concept of 'the childlike' makes unique contributions to philosophy, theology and the history of ideas, and, as a result, helps navigate a third way for children's literature.

Of course, if MacDonald was a late Romantic, he was philosophically a late German Romantic. In the same way that Lewis acknowledged MacDonald as his spiritual master, MacDonald looked to Novalis as his aesthetic and spiritual guide. Yet the German Romantic view of childhood is slightly different from Rousseau and the English Romantics. Friedrich Schiller says that what moves us about the ideal child is not 'its poverty and limitation' but 'its pure and free strength, its integrity, its eternality'.[31] He also famously claimed that children 'are what we were, they are what we want to be again'.[32] This is almost identical to MacDonald's criticism of Wordsworth in *England's Antiphon*: 'what we feel is wanting in Wordsworth is the hope of return to the bliss of childhood'. He continues:

> Life is, as it were, a constant repentance, or thinking of it

---

29 Lewis, 'On Three Ways of Writing for Children', p. 514.

30 Roderick McGillis, 'Childhood and Growth: George MacDonald and William Wordsworth' in *Romanticism and Children's Literature in Nineteenth Century England*, edited by James Holt McGavran (Athens: University of Georgia Press, 2009), p. 150.

31 Quoted in, *Kümmerling-Meibauer*, 'Images of Childhood', p. 185.

32 Ibid., p. 187.

again: the childhood of the kingdom takes the place of the childhood of the brain, but comprises all that was lovely in the former delight. The heavenly children will subdue kingdoms, work righteousness, wax valiant in the fight, merry of heart as when in the nursery of this world they fought their fancied frigates, and defended their toy-battlements.[33]

The child is thus neither an incomplete adult nor a strange and separate being isolated from the adult but something eternal and universal in humanity. MacDonald juxtaposes the battle imagery of 'subduing kingdoms' and 'waxing valiant in the fight' with being 'merry at heart', suggesting that whatever else childhood is, it is not anxious. Childhood for MacDonald, as Chad Schrock comments, 'is power, is potency'.[34] It is fearlessness, or at least bravery in the face of fear.

Childhood is also what we are all striving towards:

There is a childhood into which we have to grow, just as there is a childhood we must leave behind; a childlikeness which is the highest aim of humanity, and a childishness from which but few of those who are counted the wisest among men, have freed themselves in their imagined progress towards the reality of things.[35]

Following Novalis, who said that 'where there are children, there is a golden age' and that 'every stage of education begins with childhood and that is why the most educated person on earth so much resembles a child', MacDonald imagines childhood as both origin and goal, and therefore that which must be continually renewed in the present.[36]

Furthermore, MacDonald also seems to have resonated with Novalis's idea that a good fairy tale expressed the 'confessions of a true synthetic child, an ideal child'.[37] Childlikeness, in other words, was naturally at home in fairytales, because fairytales somehow evoke the atmosphere and aura of ideal childhood. Chesterton goes so far as

---

33 George MacDonald, *England's Antiphon* (Whitehorn: Johannesen, 1996), p. 256.

34 Chad Schrock, 'From Child to Childlike: The Cycle of Education in Novalis and George MacDonald' *North Wind* 25 (2006), p. 60.

35 George MacDonald, *David Elginbrod* (Whitehorn: Johannesen, 1995), p. 33.

36 Quoted in Schrock, 'From Child to Childlike', p. 60, 59.

37 Quoted in Kümmerling-Meibauer, 'Images of Childhood', p. 189.

to say that MacDonald's entire vision of reality was shaped by fairy tales to such an extent that the fairy tale structure pervades even his realistic novels: 'It is not that he dresses up men and movements as knights and dragons, but that he thinks that knights and dragons, really existing in the eternal world, are dressed up here as men and movements'.[38] He adds that 'MacDonald enters fairyland like a citizen returning to his home' and that his 'world of extravagance is penetrated through and through with a warmth of world-love, the cosmic camaraderie of the child'.[39] Childlikeness, in other words, is not a footnote to MacDonald's fairy tales, it is the beating heart, the 'entire cast of mind' that gives shape and structure to every character, symbol and sentence.

This is a large claim and one that is difficult to demonstrate, particularly given how many different attributes MacDonald ascribes to the childlike in his various writings, so I will only gesture to two ways in which his idea of the childlike manifests itself *structurally* in his fairy tales. The first is fearlessness, and the second is the potency of goodness and beauty.

Describing Jesus being found in the temple by Mary and Joseph, MacDonald says that 'the world was his home because his father's house [...] he was no lost child, but with his father all the time'.[40] As the perfect divine child, Jesus could rejoice and wonder at even the commonest things because 'the world has for him no chamber of terror'.[41] We on the other hand are not yet 'at home in this great universe' because we are not yet 'true children' and 'hence, until then, the hard struggle, the constant strife we hold with *Nature*'.[42] Unlike the rest of humanity, Jesus 'has never lost his childhood, the very essence of childhood being nearness to the Father and the outgoing of his creative love'.[43] As such, Jesus has no fear of demons, storms, sufferings or insults. Nor does he fear misinterpretation. In his sermon 'The Final Unmasking' MacDonald says that because all things shall ultimately be revealed (Matt 10.26) Jesus teaches 'fearlessness as to

---

38 G. K. Chesterton, 'George MacDonald and His Work', *The Daily News* (June 11, 1901), p. 6.

39 Ibid.

40 George MacDonald, *Hope of the Gospel* (Whitehorn: Johannesen, 2000), p. 55.

41 Ibid., p. 53.

42 Ibid., p. 52.

43 Ibid., p. 58.

the misinterpretation of our words and actions'.[44]

As we have seen both the moralistic and the aesthetic traditions of children's literature are in different ways anxious about their works being misinterpreted by children: the moralists that a child might miss the practical or ethical meaning of a text—or worse, have their imaginations 'inflamed'—and the aesthetes of innocence that a child might be tainted by adult seriousness. This fear of misinterpretation often emerges in forewords, afterwords, dedications and other paratextual apparatus. Indeed, Victorian paratexts in books intended for children display a continual anxiety about misinterpretation. Two brief examples will have to suffice. After concluding the narrative of *The Water-Babies* Charles Kingsley appends a final section headed simply 'Moral'. The authorial voice is light and playful, but it conceals a sincere concern about his son's education:

> And now, my dear little man, what should we learn from this parable? We should learn thirty-seven or thirty-nine things, I am not exactly sure which.

He then digresses for over a page on the spiritual evolution of things as a way of explaining his children's parable before more directly giving fatherly guidance in interpreting both the story and life:

> If my story is not true, something better is; and if I am not quite right, still you will be, as long as you stick to hard work and cold water. But remember always, as I told you at first, that this is all a fairy tale, and only fun and pretense; and therefore you are not to believe a word of it, even if it is true.[45]

In his final words to his readers, Kingsley twice suspends the category of truth with conditional clauses ('if my story is not true', 'even if it is true').[46] The hesitation and uncertainty of how to speak of

---

44 George MacDonald, *Unspoken Sermons* (Whitehorn: Johannesen, 2004), p. 594.

45 Charles Kingsley, *The Water-Babies* (London: Macmillan and Co, 1903), pp. 201, 202.

46 Kingsley's assertion here initially seems similar to MacDonald's toward the end of *At the Back of the North Wind* in which Diamond asks the narrator, 'Could it be all dreaming, do you think, sir?' The narrator replies: 'I daren't say, Diamond, but at least there is one thing that you may be sure of, that there is a still better love than that of the wonderful being you call North Wind. Even if she be a dream, the dream of such a beautiful creature could not come to you by chance.' But whereas Kingsley speaks

that which is not true according to the standards of Victorian realism suggests that Kingsley is somewhat conflicted and anxious about how his story will be received. That his son and children more generally might have their gullible imaginations inflamed and actually believe there are such things as water-babies, is an unsettling thought to the naturalist in Kingsley. But he is also potentially anxious about how adults will perceive his foray into fantasy. By suspending the truth status of his story he simultaneously seems to be trying to protect the child from an incursion of too much adult seriousness much like the romantic aesthetic tradition, whilst also appeasing adult moralists by acknowledging that his story is 'only fun and pretense'.

In a similar way, Lewis Carroll provided several prefatory poems and dedications to his various editions of *Alice in Wonderland* and *Through the Looking-Glass*, which attempt to guide the reader's interpretation of the stories. Speaking to his child audience, but also cryptically to Alice Liddell, Carroll writes:

> Child of the pure unclouded brow
> And dreaming eyes of wonder!
> Though time be fleet, and I and thou
> Are half a life asunder,
> Thy loving smile will surely hail
> The love-gift of a fairytale.[47]

The Romantic aesthetic view of the child here is in full force—the child's brow is 'pure' and 'unclouded', a symbol of the innocence and naiveté of the child, while Carroll's life is largely 'sundered' from the world of a child. But fear becomes pervasive at the end of the poem:

> Come, hearken then, ere voice of dread,
> With bitter tidings laden,
> Shall summon to unwelcome bed
> A melancholy maiden!
> We are but older children, dear,

with an unmasked authorial voice, MacDonald's statement comes through the intradiagetic narrator, preserving MacDonald's authorial distance and neutrality. Moreover, unlike Kingsley's final sentence exhorting disbelief in his entire story, the narrator of *North Wind* ends with confident belief in Diamond's stories: 'They thought he was dead. I knew that he had gone to the back of the north wind.' George MacDonald, *At the Back of the North Wind* (Whitehorn: Johannesen, 2002), pp. 376, 378.

47   Lewis Carroll, *The Complete Works*, p. 123.

Who fret to find our bedtime near.

Without, the frost, the blinding snow,
The storm-wind's moody madness—
Within, the firelight's ruddy glow,
And childhood's nest of gladness.
The magic words shall hold thee fast:
Thou shalt not heed the raving blast.[48]

All around the child are threats, dangers and burdens. The adult 'voice of dread' is ever seeking to invade and interrupt 'childhood's nest of gladness'. Frost, snow, death and even the wind's 'moody madness' all loom outside the safe, warm realm of childhood. As he did with Lilia MacDonald, Carroll nervously seeks to assure his child reader that his story will not let in any drafts from the cold and ruthless adult world. Rather the 'magic words shall hold thee fast'—do their best to freeze the development of the child so that she can remain eternally innocent. Don't worry, he seems to say, I won't impose moral virtue or practical correction upon you like all other adults. Both Carroll and Kingsley shared MacDonald's Christian beliefs and could also be described as Victorian Romantics, yet both retain underlying anxieties about how their stories for children are interpreted and the danger of misinterpretation.

MacDonald, however, rarely gives paratextual guidance as to how to interpret his stories. He dedicates *Dealings with the Fairies* to his children saying:

> You know I do not tell you stories as some papas do. Therefore, I give you a book of stories. You have read them all before except the last. But you have not seen Mr. Hughes's drawings before.[49]

Unlike Kingsley and Carroll who first told their stories spontaneously to specific children and later crafted them for publication, MacDonald seems to have written his stories in creative isolation. This suggests a very different attitude to fairy tales than Carroll or Kingsley. They are not 'just fun and pretense' written merely to please a child, but are deeply and personally meaningful to MacDonald. Moreover, MacDonald seems strangely nonchalant about letting his children read his fairy tales on their own without

---

48 Ibid.

49 George MacDonald, *Dealings With the Fairies* (London: Alexander Strahan, 1867).

his parental, authorial presence to help guide their interpretation. In comparison with his Victorian contemporaries he comes across as relatively fearless of misinterpretation. Indeed, unlike other Victorians MacDonald gives his childlike audience almost no paratextual guidance. When asked by an American publisher for an introduction to his fairy tales, MacDonald produced 'The Fantastic Imagination', an essay that in many ways is a refusal to answer the basic question: 'What is a fairy tale?' MacDonald continually frustrates and deflects the hermeneutical inquiries of his hypothetical reader who anxiously and repeatedly questions:

> You write as if a fairytale were a thing of importance: must it have a meaning?
> How am I to assure myself that I am not reading my own meaning into it, but yours out of it?
> Suppose my child ask me what the fairytale means, what am I to say?
> But words are not music; words at least are meant and fitted to carry a precise meaning?
> But a man may then imagine in your work what he pleases, what you never meant!
> But surely you would explain your idea to one who asked you?[50]

Essentially, the nervous, baffled speaker repeats the same question six times—what does it *mean*? Even when he threatens MacDonald with misinterpretation—a great fear of most writers—MacDonald blithely and humbly returns: 'it may be better that you should read your meaning into it. That may be a higher operation of your intellect than the mere reading of mine out of it: your meaning may be superior to mine'.[51] It is easy to miss how radical a statement this is in any age or context, but particularly in the Victorian era and in the preface to a book intended for the 'childlike'. Neither Locke nor Rousseau would have approved. MacDonald not only trusts the interpretative abilities of children, but he even seems to condone and encourage their misinterpretation as a potentially higher and superior operation of their intellect and development.

MacDonald's fearlessness of misinterpretation also informs the style of his stories 'for the childlike'. Unlike his realistic novels in which

---

50 George MacDonald, *A Dish of Orts* (Whitehorn: Johannesen, 1996), pp. 316, 317, 318, 320, 321.

51 Ibid., p. 316.

digression and authorial commentary can go on for pages, in his fairy tales MacDonald's prose is lucid and paired down. The Germanic compound-complex sentences piled with dependent sub-clauses and restrictive phrases that we often encounter in the novels, essays and sermons give way to the brevity and rapidity of simple sentences. He quells his desire to rhapsodize on the meaning of the twilight, the stars or human wickedness, and allows fantastic images to shine in all their radiant splendor. He also plays more in his fairytales, making his tone light and introducing an added layer of ambiguity that grants readers space to imagine and interpret on their own.

Fearlessness also gives structural shape to aspects of MacDonald's fairytales. In a letter from 1863 John Ruskin anxiously warns MacDonald about the sexuality of 'The Light Princess':

> It is too amorous throughout—and to some temperaments would be quite mischievous. You are too pure-minded yourself to feel this—but I assure you the swimming scenes and love scenes would be to many children seriously harmful.[52]

Ruskin takes the standard Romantic, aesthetic view of the child as a creature to be protected from adult taints, but MacDonald was not affected by Ruskin's fear and unconcernedly published the story without alteration in *Adela Cathcart* (1864), putting Ruskin's objections into the mouth of a crabby, selfish aunt. Furthermore, MacDonald's fairytales almost always have one boy and one girl who enter fairyland separately but who then meet and become close companions, and frequently marry (Richard and Alice, Mossy and Tangle, Photogen and Nycteris). Unlike many of his contemporaries, MacDonald was not afraid of exposing children to the grown-up world of sexual attraction at an early age. In this, C. S. Lewis was slightly more tentative than MacDonald for while Lewis maintains gender parity almost perfectly throughout the Narnia stories, in many of the books he avoids or marginalizes love interests and sexuality, not least by making most of the children related to one another.

MacDonald argues that one of the reasons childlikeness is fearless of misinterpretation is because of the living power of goodness. In his first published essay, on Robert Browning's poem 'Christmas Eve', MacDonald says that 'the child-like heart' is particularly gifted at receiving 'the revelation of the true through the beautiful'.[53] He

52 Quoted in U. C. Knoepflmacher, *Ventures into Childland* (Chicago and London: University of Chicago Press, 1998), p. 138.
53 MacDonald, *A Dish of Orts*, pp. 195-6.

adds that 'exhibiting truth' and 'unveiling beauty' is more potent than 'exposing error' or 'critical dissections of deformity'. 'Let the true and the good destroy their opposites', he says, 'it is only by the good and beautiful that the evil and ugly are known. It is light that makes manifest'.[54] The childlike soul does not need to spend time directly fighting evil and depravity because if they are delighting in and drawing attention to the True, the Good and the Beautiful, then evil will deconstruct itself when confronted with the presence of something infinitely greater. 'Our light', says MacDonald in *Hope of the Gospel*, 'must shine in cheerfulness, in joy, yea, where a man has the gift, in merriment; in freedom from care [...] in fearlessness and tenderness, in courtesy and graciousness.'[55] Positive attributes partake in the goodness and beauty of God the Father and therefore far outshine shadowy traits often praised by adults such as cynicism, skepticism and wariness.

Instances of the potency of beauty and goodness are easy to find in the fairytales. Alice and Richard in 'Cross Purposes' discover in the midst of darkness that their budding love for each other gives them light to see the obstacles along the path. In 'The Golden Key' Mossy's rapturous encounter with the beautiful rainbow reveals to him the hiding place of the golden key, which ultimately gives him and Tangle access to the stairway to the land whence the shadows fall. The self-sacrificial goodness of the prince in 'The Light Princess' is what finally penetrates through the curse of heartless levity to the true loving heart of the princess. But in addition to these plot incidents, I think MacDonald's concept of how the childlike soul should champion beauty rather than attack falsehood imbued his fairyland with an aura of aesthetic goodness. W. H. Auden writes: 'George MacDonald's most extraordinary, and precious, gift is his ability, in all his stories, to create an atmosphere of goodness about which there is nothing phony or moralistic. Nothing is rarer in literature'.[56] MacDonald is almost unique in this ability to make goodness thrilling and enticing and evil paltry, petty and boring. Fairytales are perhaps the genre in which this atmosphere of goodness works best because of their ability to draw upon luminous curiosities and exotic oddities along with their proclivity for journeys, adventures and eucatastrophic endings. Thus,

---

54 Ibid., pp. 196-7.

55 MacDonald, *Hope of the Gospel*, p. 186.

56 W. H. Auden, 'Afterword' in *The Golden Key* (New York: Farrar, Straus and Giroux, 1967), p. 86.

when MacDonald says that he writes 'for the childlike', I think he means that he writes his fairytales and fantasies to awake the childlike in everyone willing to enter fearlessly into his beneficently beautiful world of once-upon-a-time. In this way, the childlike provides a third way for children's literature. It neither fears inflaming the imagination nor the danger of adult morals, because the childlike vision unites the two in a higher harmony. In *The Hope of the Gospel*, MacDonald comments: 'guided in dance inexplicable of prophetic harmony, move the children of God, the lights of the world, the lovers of men, the fellow-workers with God'.[57] Childlikeness means engaging and participating in this 'dance inexplicable' and seeking the 'prophetic harmony' of contraries like innocence and experience.

For this reason, MacDonald's stories constantly strive for a higher unity of conventional dichotomies. In 'The Carasoyn', for example, after saying 'all the time that [Colin] was working, he was busiest building castles in the air', the narrator comments, 'I think the two ought always to go together'.[58] The unity of working and dreaming then becomes the structural principle of the first half of the story. In good fairytale fashion, Colin has three tasks to perform before he can produce the magical Carasoyn and save his future wife: to dream three days without sleeping, work three days without dreaming, and work and dream three days together. The isolated tasks of dreaming and working are necessary, but it is the third task of uniting the two in a higher unity that ultimately yields the grapes that become the magic wine.

This structural strategy of transcending opposites is, of course, not original to MacDonald, and is likely drawn from the mystical tradition of writers like Swedenborg and Jacob Boehme or perhaps from William Blake who MacDonald calls a 'genius' displaying a kind of 'mysticism run wild' in his poetry. Blake for instance claimed 'without contraries is no progression' and 'there is a place where contraries are equally true'.[59] He called the state beyond the mere opposition of innocence and experience 'organised innocence', the place 'where innocence dwells with Wisdom'.[60]

---

57   MacDonald, *Hope of the Gospel*, p. 128.

58   George MacDonald, *The Light Princess and Other Fairy Tales* (Whitehorn: Johannesen, 2001), p. 217.

59   William Blake, *The Complete Poems* (London: Penguin, 1977), pp. 181, 580.

60   Inscription in the manuscript of *The Four Zoas*.

Something akin to this paradoxical vision seems to inform and indwell MacDonald's fairytales. Even the title of 'The Day Boy and the Night Girl' discloses the dialectic tension of the story. The ultimate marriage of Photogen and Nycteris thus symbolizes the harmonious synthesis of opposites (day/night, girl/boy, power/weakness, rationality/imagination). Likewise, 'The Light Princess' seems to have a similar tripartite structure, beginning with innocent but heartless laughter (chapters 1-7), proceeding through the grim experience of pain and suffering (9-14), and culminating in the simultaneous delight and seriousness of marriage symbolized in the princess' paradoxical sobbing for joy (15).[61] In other words, the story brings play and seriousness into a higher unity—a kind of ecstatic gravity or earnest levity.

So how did all of this affect C. S. Lewis? It seems unlikely that such an avid disciple of MacDonald's works could have come away with his 'cast of mind' unaffected by MacDonald's concept of the childlike. In addition to 'On Three Ways of Writing for Children', Lewis wrote a curious essay called 'Talking of Bicycles' in which something akin to the childlike emerges. In a kind of lighthearted Platonic dialogue, Lewis discusses how our experiences of things go through four different ages. In early childhood, bicycles meant nothing, says Lewis's imagined friend, but then came the time when having and riding a bicycle 'was like entering Paradise' and it seemed somehow to communicate something of 'the secret of life'.[62] But then habitual need to ride the bicycle daily and in all weathers and seasons makes riding the bicycle seem like being 'a galley slave'. Lewis names these ages: Unenchantment, enchantment and disenchantment. In the fourth age 'the mere fact of riding brings back a delicious whiff of memory' so that 'he recovers the feeling of enchantment' and also realizes how true and even philosophical those feelings were.[63] This is the age of re-enchantment. All of this sounds very similar to MacDonald's spiral of development in which we return to the feelings of childhood on a higher plain, or William Blake's 'organised innocence'. We return

---

61 MacDonald's structure follows almost exactly Blake's progression in his 'Introduction' to Songs of Innocence in which the child who hears the Piper's songs first 'laughs', then 'weeps' and finally 'weeps with joy'. Blake, *Complete Poems*, p. 104.

62 C. S. Lewis, 'Talking about Bicycles', in *Essay Collection & Other Short Pieces* (London: HarperCollins, 2000), p. 689.

63 Ibid., p. 690.

to the joys and delights of childhood, but with the vital difference of having passed through the veil and travail of experience, uniting both enchantment and disenchantment in a higher prophetic harmony.

I think there was also a certain childlike fearlessness in Lewis's decision to write fairy tales as an Oxbridge don post WWII in a literary atmosphere steeped in Freudian criticism. He opened himself to mockery and ridicule by his colleagues, and, what would have been even more terrifying to him—psychoanalysis. A century earlier another Oxford don created an alternate name and persona in an attempt to keep his play separate from his work. Charles Dodgson to the end of his life often refused to acknowledge that he was the author of the *Alice* stories when he was at Christ's Church returning letters addressed to 'Lewis Carroll, Christ Church' saying no such person lived there, in an anxious attempt to preserve his professional dignity. In contrast, C. S. Lewis even claimed that fairytales helped check his 'expository demon'. That is, the form's 'inflexible hostility to all analysis, digression, reflection and "gas"' attracted Lewis and gave him permission to let go of the desire of the critic and public speaker to explain the meanings of things unambiguously.

Lewis also follows aspects of MacDonald's harmonic structuring in his Narnia stories. Lewis's decision to mix Norse, Greek and Roman mythologies along with talking animals famously upset Tolkien's purist aesthetic sensibility, but it also is a synthetic enterprise, the seeking of a higher unity in apparent disparates. The talking animals, likewise, combine animalness with human intelligence without sacrificing the individuality of either. Meanwhile, *The Voyage of the Dawn Treader*, a story about journeying toward the sun, is followed by *The Silver Chair*, a moon-inspired story about night, darkness and shadowy places.[64] However, perhaps the most MacDonald-like story of all is *The Horse and His Boy*—the only story that ends with the marriage of two of its protagonists, Shasta and Aravis, who are in many ways diametrical opposites (low vs. high class, Northern vs. Southern, light vs. dark, boy vs. girl).

In these and many other ways, Lewis carries on MacDonald's project of organizing innocence. Both authors fearlessly refuse to treat children either as simpletons (like the moralistic tradition) or idols (like the Romantic tradition). Instead they daringly trust the childlike reader, relying on the potency of fairytales to speak truth and goodness enticingly through the medium of beauty. You should

---

64 See Michael Ward, *Planet Narnia* (Oxford: Oxford University Press, 2008), pp. 100-39.

'let the pictures tell you their own moral', says Lewis, 'but if they don't show you any moral, don't put one in'.[65] Artificially attempting either to insert or exclude morals is to assume 'too superior an attitude' to the child. Instead writers 'must meet children as our equals in that area of our nature where we are their equals'.[66] This 'area' is likely humanity's spiritual nature, which is why morals must 'rise from whatever spiritual roots' a person has struck during 'the whole course of life'.[67] For both Lewis and MacDonald, therefore, innocence should not be fearfully guarded by dainty aesthetes nor anxiously marshalled by zealous didacts, but organically nurtured by beauty and wisdom.

---

65   Lewis, 'On Three Ways of Writing For Children', p.513.
66   Ibid., p. 514.
67   Ibid., p. 513.

BIBLIOGRAPHY

Auden, W. H., 'Afterword', in George MacDonald, *The Golden Key*, New York: Farrar, Straus and Giroux, 1967. Print.

Blake, William, *The Complete Poems*, London: Penguin, 1977. Print.

Bunyan, John, *A Book for Boys and Girls*, London: Elliot Stock, 1889. Print.

Carroll, Lewis, *The Complete Works of Lewis Carroll*, New York: Barnes and Noble, 1994. Print.

Chesterton, G. K., 'George MacDonald and His Work', *The Daily News* (June 11, 1901), p. 6. Print.

Cohen, Morton N. (ed), *The Letters of Lewis Carroll*, 2 vols., London: Macmillan, 1979. Print.

Edgeworth, Maria, *Moral Tales*, New York: W. B. Gilley, 1819. Print.

Edgeworth, Maria, *Practical Education*, New York: Harper & Brothers, 1855. Print.

Kingsley, Charles, *The Water-Babies*, London: Macmillan and Co, 1903. Print.

Knoepflmacher, U. C., *Ventures into Childland*, Chicago and London: University of Chicago Press, 1998. Print.

Kümmerling-Meibauer, Bettina, 'Images of Childhood in Romantic Children's Literature', in Gerald Gillespie, Manfred Engel and Bernard Dieterle (eds), *Romantic Prose Fiction*, Amsterdam: Benjamins, 2008. Print.

Lamb, Charles, *The Best Letters of Charles Lamb*, edited by Edwin Gilpin Johnson, *Project Gutenberg* <http://www.gutenberg.org/files/10125/10125-8.txt> [accessed 29 November 2014].

Lewis, C. S., *Essay Collection & Other Short Pieces*, London: HarperCollins, 2000. Print.

Locke, John, *Some Thoughts Concerning Education*, London: J. Hatchard and Son, 1836. Print.

MacDonald, George, *At the Back of the North Wind*, Whitehorn: Johannesen, 2002. Print.

MacDonald, George, *David Elginbrod*, Whitehorn: Johannesen, 1995. Print.

MacDonald, George, *Dealings With the Fairies*, London: Alexander Strahan, 1867. Print.

MacDonald, George, *A Dish of Orts*, Whitehorn: Johannesen, 1996. Print.

MacDonald, George, *England's Antiphon*, Whitehorn: Johannesen, 1996. Print.

MacDonald, George, *Hope of the Gospel*, Whitehorn: Johannesen, 2000. Print.

MacDonald, George, *The Light Princess and Other Fairy Tales*, Whitehorn, Johannesen, 2001. Print.

MacDonald, George, *Unspoken Sermons*, Whitehorn: Johannesen, 2004. Print.

McGillis, Roderick, 'Childhood and Growth: George MacDonald and William Wordsworth', in *Romanticism and Children's Literature in Nineteenth Century England*, James Holt McGavran (ed), Athens: University of Georgia Press, 2009. Print.

Milbank, John, 'Fictioning Things: Gift and Narrative', *Religion & Literature* 37.3 (2005). Print.

Rose, Jacqueline, *The Case of Peter Pan: The Impossibility of Children's Fiction*, Philadelphia: University of Philadelphia Press, 1984. Print.

Rousseau, Jean Jacques, *Emile*, translated by William H. Payne, New York and London: D. Appleton and Company, 1918. Print.

Schrock, Chad, 'From Child to Childlike: The Cycle of Education in Novalis and George MacDonald', *North Wind* 25 (2006). Print.

Tolkien, J. R. R., *A Tolkien Miscellany*, New York: SFBC, 2002. Print.

Trimmer, Sarah, *Fabulous Histories*, London: J. G. & F. Rivington, 1838. Print.

Ward, Michael, *Planet Narnia*, Oxford: Oxford University Press, 2008. Print.

Wilde, Oscar, *The Happy Prince and Other Stories*, London: Penguin, 1994. Print.

Fantasy, Fear and Reality:
Tracing Pathways Between Kingsley, Carroll, and MacDonald Leading to the Inklings

Jean Webb

One of the advantages of being an academic is possessing hindsight; that is, being in a position to perceive the 'significance and nature of events after they have occurred'.[1] Perception suggests subjectivity, a particular view held at a particular time. In her essay 'Mr. Bennett and Mrs. Brown' Virginia Woolf posited that 'in or about December, 1910, human character changed.'[2] She continued: 'The change was not sudden and definite. But a change there was, nevertheless; and, since one must be arbitrary, let us date it about the year 1910.'[3] Woolf's seminal essay on the subject of characterization in literature argued for a shift in literary thinking and a reassessment of how writers might interpret subjectivity and the representation of life. Woolf was contributing to Modernist thinking in literature. As she rightly said any such dating is arbitrary, yet for convenience the impression is given that there are distinct shifts from, for example, Romanticism to Modernism to Postmodernism. No literary and/or philosophical movement begins or ends abruptly nor in a singular way, for thinking develops and crosses over. This thought can also be expressed more eloquently in the words of C.S. Lewis from the beginning of *The Allegory of Love* where he stated: 'Humanity does not pass through phases as a train passes through stations: being alive, it has the privilege of always moving yet never leaving anything behind.'[4] The intention in this discussion is not to take the train but to trace pathways. By doing so one can look back, sideways, or occasionally perhaps deviate, however I cannot promise not to be guilty of 'leaving anything behind'. My pathways are between some of the most influential writers of fantasy in English nineteenth and early twentieth century literature, they being Charles Kingsley, Lewis

---

1 http://www.collinsdictionary.com/dictionary/english/hindsight [accessed June 1 2015]

2 Peter Faulkner, *A Modernist Reader: Modernism in England* 1910-1930 (London: Batsford, 1986), p. 113.

3 Ibid., p. 113.

4 C.S. Lewis, *The Allegory of Love* (Cambridge: Cambridge University Press, 2013), p. 2.

Carroll, George MacDonald, J.R.R. Tolkien and C.S. Lewis—Tolkien and Lewis being key figures in the Inklings.

The epigraph to Charles Kingsley's *The Water-Babies* (1863) is: 'Come read me my riddle, each good little man: If you cannot read it, no grown-up folk can.'[5] Literature is a way of working out puzzles and ideas, to find a way to 'solidify' and to give shape through language and form to that which is abstract and intangible but which does reflect upon, influence and affect culture and society. The argument pursued here is that in the forms of fantasy employed by the above authors there are connections which relate to concerns, or more deeply, fears about their present and future societies in a period of rapidly increasing change: fears and concerns which would eventually be voiced and 'formalised' as Modernist thinking in the early decades of the twentieth century. The fantasy works of these writers all had a relationship with a reality that they perceived in their own individual ways. Stephen Prickett, in *Victorian Fantasy* has clearly defined and demonstrated the differences in the relationships to the real world of the Victorian era established by Kingsley, Carroll and MacDonald. As Prickett states in *The Water-Babies* 'Kingsley's world is, and remains, this world.'[6] My first steps on the pathway therefore begin in considering this, or rather Kingsley's perception of his world through a focus on *The Water-Babies*.

Kingsley's *The Water-Babies* is principally known for the story of Tom the chimney sweep's boy and Kingsley's Rabelaisian reflection on Victorian life and society. The text is a combination of a critique of the working conditions of chimney sweep children written in a realist mode; a surreal morally didactic fantasy; a fairy tale; an advocacy for engagement with nature and science and a philosophical exploration of creation amongst other ways one might try to define this text, for *The Water-Babies* defies a singular encompassing definition. *The Water-Babies* thus reverberates with Victorian society. In commenting upon Victorian thinking through *The Water-Babies* and in his distinctive mixing of forms combining realism, fantasy, fairytale, sermonising, critical commentary on Victorian society and science and an echoing of Swift's Gulliver's Travels, Kingsley had had to 'make it new' and in doing so pre-shadows Ezra Pound's Modernist dictum to 'Make it

---

5   Charles Kingsley, *The Water-Babies* (Oxford: Oxford University Press, 2013), unpaginated.

6   Stephen Prickett, *Victorian Fantasy* (Waco: Baylor University Press, 2005), p. 162.

new!'

The text falls into those works which are defined as being Romantic with the emphasis on alternative imagined worlds, the innocence of the child, the journey from innocence to experience and the close relationship with nature, which Kingsley takes further, for Tom is educated about nature in a scientific way. He is taught to observe, with Kingsley making analogies to the industrialized world. Kingsley's Tom is not, however, the epitome of the idealized Romantic child later portrayed by Frances Hodgson Burnett in *Little Lord Fauntleroy*. *The Water-Babies* portrays a darker side of life that can be seen to contain elements similar to those that will be attributed to Modernist literary thinking some forty years later. Comparing *The Water-Babies* with the Modernist concerns about industrialization and urbanization it is clear that Kingsley is trying to find a way to respond to the fast changing pace of life and the turmoil which he had identified in his series of 'Sermons on National Subjects' preached in 1849 when he said:

> It was not sixty years ago, that a nobleman was laughed at in the House of Lords for saying that he believed that we should one day see ships go by steam; and now there are steamers on every sea and ocean in the world. Who expected twenty years ago to see the whole face of England covered with these wonderful railroads?[7]

Kingsley is not against industrial progress *per se* as Colin Manlove has eruditely discussed in his article on the machine in the work of Kingsley and H.G. Wells.[8] A clergyman and a naturalist with strong scientific interests, Kingsley appreciated and saw the need for progress and social change in accord with the new world that was fast emerging. The concern Kingsley has is the effect that industrial progress has upon society and the ways in which society responded to the changing culture, a stance that mirrored the government's alliance of the state of childhood and the state of the nation which had stimulated the Sadler enquiries.[9] Tom's early years have been corrupted by the effects

---

7   Charles Kingsley, 'Sermons on National Subjects' (1849) <http://www.gutenberg.org/files/8202/8202-h/8202-h.htm accessed> [June 1, 2015], p. 2.

8   Colin Manlove, 'Charles Kingsley, H. G. Wells, and the Machine in Victorian Fiction', (*Nineteenth-Century Literature* 1993), pp. 212-239.

9   Levene, A. and Webb Jean, 'Depictions of the 'ideal child' in nineteenth-century British literature and legislature,' *Journal of the History of Childhood*

of industrialisation and a society which saw the child as part of the wider economic machine. As a working child, his mother dead and his father transported to Botany Bay, Grimes, the chimney sweep master is his role model. Grimes drinks to excess, is violent, flirtatious (although dealt with efficiently by the Irishwoman) a poacher and a criminal. Tom's vision of the future is to be like his master. Tom:

> thought of the fine times coming, when he would be a man, and a master sweep, and sit in the public-house with a quart of beer and a long pipe, and play cards for silver money, and wear velveteens and ankle-jacks, and keep a white bull-dog with one grey ear, and carry her puppies in his pocket, just like a man. And he would have apprentices, one, two, three, if he could. How he would bully them, and knock them about, just as his master did to him; and make them carry home the soot sacks, while he rode before them on his donkey, with a pipe in his mouth and a flower in his button-hole, like a king at the head of his army. (Kingsley, 2013: 6)

Tom is compared with animals on more than one occasion, being likened to the donkey in the field, an ape and a gorilla as when on the way to Harthover House 'he paddled up the park with his little bare feet, like a small black gorilla' (Kingsley, 2013: 19). Illiterate and uneducated he has no knowledge of Christianity. In fact Kingsley notes: 'he was as much at home in a chimney as a mole is underground'. Tom is an urbanized child who is, unbeknownst to him, on a journey of great discovery. His journey takes him out of the urban into discovery of the rural and nature as signified by Kingsley recording the beginning of the visit to Harthover where Tom is to sweep the chimneys of the great house.

> They passed through the pitmen's village, all shut up and silent now, and through the turnpike; and then they were out in the real country, and plodding along the black dusty road, between black slag walls, with no sound but the groaning and thumping of the pit-engine in the next field. But soon the road grew white, and the walls likewise; and at the wall's foot grew long grass and gay flowers, all drenched with dew; and instead of the groaning of the pit-engine, they heard the skylark saying his matins high up in the air, and the pit-bird warbling in the sedges, as he had warbled all night long.[10]

Tom is beginning his journey from urban savagery to the

---

and Youth, Unpublished Paper.

10 Kingsley, *The Water-Babies*, p. 8.

Romantic child in tune with nature, yet he still has far to go. When on the way to Harthover House the countryside is so unfamiliar to the boy that he thinks deer to be monsters, whilst on his flight from the mansion the way that he is able to negotiate the rocky face is to treat it like a chimney.

Kingsley's intention is certainly to educate Tom (and the reader) into understanding and appreciating nature and science to enable social progress, however the text can also be read as a moral education which will produce a good subject and calm the fears of revolution of which Kingsley was all too well aware. The 1830s and 1840s were periods of tension and potential violent revolution coming from the suppressed and unfranchised poor. As Kingsley again demonstrated in his 'Sermon On National Subjects' in 1849, England was not a peaceful and untroubled sceptered isle:

> Who expected on the 22nd of February last year, that, within a single month, half the nations of Europe, which looked so quiet and secure, would be shaken from top to bottom with revolution and bloodshed—kings and princes vanishing one after the other like a dream—poor men sitting for a day as rulers of kingdoms, and then hurled down again to make room for other rulers as unexpected as themselves? Can anyone consider the last fifty years?—can anyone consider that one last year, 1848, and then not feel that we do live in a most strange and awful time? a time for which nothing is too surprising—a time in which we all ought to be prepared, from the least to the greatest, to see the greatest horrors and the greatest blessings come suddenly upon us, like a thief in the night?[11]

The fear of revolution went back deeply into his teenage years, for when he was thirteen Kingsley had witnessed the Bristol Riots of 1832, a subject on which he would reflect in his sermons and in his writings. He recounted the awfulness of the drunken rioters supping in the gutters the spirits which had gushed and flowed from broken caskets and then caught alight turning the rioters into charred corpses (Kingsley, 1883: 159). His wife Fanny noted the conversation they had following his telling her of this episode and her asking whose fault lay behind these dreadful episodes. Kingsley's answer was 'Mine [...] and yours.'(Kingsley, 1883: 159). His authentic response to the threat of the uprising poor and working classes was to adopt a position of responsibility through his educative preaching and

---

11   Charles Kingsley, 'Sermons on National Subjects', p. 2.

writing. Although a supporter of the Chartists in their wanting better living and working conditions he was not in favour of their mode of achieving such, for his belief was that the vote would not be of use until the lower classes knew how to use it, until they had clean water, improved living conditions, were literate and morally sound Christian subjects. Whereas the Modernists would see life as being without purpose and imbued with a sense of hopelessness, for Kingsley the driving force was to take society out of the moral and social chaos through a combination of hope, education and faith. The final item Kingsley's Mother Carey identifies at the bottom of Pandora's box is hope. His view on life was one which was very much in contact with reality and the fusion of the spiritual and the lived experience.

Kingsley's curiosity about life was exemplified by his interest in the natural sciences. He and Darwin met in 1854 (Kingsley, 1883: 210) and subsequently wrote to each other for ten years. His life-long interests and subsequent experiences engaged him in debates on Natural Theology on which he spoke at Sion College in 1871. Kingsley did not seek, nor believe in a singular absolute answer but rather understanding, seeing God in the beauty of nature. He also realized that it was the responsibility of human beings to care for nature and not to create a desert from fertile land by misuse, as in the following quotation from his lecture on 'The Natural Theology of the Future':

> Man's work is too often the curse of the very planet which he misuses. None should know that better than the botanist, who sees whole regions desolate, and given up to sterility and literal thorns and thistles, on account of man's sin and folly, ignorance and greedy waste.[12]

Kingsley's theological position is subtly inserted into the text from the onset of Tom's journey to Harthover. Nature, industry and the awareness of faith come together with 'the skylark saying his matins high up in the air, and the pit-bird warbling in the sedges'. The melding together of Christian faith, science and industry underpins the text reappearing as a constant trope throughout. For example, returning to Mother Carey's story of Pandora's box, it is Epimetheus who is the practical hard-working figure admired by Kingsley, for it is Epimetheus who looks to the past to improve the future for in Mother Carey's words, which are approved of by the narrator Kingsley:

---

12 Charles Kingsley, 'The Natural Theology of the Future' (1871) <http://www.gutenberg.org/files/10427/10427-h/10427-h.htm> [June 1, 2015], p. 3.

his children are the men of science, who get good lasting work done in the world; but the children of Prometheus are the fanatics, and the theorists, and the bigots, and the bores, and the noisy windy people, who go telling silly folk what will happen, instead of looking to see what has happened already.[13]

Tom looks to see if he can observe what it is that Mother Carey is doing as she is creating life, yet there is nothing to be seen for she allows life to make itself, which leads Tom to journey to Kingsley's ultimate image of creation for:

Then he came to a very quiet place, called Leaveheavenalone. And there the sun was drawing water out of the sea to make steam-threads, and the wind was twisting them up to make cloud-patterns, till they had worked between them the loveliest wedding veil of Chantilly lace, and hung it up in their own Crystal Palace for any one to buy who could afford it; while the good old sea never grudged, for she knew they would pay her back honestly. So the sun span, and the wind wove, and all went well with the great steam-loom; as is likely, considering—and considering—and considering—.[14]

This is nature in harmony with industry, invention and commerce so vital to Victorian society and the expanding Empire. The images are delicate, vivid and peaceful, working as one continuous effort without effort. The puzzle set by this passage is the unfinished sentence, the only one in the book, the phrase: 'considering—and considering—and considering—' divided by dashes representing a mood of contemplation. The unfinished sentence combined with the name of the place, 'Leaveheavenalone', presents a number of considerations, with Kingsley perhaps setting a riddle for the reader. In one way it can be read as representing a wavering and possible loss of faith in Kingsley who was a minister of the Church and also an ardent follower of Darwin. It also represents the tenor of the work: contemplation and continuing thinking and puzzling—the place which writing affords Kingsley, the stillness at the centre of Rabelaisian thought. Finally Tom becomes Kingsley's champion making him a representative of the creator of the new world emerging as a Great Man of Science, an identity for the Victorian Age.

The question of identity is one matter which Alice is pursuing through Lewis Carroll's surreal fantasy *Alice in Wonderland* (1865). For on falling down the rabbit-hole things are changing:

13 Kingsley, *The Water-Babies*, p. 150.
14 Ibid., p. 169.

> Dear, dear! How queer everything is to-day! And yesterday
> things went on just as usual. I wonder if I've been changed
> during the night? Let me think: was I the same when I got up
> this morning? I almost think I can remember feeling a little
> different. But if I'm not the same, the next question is, who in
> the world am I? Ah, that's the great puzzle![15]

Unlike Tom, whose identity has been fixed for him by Kingsley,
Alice's identity is unpredictable and changing. Kingsley's tale is
a moral venture, whilst Carroll sets Alice on a journey through an
illogical and surreal world in which she tries to employ logic that
increasingly slips away from her as meaning and syllogism collide.
Tom begins in a state of moral illiteracy whereas Alice is an educated
middle-class child with a clear sense of right and wrong.

The artist George Cruikshank's Beehive etching of British
society in 1867 gave an image of a seemingly fixed society, yet this
was a period when society was changing with the increasing wealth
of empire and industry which resulted in social mobility for some. A
rapidly changing society combined with Romantic ideas of the sense
of individuality come together in Alice's experience. The characters
she meets such as the Caterpillar, the White Rabbit or the Red
Queen, would have existed in different form as insects, animals or
playing cards in the real world, yet here they retain enough for Alice
to identify them whilst being also, to borrow W.B. Yeats's phrase,
'changed utterly'. (Yeats, 1962: 95) Not surprisingly in this world of
question Alice tries to identify who she is and wonders if she has been
changed into Mabel when she assesses her knowledge that is now out
of place underground. Mabel is the potential model, since she is a
child who knows little.

> I must be Mabel, after all, and I shall have to go and live in
> that poky little house, and have next to no toys to play with,
> and oh! ever so many lessons to learn! No, I've made up my
> mind about it; if I'm Mabel, I'll stay down here! It'll be no use
> their putting their heads down and saying, 'Come up again,
> dear!' I shall only look up and say, 'Who am I then? Tell me
> that first, and then, if I like being that person, I'll come up: if
> not, I'll stay down here till I'm somebody else. (Carroll, 1992:
> 16)

There is an implication of class association with personal identity
here, as Alice is concerned that if she is Mabel then she will have

---

15 Lewis Carroll, *Alice in Wonderland & Through the Looking-Glass* (New
York: W.W. Norton & Company, 1992), p. 15.

to live in a small house with less trappings of affluence, in short, downward social mobility, a circumstance which she would avoid by staying in Wonderland. Carroll is reflecting the anxieties of class and identity for with middle class expansion, the rise of the bourgeoisie, came an uncertainty about a sense of identity, a problem of identity which would later be overtly pursued by the Modernists, but which is rooted in the nineteenth century. As Mihaela Dumitrescu observes in her article 'Modernism, Postmodernism and the Question Of Identity' (*Repères Théoriques Theoretical Considerations*, Dialogos 3, 2001): 'The very paradigm of modernity relies heavily on the idea of universal reason and of social progress achievable through advances in knowledge, as illustrated by the "grand narratives".' (Dumitrescu, 2001: 11) For Alice her knowledge of Victorian grand narratives into which she has been inculcated at school is slipping away. Mathematical and geographical facts are no longer absolute certainties for her when she tests her own knowledge:

> I'm sure I can't be Mabel, for I know all sorts of things, and she, oh! she knows such a very little! [17] Besides, she's she, and I'm I, and—oh dear, how puzzling it all is! I'll try if I know all the things I used to know. Let me see: four times five is twelve, and four times six is thirteen, and four times seven is—oh dear! I shall never get to twenty at that rate! However, the Multiplication Table doesn't signify: let's try Geography. London is the capital of Paris, and Paris is the capital of Rome, and Rome—no, that's all wrong, I'm certain! I must have been changed for Mabel![16]

Interestingly Alice/Carroll uses the term 'signify'. Alice's problem is that what she knows, or thinks she knows, does not have a correlation between signifier and signified. Her process of identification, of the realization of her subjectivity, through Wonderland is by opposition. She is defined and defines what she is by what she is not. Carroll sets this up from the point of her landing at the bottom of the rabbit hole and trying to decide where she is, thinking that she has fallen so far that she has probably gone through to the other side of the earth and landed in the Antipodes. However, Alice uses the term 'The Antipathies' which ironically is apt for this is a world where there is opposition to her and she is in opposition to it; where she is questioned and moves on until she finds an answer.

Lewis Carroll's *Alice in Wonderland* and *Alice Through the Looking-Glass* are satirical views on Victorian society, surreal creations which

---

16 Ibid., p. 16.

are his mixture of fact and fantasy. Alice is, as it were, caught in a Modernist conundrum ahead of her time. Whilst Alice endeavours to understand Wonderland and the Looking-Glass World through her perceptions and interactions she is thwarted by the characters she meets, for what is 'truth' is what they say it to be and not what Alice knows or decides. The conversations with the Caterpillar and Humpty Dumpty epitomize Alice's position.

> The Caterpillar and Alice looked at each other for some time in silence: at last the Caterpillar took the hookah out of its mouth, and addressed her in a languid, sleepy voice.
>
> "Who are you?" said the Caterpillar.
>
> This was not an encouraging opening for a conversation. Alice replied, rather shyly, "I hardly know, sir, just at present—at least I know who I was when I got up this morning, but I think I must have been changed several times since then."
>
> "What do you mean by that?" said the Caterpillar sternly. "Explain yourself!"
>
> "I can't explain myself, I'm afraid, sir," said Alice, "because I'm not myself, you see."
>
> "I don't see," said the Caterpillar.
>
> "I'm afraid I can't put it more clearly," Alice replied very politely, "for I can't understand it myself to begin with; and being so many different sizes in a day is very confusing."
>
> "It isn't," said the Caterpillar.
>
> "Well, perhaps you haven't found it so yet," said Alice, "but when you have to turn into a chrysalis—you will some day, you know—and then after that into a butterfly, I should think you'll feel it a little queer, won't you?"
>
> "Not a bit," said the Caterpillar.
>
> "Well, perhaps your feelings may be different," said Alice; "all I know is, it would feel very queer to me."
>
> "You!" said the Caterpillar contemptuously. "Who are you?"
>
> Which brought them back again to the beginning of the conversation. Alice felt a little irritated at the Caterpillar's making such very short remarks, and she drew herself up and said, very gravely, "I think you ought to tell me who you are, first."
>
> "Why?" said the Caterpillar.

Here was another puzzling question; and as Alice could not

think of any good reason, and as the Caterpillar seemed to be in a very unpleasant state of mind, she turned away.[17]

In his fantasies Carroll has removed an absolute sense of meaning; truth and meaning are defined as a matter of relativity, an approach to meaning that is developed through Modernism. The power of language and the contest for power is repeated in *Through the Looking-Glass* in the conversation with Humpty Dumpty:

> "When I use a word," Humpty Dumpty said in rather a scornful tone, "it means just what I choose it to mean—neither more nor less."
>
> "The question is," said Alice, "whether you CAN make words mean so many different things."
>
> "The question is," said Humpty Dumpty, "which is to be master—that's all."[18]

Alice's journeys of both through Wonderland and the Looking-Glass world take her into contact with another seat of power, that of royalty. In *Wonderland* she is finally in the court and in *Looking-Glass* her intention is to become a queen. In both cases these are challenges to the established authority, the challenge of the younger generation who will make the new world. Alice overturns the power of the royal court when she grows to her full size and they flutter down as 'nothing but a pack of cards!' Her realization is that this world has been but a game and as a more experienced character in *Through the Looking-Glass* her determination is to become a Queen in the game of chess where she will be arguably the most powerful piece, as she has the most moves.

Lewis Carroll stands out from my selected authors because he is intent on playing with language, subverting and satirizing Victorian society and culture, challenging authority—a subject which will be returned to later. Carroll is playing with the elements of subjectivity, the perception of the world through the subject in relation to other. The text has very little in terms of description of landscape; there is no reliance on a realist mode of convincing the reader that this is a real world through description, history or landscape detail. The driving forces are language and understanding for this is the interior world which defines a human being, it is an intellectual landscape. In contrast the work of Charles Kingsley and George MacDonald has greater affinity in that their fantasy worlds interact more directly

---

17 Ibid., p. 35.

18 Ibid., p. 163.

with the social realities of the period, which was an increasing trend. Earlier in the nineteenth century there was a sense of distance between the realities of the poor and middle class characters. For example in Charlotte Yonge's realist *The Daisy Chain* (1856), the middle-class family would decide that their contribution to relieving the plight of the impoverished was to build a church.[19] By the 1870s the movement in literary representations of the poor and working class was towards greater understanding with the poor and working child being the focus of the literature as in Hesba Stretton's *Pilgrim Street* (1886). This was a considerable move forward from the early part of the century, moreover, MacDonald's fantasies produced a more complex representation whilst retaining the emphasis on morality and moral education.

Whereas Kingsley's Tom is very much a child of the world, MacDonald's Diamond in *At the Back of the North Wind* is both a child of this world and of the spirit and the spirit of nature. He co-exists and interacts between both worlds, the world of now and that of the imagination, which is another reality for him and for the reader: both are 'true'. The relationship of the central character to the imaginary worlds differs across the texts: Tom has no recollection of his world of the chimney sweep boy once he enters the waters and becomes a water-baby. His transition up the back stairs to re-enter the real world as a Great Man of Science is engineered by the Irish Fairy who covers his eyes. The worlds are kept as separate consciousnesses. Alice gradually loses contact with her world outside her dream as she becomes more deeply engaged and immersed in Wonderland until she can break free and awake. MacDonald certainly does not want either Diamond or his reader to perceive the worlds as separate: for MacDonald the imagination is vital to reality.

At the Back of the North Wind takes the reader from the known to the unknown to the unknowable. Nature is an ever present force in the text and is realized through the North Wind. For Diamond dream, reality and experiencing an intimacy with nature are fused:

> As he stood there he remembered how the wind had driven him to this same spot on the night of his dream. And once more he was almost sure that it was no dream. [...] Not a flower was to be seen in the beds on the lawn. Even the brave old chrysanthemums and Christmas roses had passed away before the frost. What? Yes! There was one! He ran and knelt

19 Charlotte M. Yonge *The Daisy Chain, Or Aspirations* (1856) <http://www.gutenberg.org/files/3610/3610-h/3610-h.htm> [June 1, 2015], p. 32.

down to look at it.

It was a primrose—a dwarfish thing, but perfect in shape—a baby-wonder. As he stooped his face to see it close, a little wind began to blow, and two or three long leaves that stood up behind the flower shook and waved and quivered, but the primrose lay still in the green hollow, looking up at the sky, and not seeming to know that the wind was blowing at all. It was just a one eye that the dull black wintry earth had opened to look at the sky with. All at once Diamond thought it was saying its prayers, and he ought not to be staring at it so. He ran to the stable to see his father make Diamond's bed. Then his father took him in his arms, carried him up the ladder, and set him down at the table where they were going to have their tea.[20]

The passage seamlessly brings together all of the elements of Diamond's life: nature, the passing of the seasons, the courage of nature in all weathers, the need to realize the source of such creations in God, and the closeness of his family. Diamond will face the harsher realities in the world of work when he takes over running the cab when his father is ill. Yet it is this child of God who stands against the inhumanities of poverty and cruelties of life in the Victorian city. He has learnt from his time with the North Wind when she took him on the ledge of the cathedral that faith can give courage. Diamond's adventures and contemplative times spent with North Wind and at the back of the North Wind defy the constructions of linearity. The experiences at the back of the North Wind can only be recalled in poetry and music; poetry which celebrates the harmony and rhythms of nature, and music which goes beyond words. MacDonald's response to a fast changing world was to embody the power of faith and trust in the figure of a child who, although he could not continue in this world, did have such an effect that it reverberated through the lives of others for better. The Modernist roots stirring in MacDonald's work are implicit. The Romantic child is a foil to the deprivation and evils of urbanization, yet there are no absolute answers, no manifestoes; Diamond will shine through the future with his inner strength and that which the memory and experience of him gives to others. *At the Back of the North Wind* neither relies upon, nor draws on grand narratives or tradition. The story of Diamond is in the 'here and now' of domesticity and the world of work in Victorian England where it

---

20 George MacDonald, *At The Back Of The North Wind* (Guelph: Broadview, 2011), p. 64.

is up to those who have known Diamond to make a better world, it is their individual responsibility. Diamond is not a hero in the grand tradition of nineteenth century adventure stories, for MacDonald saw no need for such, a different perception of need from that which would come some four decades later in World War I.

Had Virginia Woolf had the gift of foresight she might well have altered her statement in 'Mr. Bennet and Mrs. Brown' to: 'The change was sudden and definite [...] a change there was, nevertheless; and, since one cannot be arbitrary, let us date it as July 28th 1914', the day which set Europe on a path of destruction and irrevocable change when war was declared. Both J.R.R. Tolkien and C.S. Lewis fought in the war and *The Hobbit*, *The Fellowship of the Rings* and the Narnia series reflect a shift in thinking. Kingsley, Carroll and MacDonald can be referred to as pre-Modernist writers with the stirring of what would be known as Modernism in their fantasies. Tolkien and Lewis are what can be called 'Retro-Victorians' looking for the re-establishment of social paternalist order and tradition which had been blown across the fields of France and later the battlefields of Europe in World War Two.

Tolkien's work creates a mythic grand narrative as does Lewis's Narnia series. By the mid-nineteen fifties the power of the British Empire was fast fading. India, the jewel in the crown of the Empire had independence and African countries were fast following. Britain had infamously won the war and lost the peace as post-war austerity and rationing continued. The Festival of Britain in 1951 was to showcase to an exhausted nation the power of their invention and creativity, the ability to revive and succeed after prolonged attack, loss and grinding down; the ability to resist and win. Tolkien and Lewis provided the new myths, the belief that evil could be defeated. Tolkien proved through his stories that even a small Hobbit could be a hero against immeasurable and unseen forces and that the idyll of the landscape of Middle Earth, the landscape fought for in both world wars, would be preserved. Narnia is a land imbued with imperialist values. The children become apprentices and then Kings and Queens, heroes and heroines in the fight against evil. Both the worlds of Middle Earth and Narnia have that clear battle, the division between Good and Evil. Eliot's 'Wasteland'(1922) fractured and exhausted with a disappearing Fisher King obscured by fragmented references was not to be the model. Here both Tolkien and Lewis created mythical worlds which were solid in materiality and in faith. Their pathways would lead to glory and to rest. There would always be a saviour and there would always be the hard working faithful. There would always be more than one can see on the surface of life.

In conclusion as Eliot reflected in 'Burnt Norton'

> Time present and time past
> Are both perhaps present in time future
> And time future contained in time past.
> If all time is eternally present
> All time is unredeemable.
> What might have been is an abstraction
> Remaining a perpetual possibility
> Only in a world of speculation.[21]

Fantasy is a means of speculation. The work of the children's authors discussed is simultaneously playful and deeply serious contemplating matters such as identity, environment, the place of and nature of humanity, the structures of society which continue to be the subjects of contemporary writers in an everlasting and overlapping literary conversation.

---

21 T.S. Eliot, 'Burnt Norton', *Collected Poems 1909-1962* by T.S. Eliot (London: Faber and Faber Limited, 1963), p. 189.

BIBLIOGRAPHY

Carroll, Lewis, *Alice in Wonderland & Through the Looking-Glass*, New York: W.W. Norton & Company, 1992. Print.

Dumitrescu, Mihaela. 'Modernism, Postmodernism and the Question Of Identity', *Repères Théoriques Theoretical Considerations*, Dialogos 3 (2001). Print.

Faulkner, Peter, *A Modernist Reader: Modernism in England 1910-1930*, London: Batsford, 1986. Print.

Eliot, T.S., 'Burnt Norton', *Collected Poems 1909-1962 by T.S. Eliot*, London: Faber and Faber Limited, 1963. Print.

Kingsley, Charles, 'Sermons on National Subjects' (1849) <http://www.gutenberg.org/files/8202/8202-h/8202-h.htm accessed> [June 1, 2015.]

Kingsley, Charles, 'The Natural Theology of the Future' (1871) <http://www.gutenberg.org/files/10427/10427-h/10427-h.htm> [June 1, 2015.]

Kingsley, Charles, *The Water-Babies*, 2013, Oxford: Oxford University Press. Print.

Kingsley, Frances E.G. (ed), *Charles Kingsley: His Letters and Memories of His Life*, New York: Charles Scribner's Sons, 1883. Print.

Levene, A. and Webb Jean, 'Depictions of the 'ideal child' in nineteenth-century British literature and legislature,' *Journal of the History of Childhood and Youth*, Unpublished Paper.

Lewis, C.S., *The Allegory of Love*, Cambridge: Cambridge University Press, 2013. Print.

MacDonald, George, *At The Back Of The North Wind*, Guelph: Broadview, 2011. Print.

Manlove, Colin, 'Charles Kingsley, H. G. Wells, and the Machine in Victorian Fiction', *Nineteenth-Century Literature*, Vol. 48, No. 2 (Sep., 1993), pp. 212-239. Print.

Prickett, Stephen, *Victorian Fantasy*, Waco, Texas: Baylor University Press, 2005. Print.

Stretton, Hesba, *Pilgrim Street*, London: The Religious Tract Society, 1886. Print.

Yeats, W.B., 'Easter 1916', *W.B. Yeats Selected Poetry*, London: Macmillan, 1962. Print.

Yonge, Charlotte M., *The Daisy Chain*, Or Aspirations (1856) <http://www.gutenberg.org/files/3610/3610-h/3610-h.htm> [June 1, 2015]

'The Leaven Hid in The Meal':
George MacDonald, C.S. Lewis, and the Practice of Literary Criticism

Bethany Bear Hebbard

In *The Allegory of Love* (1936), C.S. Lewis heads his chapter on Spenser with an epigraph from George MacDonald's 1867 novel, *Annals of a Quiet Neighborhood*: 'The quiet fulness [sic] of ordinary nature.'[1] While MacDonald is a frequent guide in Lewis's autobiographical, theological, and fantastical writings, it may seem more surprising to meet him in Lewis's scholarly work. MacDonald did publish several anthologies and critical essays, but at first glance his approach to literature seems remarkably different from that of Lewis. MacDonald's most extensive critical exercise is *England's Antiphon* (1868), an anthology of religious verse. Here, in his own chapter on Spenser, MacDonald makes a claim that resonates throughout *Antiphon*, namely, that when studying religious writers, 'we cannot speak of their words without speaking of themselves'.[2] On the other hand, from 1934-1936, Lewis and E.M.W. Tillyard published a series of articles (collected in 1939 as *The Personal Heresy*), in which Lewis maintains, against Tillyard, that discussing an author's personality is not a legitimate end for literary criticism. Why then would Lewis begin his chapter on *The Faerie Queene* with a line from MacDonald, who seems to practice the very form of criticism Lewis disavows?

One answer to this question may lie in MacDonald's concept of a hidden tradition, which surrounds and surpasses any single poet, and which it is the critic's duty to herald and sustain. Thus, while he may seem to practice the 'personal heresy' Lewis condemns, MacDonald is actually a fitting patron of Lewis's criticism. In his own critical works, MacDonald models a paradox that emerges not only in *The Personal Heresy*, but also in Lewis's mature literary criticism: that it is through a tradition of shared poetic experiences, not biographical analysis or hero-worship, that a reader can enjoy a true encounter with an author.

Admittedly, *The Personal Heresy* is an unusual choice for examining Lewis's contributions to literary criticism. The book

---

1   C.S. Lewis, *The Allegory of Love*. (London: Oxford University Press, 1972), p. 297.

2   George MacDonald, *England's Antiphon*, (Whitehorn: Johannesen, 1996), p. 63.

itself is difficult to obtain, and was out of print from 1965 to 2008.[3] Furthermore, as Charles Beach observes, when Lewis published the first of the *Heresy* essays in 1934, he had not yet published a major work of literary criticism or scholarship.[4] Rather than a carefully planned manifesto, the work has the energy and, at times, the obscurity, of someone thinking out loud. As one editor has noted, Lewis is 'clearly constructing [his argument] on the fly'.[5] Nevertheless, *Heresy* is valuable, for it shows Lewis working through questions and practices that would shape the rest of his writing career. Additionally, in 1936, as the *Heresy* controversy continued, Lewis published the first of his substantial critical works, *The Allegory of Love*. Together, then, these two early works offer a glimpse of the foundations of Lewis's career as a critic. More specifically, references to MacDonald in both works suggest that the elder writer played an important role in Lewis's scholarly development, congruent with his more commonly-heralded importance as imaginative and spiritual guide.

In the early essays of *Heresy* Lewis attempts to draw a fairly hard line against the idea that reading—whether as a critic or layman—is primarily valuable for what it reveals about the author's personality. He summarizes his objections in the opening lines of his first essay. 'Poetry', he writes, 'is widely believed to be the "expression of personality": the end which we are supposed to pursue in reading it is a certain contact with the poet's soul' (*Heresy* 2). He does not deny that it is possible to 'extract' an idea of the poet's identity from the poem, but he does argue (at least in the first essay), that such analysis is not part of true 'poetical experience' (5). He claims that those who focus on explicating an author's temperament and biography, such as E.M.W. Tillyard, represent a 'psychological' or 'Romantic' school of criticism. In the essay dialogue that follows, Lewis and Tillyard spend

---

3   In 1965 Oxford University Press issued a reprint of their original 1939 edition. The 2008 edition was edited by Joel Heck (Austin, TX: Concordia University Press). Since the late 1970s, *The Bulletin of the New York C. S. Lewis Society* has published several summaries of the book's contents, including one by Heck. For readers who have difficulty finding a copy of *Heresy*, the most thorough summary available is Charles Beach's "C.S. Lewis vs. E.M.W. Tillyard: *The Personal Heresy*."

4   Charles Beach, 'C.S. Lewis vs. E.M.W. Tillyard: *The Personal Heresy*' (*CSL*, 2007), p. 1.

5   Michael I. Edwards and Bruce L. Edwards, '"Everyman's Tutor": C.S. Lewis on Reading and Criticism' (*C. S. Lewis: Life, Works, and Legacy*, Westport: Praeger, 2007), p. 168.

a great deal of time debating the word 'personality', but whether we prefer Tillyard's 'pattern of mind' or Lewis's 'personality', the crux of their dispute is not the word itself. Rather, Tillyard wants to look at the author's personality as an object of poetic study, while Lewis wants to look with, or perhaps even through the author, toward the objects described in the literary text. As an example of this process, Lewis describes how he might read a poem by Herrick: [6]

> It may be true that what I am aware of in reading Herrick's poem is silk, but it is not silk as an object in rerum natura. I see it as Herrick saw it; and in so doing, it may be argued, I do come into contact with his temperament in the most intimate—perhaps in the only possible—way. [...] Let it be granted that I do approach the poet; at least I do it by sharing his consciousness, not by studying it. I look with his eyes, not at him. He, for the moment, will be precisely what I do not see; for you can see any eyes rather than the pair you see with, and if you want to examine your own glasses you must taken them off your own nose. The poet is not a man who asks me to look at him; he is a man who says, "look at that" and points; the more I follow the pointing of his finger the less I can possibly see of him. (11)

Lewis reiterates this point, even more memorably, a page later:

> To see things as the poet sees them I must share his consciousness and not attend to it; I must look where he looks and not turn round to face him; I must make of him not a spectacle but a pair of spectacles: [...] I must enjoy him and not contemplate him. Such is the first positive result of my inquiry. (12)

The distinction between enjoyment and contemplation comes from Samuel Alexander's *Space, Time and Deity* (1920), and, as Stephen Logan observes, in *Heresy* Lewis uses Alexander's terms to frame his perennial challenge to self-consciousness in both art and criticism. Thus, to enjoy a reading experience 'means participating fully in the results of attending to its object', whereas to contemplate entails 'consciously examining those results'.[7] According to this distinction, Lewis disapproves of psychological criticism not only because it can create an idolatrous fascination with the poet's biography, but

---

6   The poem Lewis references here is Herrick's 'Whenas in silks my Julia goes'.

7   Stephen Logan, 'Old Western Man for Our Times' (*Renascence: Essays on Values in Literature*, 1998), p. 72.

because it teaches readers to contemplate the personal results of a poetic experience, rather than facilitating the reader's disinterested enjoyment of the experience itself.

As a reader and critic, in other words, Lewis has little interest looking at an author's portrait, no matter how accurate. Rather, he wants to help readers surrender to a poetic experience, an experience mediated by the poet. The enjoyment Lewis hopes to facilitate between author and reader ought to sound familiar, for it anticipates a distinction Lewis would make almost twenty-four years later in *The Four Loves* (1960). In this later work, Lewis is attempting to distinguish between lovers and friends. He writes, 'Lovers are always talking to one another about their love; Friends hardly ever about their Friendship. Lovers are normally face to face, absorbed in each other's; Friends, side by side, absorbed in some common interest.'[8]

One might reasonably argue, then, that when Lewis says he must 'share [an author's] consciousness and not attend to it', he is upholding a kind of critical friendship between readers/critics and authors. Some readers have used similar language to describe Lewis's own criticism. Noting that Lewis's practice of criticism was somewhat at odds with mainstream practices even in his own day, Bruce Edwards and Michael Edwards suggest that the most apt phrase to describe Lewis's academic work is not 'critic', but rather, 'literary companion, a knowledgeable traveler and navigator, drawing our attention from time to time to landmarks of the textual journey we might miss'.[9] Lewis asserts the virtues of such a companionate relationship among writers, critics and readers later in *Heresy*, when he charges the 'Romantic' school with committing a form of 'poetolatry': that is, he accuses them of devotion to poets as 'great men' whose personalities are somehow specially worthy of observation, even reverence or adoration.[10] In other words, he casts these analysts as he would later describe lovers: staring intently at the poet, perpetuating self-consciousness by channeling this contemplation into some insight about his (the critic's) own soul. The analogy is not perfect, of course, but it does provide a useful framework for talking about the kind of critic Lewis hopes to inspire in *Heresy*: not one who denies the presence of personality in literature, but one who refuses to make a writer's self-revelation the point of critical inquiry.

---

8   C.S. Lewis, *The Four Loves*, (London: Harcourt, 1971), p. 60.

9   Edwards, "Everyman's Tutor", p. 165.

10   Beach, 'C.S. Lewis vs. E.M.W. Tillyard: *The Personal Heresy*,' p. 96.

One of the main problems with this idolatrous form of criticism is that it artificially isolates literary texts, excluding other readers. A lovers' meeting by its very nature excludes others, as Lewis himself notes in *The Four Loves*. Friendship, on the other hand, is more generous, admitting to its fellowship any who are willing to enjoy or suffer the same thing.[11] In the context of literature, this kind of friendship would mean that it is only in such a company—friends seeing or seeking a common object—that one has access to a writer's consciousness. Not a tryst, but a tradition could bring readers and writers into meaningful contact. In other words, Lewis argues that in having an 'imaginative experience' with a text, 'we do come to share or enjoy a new kind of consciousness, but that consciousness is not the consciousness of any single individual'.[12] He means a number of things by this statement. First of all, a poet may use poetic devices 'which are the offspring of no human temperament', such as epithets or meters.[13] Additionally, after a poem exists, it will inevitably take on 'new colours which the artist neither foresaw nor intended'.[14] While critics may attempt to parse these accretions from whatever the author intended, Lewis maintains that these traditional colours—echoes of exchange between generations of readers and authors—are inseparable from a reader's experience of the text.[15]

Finally, Lewis insists that when writing, even according to the impulses of temperament, a poet is not experiencing the same kind of consciousness he or she always possesses. Reading a poet's sonnet and conversing with her in the grocery store, for example, would give one quite different senses of the poet's consciousness. Rather, the consciousness that produces a poem is inseparable from tradition, as individual poets sustain and recreate conversations with other poets, texts, and objects. Lewis's argument on this point is a bit muddy in the early essays, but in his postscript to *Heresy*, he attempts to clarify his position:

> All I have a right to say in the poetic speech-thought uses such memories, associations, and values as are widely distributed among the human family in space and time, and rejects what is merely idiosyncratic; and that no human being permanently

11 Lewis, *The Four Loves*, p. 61-2.

12 Ibid., p. 15.

13 Ibid., p. 15.

14 Ibid., p. 16.

15 Ibid., p. 16.

enjoys poetic speech-thought. Perhaps I can still say that if any being did, he, or it, would be an angel.[16]

As his dialogue with Tillyard forces Lewis to refine his argument, Lewis reveals that his theories of criticism build upon the premise that the greatest literature 'communicates such experiences as all men have had'.[17] This definition reinforces the futility of personality-based reading. If Chaucer, Shakespeare, and Milton create great poetry because they attempt to express universal experiences, not idiosyncratic perspectives, then enjoying a meaningful encounter with the poet cannot be *essential* to the practice of criticism. However, in a curious concession, Lewis admits that there is a second kind of poetry, one that deals not in familiar experiences, but which startles readers with 'a new and nameless sensation, or even a new sense, to enrich me with experience which nothing in my previous life had prepared me for'.[18] Even more surprisingly, Lewis concedes that in works such as this, 'I do not deny that we are sharing something peculiar to the poet'.[19] He finds these nameless wonders most often, he writes, in the prose fiction of George MacDonald. In *Heresy*, Lewis hastily dismisses this kind of encounter, arguing that it is not essential to any definition of imaginative literature, and implying, likewise, that it should not inform critical practice. He insists that even when he is able to share 'something peculiar to the poet,' this encounter is less important than the objects of the text. 'I do not care for these things because they introduce me to the men Morris and MacDonald', he maintains: 'I care for the books, and the men, because they witness to these things, and it is the message not the messenger that has my heart'.[20]

Given the distance Lewis seems to place between his own theories of poetry and the literary temper of George MacDonald, it is surprising to find that in *The Allegory of Love* (published in 1936, the same year as the first *Heresy* essay) Lewis heads his culminating chapter—his study of Spenser—with an epigraph from MacDonald

---

16   Beach, 'C.S. Lewis vs. E.M.W. Tillyard: *The Personal Heresy*', p. 147.

17   Ibid., p. 102.

18   Ibid., p. 102.

19   Ibid., p. 102.

20   Ibid., p. 103. For an even more intimate example of this kind of literary friendship, see Lewis's *A Preface to Paradise Lost* (1942). In the book's dedication to Charles Williams, Lewis writes, 'It gives me a sense of security to remember that, far from loving your work because you are my friend, I first sought your friendship because I loved your books'.

himself. In addition to the distance he places between himself and MacDonald in *Heresy*, this reference is remarkable for a number of reasons. First, compared to his imaginative fiction and sermons, MacDonald's strictly critical output was small, and his reputation has never rested on his criticism. However, during his lifetime MacDonald frequently lectured on literary subjects, and one of his most interesting early works is *England's Antiphon* (1868), an anthology of and commentary on English religious poetry. Here, in his own chapter on Spenser, MacDonald writes that '[w]hen we come to the masters of such [religious] song, we cannot speak of their words without speaking of themselves'.[21] Even more, in his preface to the collection, MacDonald announces his aim as the creation of 'intelligent and cordial sympathy' between his readers and the writers he has included.[22] MacDonald seems to take for granted that it is both possible and desirable for a reader and author to meet in a meaningful way. One must ask, then, whether MacDonald's desired sympathy is nearer the friendship Lewis enjoins or the poetolatry Tillyard allegedly practices. Is it 'enjoyment' or 'contemplation'? Friendship or infatuation?

As one looks more closely at *England's Antiphon*, it becomes clear that the sympathy MacDonald hopes to establish is quite similar to Lewis's description of critical friendship, for he draws his readers' attention to something beyond both writer and reader. In *Antiphon*, the poetic experiences and objects are religious, most often the person of Christ, his mother, or the revelation of God through nature. For MacDonald, critical sympathy depends upon writers' and readers' shared participation in the literary traditions of the Christian Church, not upon any particular writer's self-expression. It is this idea of religious literary tradition that is behind the curious closing line in MacDonald's preface. Having announced his desire to mediate towards sympathy, MacDonald cries, 'Heartily do I throw this my small pebble at the head of the great Sabbath-breaker *Schism*'.[23] In other words, the sympathy MacDonald hopes to create does not depend upon the analysis of a poet's personality, but upon mutual surrender to the objects of Christian worship.

While Lewis imagines a reader seeing through a poet's eyes, MacDonald imagines readers listening to the poet's song. He

---

21 MacDonald, *England's Antiphon*, p. 93.

22 Ibid., p. vi.

23 Ibid., p. vi.

introduces the poets in his collection as singers in an antiphonal choir, and MacDonald himself, as anthologizer, is the 'leader of the chorus' or 'master of the hearing, for my aim shall be to cause the song to be truly heard' (*Antiphon* 3). The focus of his criticism, then, is on the song, not the singers. Moreover, MacDonald hopes that with his help readers will 'join in the song of the country's singing men and singing women'.[24] For Lewis, writers share their eyes with readers; for MacDonald, their voices. As one volume of Macmillan's 'Sunday Library for Household Reading', *Antiphon* aims to extend and re-imagine reading as an experience though which '[h]earing, we worship with them'.[25]

In practice, MacDonald's vision of the critic-as-choirmaster means that he often defers attention from the poet to the text and its object. For example, in his discussion of Spenser, MacDonald's attention to the poet's biography seems cursory at first glance. He devotes most of his chapter to examining how Spenser sustains and recreates the religious concerns of other poets in the English literary tradition. Certainly, MacDonald recognizes that an author's life and times shape his writing, but in *Antiphon*, his focus remains on the interests and objects that each writer shares with other British writers across time. Thus, while he claims that 'we cannot speak of [religious poets'] words without speaking of themselves', he implies that the most durable encounter with an author comes not from dwelling on facts concerning 'the life of the writer', but from joining the poet as he meditates upon some aspect of the poet's hidden, spiritual life—the source, MacDonald implies, of poetic utterance.[26] In his discussions of this inner life, MacDonald apparently conflates the types of poetry that Lewis would later describe in *Heresy*. On the one hand, he reads poems as a record of the poet's inner life. At the same time, he claims that only the concerns of this inner life can be universal, connecting one person's experience to another's.

In other critical exercises, it is true that MacDonald spends far more time examining the external aspects of a poet's life; his 1864 essay on Shakespeare, 'St. George's Day', is a good example of this. That piece, with its emphasis on historical and biographical facts, offers a compelling sketch of the formation of Shakespeare, national poet and genius. *Antiphon*, on the other hand, aims to dramatize the

---

24 Ibid., p. 2.

25 Ibid., p. 2.

26 Ibid., p. 63.

creation of good readers. Necessarily, then, its emphasis lies more on prompting readers to recognize in the poetry, if not also in the life of the poet, a common spiritual need. Thus, after quoting sonnet 68 from Spenser's *Amoretti*, MacDonald suggests that readers 'who have never felt the need of the divine [...] will consider this poem untrue, having its origin in religious affectation. Others will think otherwise'.[27] Without this recognition of—or perhaps, participation in—the poet's hidden spiritual life, no array of facts about a poet's life will make his poems believable to new generations of readers.

The strategy MacDonald uses with Spenser—foregrounding the poet's inner life rather than his biography—is representative of his method through the anthology. His first chapter surveys the religious lyrics of the thirteenth century. Here, MacDonald focuses on what these anonymous lyrics reveal about inner life not of any one poet, but of the English nation. He calls these works, with their tender devotion to Christ and his Mother, representative of England's 'true life', a hidden tradition that MacDonald contrasts with the history of 'wars and rumours of wars, the strife of king and barons'.[28] In these lyrics—and throughout his collection—MacDonald defines this true life as participation in 'the kingdom of God' which grows 'quietly, unperceived—the leaven hid in the meal'.[29] As with his interest in Spenser's 'inner life', MacDonald's concern with the 'true life' of England means the way in which English men and women have experienced universal truths. And for MacDonald, the only universal truths are fundamentally spiritual in nature. Thus, he can write that the 'very notion of the kingdom of heaven implies a secret growth, secret from no affectation of mystery, but because its goings on are in the depths of the human nature where it holds communion with the divine'.[30]

This 'communion with the divine', which religious poets translate into poetic experience, both grounds and surpasses individual personality. One might say that MacDonald practices a criticism that looks beyond poet's face (history, biography), for the sake of sharing a poet's eyes, voice, and his hidden heart. Readers familiar with MacDonald will recognize that this play between the surface and the depths is a paradox that appears in all his writings, from

---

27 Ibid., p. 65.

28 Ibid., p. 5.

29 Ibid., p. 5-6.

30 Ibid., p. 6.

sermons to his storytelling. His otherworlds are places where ordinary surfaces—faces, landscapes, and even words—give way as hidden spiritual realities become visible. Indeed, in MacDonald's fiction, the best friends to the protagonists tend to be those who help other characters see beyond surfaces and into the depths of spiritual truth. The best example of such a guide is Mr. Raven, from the romance *Lilith* (1895). In the company of Mr. Raven, the protagonist enters a dimension in which spiritual realities, such as prayers, are visible, while the surfaces of Vane's world, such as his house, disappear. As the passages above suggest, MacDonald takes on a role similar to Mr. Raven's when he turns to criticism. The result is something far more 'personal' than Lewis's ideal in Heresy, but it resonates in important ways with Lewis's practice in *The Allegory of Love*.

In *Allegory*, Lewis conducts his criticism in ways that invoke MacDonald's pursuit of a writer's inner—but not idiosyncratic—spiritual life. *Allegory* concludes with an introduction to Spenser's *The Faerie Queene*, completing Lewis's 'study in medieval tradition'.[31] Like MacDonald, Lewis frames his chapter on the relation between surfaces and depths, revelation and concealment. He opens with an apparent break from his earlier subject matter (English allegories of courtly love), observing that Spenser's direct models for *The Faerie Queene* are Italian epics; they are the armor in which he fights.[32] However, when Lewis turns to the opening lines of the poem—the first objects we see through Spenser's eyes—these Italian models do not help. Unlike Boiardo and Ariosto, Spenser provides no 'situation' or external context for his tale.[33] Rather, Spenser shows us an image: a woman leading a lamb and a knight with a red cross on his silver shield. These images, and the characters they introduce, have their origins not in the Italian epic but in something underneath the Italianate trappings. At the same time, the English courtly love tradition is not sufficient to explain these images, either. Rather, the reader must look both with and within Spenser. Lewis writes,

> Spenser begins like a man in a trance, or a man looking through a window, telling us what he sees. And however deep we dig in Spenser we shall never get to a situation, and never find a context in the objective world for the shapes he is going

---

31 Lewis, *The Allegory of Love*, p. 1.

32 Ibid., p. 304.

33 Ibid., p. 310.

to show us.[34]

As in *Heresy*, Lewis uses the metaphor of reading as sharing an author's eyes. However, in *Allegory* Lewis acknowledges a fact of literary creation that he largely neglects in *Heresy*, namely, that the object a poet 'sees' is often invisible, whether spiritual, intellectual, emotional, etc. Looking at something with a poet often means looking at something hidden, even if the author does not see poetry as self-expression. In the case of Una and Redcrosse, Lewis argues that the enjoyment of Una and Redcrosse demands 'the world of popular imagination: almost, a popular mythology' that Spenser shared with his first readers.[35]

In *Allegory*, then, Lewis practices what he describes theoretically in *Heresy*: he explicates Spenser's 'poetic speech-thought' in terms of the 'memories, associations, and values [that] are widely distributed among the human family in space and time', although here it is the English family, rather than the human family generally, that has Lewis's attention.[36] He goes on to argue that many of the confusing elements of this opening scene in the *Faerie Queene* make sense if we trace them to their probable sources: 'the Lord Mayor's show, the chap-book, the bedtime story, the family Bible, and the village Church'.[37] Beneath both the Italianate characters and courtly flourishes, Spenser derives much of his message and method from 'the old-fashioned service in the village church still continuing the allegorical tradition of the medieval pulpit'.[38] Furthermore, while this passage is undeniably analysis, it is analysis for the sake of the reader's experience. Readers who come to Spenser with images of fairy tales and Bible stories will be better able to enjoy the text than otherwise. For MacDonald, hidden traditions such as this are the 'leaven hid in the meal', and Lewis makes a similar claim regarding Spenser's religious mythology. He claims that Spenser draws upon English folk traditions for the sake of 'the primitive or instinctive mind, with all its terrors and ecstasies', and that this instinctive mind is 'Spenser's real concern'.[39] As MacDonald finds the 'true life' of the English people

---

34 Ibid., p. 310.

35 Ibid., p. 312.

36 Ibid., p. 316.

37 Ibid., p. 312.

38 Ibid., p. 311.

39 Ibid., p. 312.

in the anonymous lyrics of cloistered monks, so Lewis identifies Spenser's 'real concern' in the hidden traditions of English parish life.

Having traced these similarities in Lewis and MacDonald's critical practices, the epigraph Lewis borrows from MacDonald— 'The quiet fulness [sic] of ordinary nature'—sounds resonant rather than surprising.[40] Even without context, the line serves Lewis's purposes well. Compared to the rollicking Italian models, the English material does seem 'quiet', and more importantly, the line anticipates the unheralded, homely plenitude of Spenser's 'ordinary' sources. Furthermore, as it points back to MacDonald, the epigraph reasserts the possibility of friendship between readers and writers. The line comes from a novel MacDonald published only one year before *England's Antiphon*, entitled *Annals of a Quiet Neighborhood* (1867). The narrator, Revd Harry Walton, is describing the 'quiet fulness of ordinary nature' he senses in a rural landscape. To Walton, perceiving this fullness is a sign of spiritual health:

> [...] over all, the sun hung in the sky, pouring down life; shining on the roots of the willows at the bottom of the stream; lighting up the black head of the water-rat as he hurried across to the opposite bank; glorifying the rich green lake of the grass; and giving to the whole an utterance of love and hope and joy, which was, to him who could read it, a more certain and full revelation of God than any display of power in thunder, in avalanche, in stormy sea.[41]

Walton goes on to contrast those who 'could read' the landscape with '[t]hose with whom the feeling of religion is only occasional'.[42] These occasional Christians miss "quiet fulness" and must wait for grand displays of providence in life and nature. Although a minister himself, Walton is one of these unperceiving Christians at the beginning of the novel. Narrating his first day in his new parish, he actually devotes several paragraphs to describing the dreariness of the landscape.[43] What changes between these first and third chapters? Very little, except that Walton takes a number of walks and begins to meet his parishioners. These encounters are in turn sweet and disheartening, but the fact that they happen at all changes Walton's

---

40 Ibid., p. 297.

41 George MacDonald, *Annals of a Quiet Neighbourhood* (New York: Harper and Brothers, 1867), p. 22.

42 Ibid., p. 22.

43 Ibid., p. 5.

relationship to the physical as well as the spiritual community in his charge. He becomes a different kind of reader, in other words, because of personal encounters that redirect his attention.

Fittingly, from the novel's opening lines, Walton has implied that a similarly personal and spiritual encounter ought to be occurring between himself and his readers if they are going to find any value in his narrative. In the opening paragraph, Walton insists that he must 'introduce myself to your acquaintance, and I hope coming friendship'.[44] Explicitly, then, this narrator's goal is friendship with the reader, just as the goal of his walks is friendship with the parishioners. Surely Walton's invitation invites a kind of personal heresy? In fact, Walton forestalls the heresy by refusing to let readers look *at* him. 'I remain concealed behind my words', he writes.[45] If the face of the narrator is concealed, what then, is this friendship? First, readers experience, through Walton's writing, a universal spiritual need for community and redemption. At the same time, readers also come to share Walton's particular and local love for his neighborhood. His words conceal him not because he aspires to anonymity or objectivity, but because Walton, at his best, is more interested with his neighbors than with himself. For us, Walton is not the preacher in the pulpit, physically present and meeting the eyes of the congregation. Rather, he is a storyteller, conscious that he is writing a *book* for *readers*. Thus, Walton continues, 'You can never look me in the eye, though you may look me in the soul. [...] I am bold behind the mask, to speak to you heart to heart; bold, I say, just so much the more that I do not speak to you face to face'.[46]

Within his narrative, Walton models a similar form of encounter when he begins to introduce the people of the parish to certain authors. He begins to offer evening lectures on writers such as Sir Philip Sidney, attempting to bring his listeners 'heart to heart' with 'this grand company'.[47] He aims to 'acquaint' his listeners with 'men great in themselves', men who model virtue in their private lives as much as in their writing.[48] Once again, this might seem like a biographical approach, but Walton makes it clear that his presentation of these great men should inspire more than curiosity or the collection of facts.

44 Ibid., p. 3.

45 Ibid., p. 3.

46 Ibid., p. 3.

47 Ibid., p. 149.

48 Ibid., p. 149.

Rather, over years and years of lectures, Walton proclaims that certain authors are part of a tradition with spiritual value and power: they form a 'cloud of witnesses to the truth in our own and other lands'.[49] Walton himself points readers to the truth of loving one's neighbor, and in the same way, he directs his fictional neighbors to speak 'heart to heart' with the noble men and talented writers who bear witness to this and other truths.

From *The Personal Heresy* alone, one might expect Lewis to dismiss the idea of speaking 'heart to heart' outright. However, in the context of Lewis's developing critical practice in *Allegory*, MacDonald's description suggests an encounter that looks not 'face to face', as lovers, but rather, as friends, points another to objects that move the human heart. Such revelatory friendship is a form of love, and it should be no surprise that *The Four Loves* is one of the places Lewis specifically refers to MacDonald as his 'master'.[50] From his rather bashful reference to MacDonald in *Heresy*, to his quiet MacDonald epigraph in *Allegory*, this later work of Lewis's boldly asserts his debt to MacDonald in all matters of human encounter, whether poetic or personal.

In both theory and practice, we have seen MacDonald and Lewis present literary criticism as a form of friendship that finds its source and sustenance in the idea of hidden traditions. MacDonald says from the beginning of *Antiphon* that if we achieve true "sympathy" with the poets included, we will 'worship with them', just as Walton claims that right readers of his novel will see him 'in the soul'. While Lewis does not demand that readers worship as Spenser did, he nevertheless insists that they direct their eyes to the objects of his devotion and imagination. While their approaches are hardly identical, examining the critical practices of George MacDonald clarifies one resounding, valuable claim from Lewis's *Personal Heresy*: that as scholars choose from among our many possible roles—biographer, fan, iconoclast, interpreter, historian—we would be wise to remember that the first and best relation is that of a friend.

---

49 Ibid., p. 149.

50 Lewis, *The Four Loves*, p. 213.

BIBLIOGRAPHY

Beach, Charles, 'C.S. Lewis vs. E.M.W. Tillyard: *The Personal Heresy*', *CSL* 38.1 (2007): 1-18. Print.

Edwards, Michael I. Edwards and Bruce L. Edwards, '"Everyman's Tutor": C.S. Lewis on Reading and Criticism'. *C.S. Lewis: Life, Works, and Legacy*. Vol. 4. Ed. Bruce L. Edwards. Westport, CT: Praeger, 2007. 163-194. Print.

Heck, Joel D., '*The Personal Heresy*: Scholars Can Be Gentlemen'. *CSL* 39.6 (2008): 1-8. Print.

Lewis, C.S., *The Four Loves*, London: Harcourt, 1971. Print.

Lewis, C.S., *The Allegory of Love*, London: Oxford University Press, 1972. Print.

Logan, Stephen, 'Old Western Man for Our Times'. *Renascence: Essays on Values in Literature* 51.1 (1998): 63-86. Print.

MacDonald, George, *Annals of a Quiet Neighborhood*, New York: Harper and Brothers, 1867. Print.

MacDonald, George, *England's Antiphon*, Whitehorn: Johannesen, 1996. Print.

MacDonald, George, *Lilith: First and Final*, Whitehorn: Johannesen, 2009. Print.

Tillyard, E.M.W. and C.S. Lewis, *The Personal Heresy: A Controversy*, London: Oxford University Press,, 1965. Print

Dreaming into Hyperspace:
The Victorian Spatial Imagination and the Origins of Modern Fantasy in MacDonald and Carroll

Kirstin A. Mills

'What is a fantasy map but a space beyond which There Be Dragons?' - Terry Pratchett

The modern fantasy genre, exemplified by the writings of the Inklings, owes much to Victorian writers, particularly as concerns one of the most fundamental and yet critically overlooked aspects of literature, culture and human perception: the spatial imagination, and in particular, the ways that it was conceived of in terms of alternative spaces of existence such as dreams, the supernatural realm, and from the mid-century onward, higher-dimensional space, or, hyperspace. Enquiries into the nature of hyperspace (what it contained, how it interacted with the three-dimensional human world and how humans could perceive and understand it) were undertaken across a vast cross-section of Victorian society right to the end of the century. It is this energetic hunt for evidence of spaces beyond our traditional three dimensions that contributed to the development of the fantasy genre, where literature of the supernatural increasingly became seen as an appropriate vehicle through which to explore the possibilities and conditions of other worlds. This paper puts forward the idea that the literary deployment of hyperspace was fundamental to the development of modern secondary-world fantasy, and that one of the most crucial turning points in the genre's evolution was the sudden and deliberate turn, following the rise of hyperspace theories, from the dream to hyperspace in the construction of the imagined world. This crucial turning point is most clearly visible in the differences between the earlier and later works of two writers who would both go on to heavily influence modern fantasy in general, and the Inklings specifically: Lewis Carroll and George MacDonald. While their earlier texts—*Alice in Wonderland* and *Phantastes: A Faerie Romance For Men and Women,* respectively—are perhaps best known for their strong evocation of dream-worlds, these novels actually engaged directly with a long literary and even scientific tradition extending back through the Romantic period, that saw dreams as liminal spaces between the natural and supernatural worlds, and therefore, as portals through which the supernatural world might be legitimately and scientifically accessed. Moreover, while this fact is very important for challenging common critical analyses of the dream frame, still more interesting and important for modern fantasy is the fact that their later fictions *Through the Looking-Glass* and *Lilith* take up the new hyperspace theories to replace the dream frame with more concrete constructions of higher-dimensional space in the conceptual organization of their imagined worlds, and in so doing, more closely approach the singular spatial constructions—the secondary worlds—that many consider central to the modern fantasy genre.

Space, and the various ways it can be configured, mapped and imagined, is central to fantasy literature, and especially to its evolution throughout the Victorian era. Robert Louis Stevenson believed that in the process of literary creation, the setting—the world—was of primary importance, and the initial construction of space and place would suggest its own narrative elements. He writes:

> It is my contention—my superstition, if you like—that who is faithful to his map, and consults it, and draws from it his inspiration [...] gains positive support [...] The tale has a root there; it grows in that soil [...] Even with imaginary places, he will do well in the beginning to provide a map; as he studies it, relations will appear that he has not thought upon [...] it will be found to be a mine of suggestion.[1]

It is this very focus on map-making, however, that has led many modern critics to discount the majority of Victorian fantasies from inclusion within the fantasy genre. Of Stevenson's quote, Peter Hunt writes, 'It is this kind of distinction which makes the worlds of *The Water-Babies* or the "Alice" books not worlds in the way in which the Discworld, or Middle Earth [...] can be said to be separate worlds. You could not *map* them.'[2] In addition, the fact that these fantasies

---

1   Robert Louis Stevenson, 'Essays in the Art of Writing' in *The Essays of Robert Louis Stevenson, A Selection* (London: MacDonald, 1950), p. 131.

2   Peter Hunt, 'Introduction', in P. Hunt and M. Lenz (eds), *Alternative Worlds in Fantasy Fiction* (London: Continuum, 2001), p. 12.

were often couched in the framing device of a dream is problematic for most modern critics who see the dream as confirmation of the unreality of its contained world. Lin Carter, for example, writes that because works like *Phantastes* 'are set in Dreamland', 'we are not expected to take their imagined landscapes seriously'.[3]

However, an examination of these fantasies in the context of the wider spatial imagination suggests that rather than indicating a weakness in the construction of these imaginary spaces, this nebulous, dream-like quality to the landscapes is a direct reflection of the contemporary spatial imagination as it stood in relation to the supernatural at the time of writing, and engages firmly with a literary tradition that extends back to the Gothic and Romantic writers at the beginning of the century, and even centuries further back to Medieval Dream Literature, and its nineteenth-century revivals. While this history of association between dreams and the supernatural extends back to Medieval, and before it Greek literature, both of which many nineteenth-century writers such as MacDonald engaged with heavily in their work, what is new across the nineteenth century is the way that fantastic literature, or literature of the supernatural, functioned as part of a close dialogue with the frontiers of science and popular culture that were deeply interested in investigating the reality and nature of the supernatural.

These investigations set out to explore and map the supernatural realm, which, in keeping with traditional folklore, was seen as a 'beyond space', the spirit world or fairyland 'beyond the veil'. Yet gaining access to supernatural space in order to explore and map it was problematic: 'crossing over' into the spirit world was generally likely to be a one-way trip. Early literary explorations of this fascination with the supernatural—the Gothic novels—hover at the limit between the natural and supernatural worlds, representing the intrusion of ghosts in an otherwise realistic, earthly setting, and often explaining them away at the end of the story. However, with the rise of Romantic interests in dreams, trance and alternative states of mind, and particularly Coleridge's conception of what he called 'Somnial or Morphean Space'[4]—the space of dreams, both within and yet beyond the natural world—literature, and with it, science, came to see a way

---

3   Lin Carter 'Introduction', in Morris, W., *The Well at the World's End, Vol. 1* (London: Pan/Ballantine, 1971): pp. i-x, x.

4   S. T. Coleridge, *The Notebooks of Samuel Taylor Coleridge*, Ed. Kathleen Coburn, Vol. 4 (London: Routledge and Kegan Paul, 1957), note 5360.

forward as dreams become equated with the kind of 'beyond' space that the supernatural was imagined to occur within. In a move that in many ways echoed the earlier Medieval and Greek conceptions of dreams with which the Romantic writers engaged, dreams, and later alternative states of consciousness like mesmeric trance, become a liminal space opened up between the natural and supernatural worlds through which consciousness might pass to access 'the other side'. The terrified steps of the Gothic writers along corridors haunted by glimpses of the supernatural, become the intrigued transgressions of the Romantic poets into dream-worlds, and it is in Romantic poetry that the dream as portal into the supernatural realm is consolidated as a profound influence that would last throughout the century to follow, taken up by writers from De Quincey to Kingsley, and the later Victorian fantasists, as each responded to the continued widespread interest in the overlapping spaces of dreams and the supernatural.

In this context of investigation into dreams, mesmerism, and the supernatural world, works such as the *Alice* books and *Phantastes* are in direct keeping with a tradition of literature that sees the dream not as a device used to explain away the magic within, but instead, as a legitimate means of access into the supernatural realm. As direct inheritors of both this fantasy and dream-world tradition, both *Phantastes* and the *Alice* books partake in the nineteenth-century's ambiguous approach to dreams and their psychological and spatial reality. In this way, these 'dream worlds' bear a much closer resemblance to the 'secondary worlds' of modern fantasy than critics have previously allowed.

Both *Alice* and *Phantastes* use the medium of the dream to transport their protagonists into supernatural space. With its tumble down the rabbit-hole into Wonderland, and 'the dream-child moving through a land / Of wonders wild and new', *Alice*—the most famous example of Victorian dream narratives—has been adopted as an example of the literary nonsense genre, where its dream frame has often been seen as an excuse to indulge in its apparent nonsense and wordplay.[5] However, the intimate way in which it engages with the developing discourses on dreams, space, spiritualism, and the imagination, as well its importance within the developing modern fantasy genre, are less widely known. Rather than a merely cerebral, nonsensical construction, as has often been argued, Carroll's Wonderland represents a neat blending of supernatural and mental

5   Lewis Carroll, *Alice in Wonderland* in M. Gardner (ed.), *The Annotated Alice: The Definitive Edition* (New York: W. W. Norton and Co., 2000), p. 7.

space, and engages with the tradition of literary fantasy developed previously by writers such as Kingsley, Thackeray and Ruskin to create an ambiguous dreaming space that teeters on the brink of reality—in the liminal space between waking and sleeping.

That Carroll's story engages specifically with a prior tradition of literary fantasy is suggested by the particular way in which it constructs space, where Wonderland is imagined as a dream space that accords, in much the same way as Charles Kingsley's *The Water-Babies*, with the notion of fairyland and its dual connotations of supernatural folklore and imaginative literature for children (a genre that Carroll's text was instrumental in establishing in Britain). In separate diary entries detailing the story's initial inspiration, Carroll refers to his story as a 'fairy-tale,' which was told to child listeners 'hungry for news of fairy-land,' and details the way in which, 'in a desperate attempt to strike out some new line of fairy-lore, I had sent my heroine straight down a rabbit-hole'.[6] Like Alice's own reference to her reading of fairytales, this constant reference to fairyland and fairytales indicates the literary heritage of Carroll's text, and serves to undermine interpretations that see the text as pure nonsense. Instead, it suggests a way of reading the text that is much more akin to the process of hesitation involved in the literary fantastic exemplified by authors from Mary Shelley to Kingsley. In this alternative way of reading, the dream serves not to discount Alice's experiences in the Somnial Space of Wonderland, but to evoke the hesitation and ambiguity so crucial to discourses of dreaming and psychology across the nineteenth century. In this context, Alice's dream is not merely an idle figment of imagination, but becomes a powerful medium through which to destabilize concepts of reality, and the boundaries between sleeping and waking.

Carroll's direction 'down the rabbit hole' in search of new 'fairy-lore' is significant in several ways. As well as recalling liminal constructions of fairyland within the earth, such as those explored by writers such as Dickens and Kingsley, and obviously symbolizing a descent into the caverns of the subconscious mind, Alice's fall down the rabbit hole mimics the process of falling asleep, and as she descends she does actually fall asleep, 'and had just begun to dream' when she suddenly lands at the bottom. From this point onward, Alice emerges within the Somnial Space of Wonderland and encounters many strange creatures there in one of literature's most

6   Cited in Martin Gardner (ed.), *The Annotated Alice: The Definitive Edition* (New York: W. W. Norton and Co., 2000), pp. 7-8.

memorable depictions of dreaming space. However, this method of entering the dreamworld, as well as several crucial elements within the story, destabilize any simplistic divisions between Alice's sleeping and waking worlds. Importantly, rather than restricting his fantastic content to the dream world, Carroll has Alice fall asleep in this hole only after she has already observed the fantastic talking rabbit with his pocket-watch, and the strange doors and cupboards in the walls of the hole as she falls down it. The timing is crucial for the sense of suspended disbelief: the occurrence of these elements before Alice's sleep is actually described (despite the assumption that she may already be asleep by this point) destabilizes the boundaries between sleep and waking in the tale, and allow it to be enjoyed with that ambiguity and hesitation so crucial to the fantastic text, as the readers 'half believe it true'.[7]

Significantly, this destabilizing of the boundaries between waking and sleeping, reality and fantasy, continues the long-running nineteenth-century discourse on dreaming and madness that authors from Mary Shelley to Charles Dickens engaged with closely in their fantastic literature. On February 9, 1856, Carroll wrote in his diary:

> Query: when we are dreaming and, as often happens, have a dim consciousness of the fact and try to wake, do we not say and do things which in waking life would be insane? May we not then sometimes define insanity as an inability to distinguish which is the waking and which the sleeping life? We often dream without the least suspicion of unreality: "Sleep hath its own world," and it is often as lifelike as the other.[8]

The spatial language of this extract is notable for its construction of a distinct dream world, as is its suggestion that Alice's inability to distinguish between reality and dream, like her reader's, play into a discourse of madness that is reflected throughout the text. The Cheshire Cat believes everyone who enters or exists in Wonderland is mad,[9] and the inverted logic and apparent nonsense of Wonderland, as well as the characters of the Mad Hatter and March Hare, perhaps support this association of madness with a conflation of dreaming and waking worlds, though the precision of the actual logic encoded within these 'nonsense' puzzles destabilizes any simple interpretation

---

7   Carroll, *Alice*, p. 7.

8   Gardner, *Annotated Alice*, p. 67.

9   Carroll, *Alice*, p. 66.

of madness in the text.[10]

While Carroll repeatedly linked his Wonderland with 'Fairyland' and fairytales in his descriptions of it, and these discourses of madness help to maintain a hesitation upon consideration of the supernatural elements in the tale, MacDonald's Fairyland is, by contrast, a deeply mystical and spiritual space. Where *Alice* maintains a humorously academic tone that has aided the critical assumption of its nonsense-value, *Phantastes* is imbued with the high seriousness of earlier Romantic writers such as Coleridge and Wordsworth to afford his secondary world a spiritual depth and philosophical gravity, and posit the dream as a liminal space through which to transition into supernatural space beyond. In characteristically Romantic fashion, the dream is privileged as a higher form of consciousness, allowing access to a space both supernatural and psychological, paradoxically both 'beyond' the natural world and within the subconscious; a space that, also paradoxically, uses the medium of sleep to afford a transcendental spiritual awakening. *Phantastes* is, therefore, the most completely realized literary exploration of Coleridge's dream-as-portal construction of 'Somnial Space', where the dream becomes a liminal pathway between two completely separate worlds. In *Phantastes*, Fairyland is a space that 'runs parallel' to the natural human world,[11] intersecting with it in ways that recall the popular phenomenon of Spiritualism that was growing in the popular Victorian imagination at this time:

> as the lights and influences of the *upper worlds* sink silently through the earth's atmosphere; so doth *Faerie invade the world of men*, and sometimes startle the common eye with an association as of cause and effect, when between the two no connecting links can be traced. (Italics mine.)[12]

The evocation of 'upper worlds' that exist beyond the earth's atmosphere, and yet 'sink silently' (invisibly) through it to interact with the natural world in ways inexplicable to 'the common eye' reflects the tradition of supernaturalism and spatial imagination developed in

---

10 See Gardner's *Annotated Alice* for explanations of the logic behind Carroll's apparent nonsense.

11 George MacDonald, *Phantastes: A Faerie Romance for Men and Women*, 1858, in *Works of Fancy and Imagination*. Vol. 6 (London: Strahan, 1871), p. 214.

12 George MacDonald, *Phantastes: A Faerie Romance*, 1858, in *Works of Fancy and Imagination*. Vol. 5 (London: Strahan, 1871), pp. 198-9.

the Gothic, Romantic and earlier Victorian works. Most significantly, the implication is that these supernatural events, and the supernatural realm itself, may be perceived by an alternative perspective to 'the common eye': by dreams and mesmeric trance.

Indeed, in keeping with the tradition, initiated by Coleridge, of scientific enquiry into 'Somnial Space', Anodos's transition both into awareness of the supernatural and physically into the supernatural space of Fairyland is occasioned by the altered perception and liminal space of both the dream and mesmeric trance. It employs a host of liminal symbols that indicate both Anodos's spiritual, mental and physical passage into fairyland via thresholds, doors, and dreamspace, and his ritual passage from childhood to manhood (the keys to these doors are given to him upon his twenty-first birthday). Significantly, Anodos's journey is initiated with his discovery of his father's desk, which is both a metafictive symbol of text and language,[13] and an interwoven collection of secreted doorways and concealed spaces that prefigure Anodos's later transition from his waking world to the secret space of fairyland: 'the door of a little cupboard in the centre especially attracted my interest, as if there lay the secret of this long-hidden world'.[14] Behind this door is a secret space that seems to operate as a threshold between the natural and supernatural worlds: 'suddenly there stood on the threshold of the little chamber, as though she had just emerged from its depth, a tiny woman-form'—a fairy—with a 'voice that strangely recalled a sensation of twilight'.[15] This fairy, accompanied by the liminal symbols of doorways, thresholds and twilight, seems to exhibit mesmeric power over Anodos, who looks 'deeper and deeper' into her eyes 'till they spread around me like seas, and I sank in their waters,'[16] the sinking and the seas both a common metaphor for trance, sleep and the subconscious, and the seas also an expansive metaphor for the kinds of landscapes that Anodos will be drawn to, and drawn into, in Fairyland. This mesmeric supernatural experience occasions Anodos's transition into Fairyland, which, while dream-like, and continuing the same symbolic use of water, is equally presented as an awakening, as Anodos 'suddenly, as one awakes to the consciousness that the sea has been moaning by him for hours [...]

---

13 Michael Mendelson, 'George MacDonald's *Lilith* and the Conventions of Ascent', *Studies in Scottish Literature* 20.1 (1985): 197-218, p. 26

14 MacDonald, *Phantastes*, vol. 5, p. 6.

15 Ibid., p. 7.

16 Ibid., p. 11.

became aware of the sound of running water near me' and realizes he has passed into a supernatural world.[17]

Critic Fred Kaplan states that 'the central mesmeric experience is that of sleep-waking,' in which we paradoxically fall asleep (or move into a trance-state) in order to awaken to a sense of higher reality—one that, most significantly, is likened by 'the everyday consciousness' to dreams.[18] Rather than a falling asleep 'into a dream',[19] as Manlove has suggested, in a context of cultural and literary mesmerism, Anodos's journey may be instead a sleep-waking in the same way that the trance-state offered by mesmerism allowed the journeyer to discover 'other lands' and new truths.[20] This sense of higher reality, particularly spiritual reality, is emphasized throughout the text and begins in the sleep-waking transition itself, where '[t]he flowering of the man-made decorations in the carpet and the carvings immediately suggests that this *other* world, "Fairyland", is to be in some sense more "real" than the one Anodos is leaving.'[21]

While these ideas are important however, most important for the gradual development of secondary-world fantasy is the physical setting that this spiritual journey is placed within, and the sense of reality that is attributed to this space. In *Phantastes* the liminal space of the dream explored within the works of the Romantic and early Victorian writers opens out into a fully realized parallel world—a luscious, intricate and distinctly corporeal setting, laden with woods and vales that 'stretched as far as the sight could reach on every side of me,' streams and seas, towers and libraries, and a focus on topological mapping and magnetic navigation—'Through them I directed my way, holding eastward as nearly as I could guess'—in an intricate creation of a space that is not the natural world, but bears even more real psychological and emotional impact on Anodos than the Victorian world in which he began.[22] For the first time we have a protagonist who moves beyond liminal dream space into the

17 Ibid., p. 13.

18 Fred Kaplan, *Dickens and Mesmerism: The Hidden Springs of Fiction* (Princeton: Princeton UP, 1975), p. 217.

19 Colin Manlove, 'The Circle of the Imagination: George MacDonald's *Phantastes* and *Lilith*,' *Studies in Scottish Literature* (1982), p. 59.

20 Kaplan, *Dickens*, p. 225.

21 Stephen Prickett, *Victorian Fantasy* (Bloomington: Indiana University Press, 1975), p. 179.

22 MacDonald, *Phantastes*, vol. 5, pp. 60-1.

supernatural secondary world beyond, and when this world begins to be mapped and charted in realistic terms, the birth of modern fantasy has truly begun.

Yet there was one more development that would truly consolidate this direction toward secondary-world fantasy, and that was the rise of hyperspace theories. The 1880s saw a marked rise in public, scientific and spiritual interest in higher-dimensional space following the publication of mathematical theories of the fourth dimension. Originally a purely mathematical construct, it was quickly adopted by the spiritualists as a scientific explanation of the kind of 'beyond' space that literature and popular science had long imagined for the supernatural world.[23] By 1888, A. T. Schofield's *Another World* claimed that:

> The spiritual world agrees largely in its mysterious laws [...] with what by analogy would be the laws, language and claims of a fourth dimension[...] Though the glorious material universe extends beyond the utmost limits of our vision [...] that does not prevent the spiritual world and its beings, and heaven and hell from being by our very side.[24]

Popularized by works such as Edwin Abbott's *Flatland*, which used one and two-dimensional analogies to explain hyperspace and the apparent ghostly phenomena of its inhabitants, awareness of hyperspace, much like the earlier access to the supernatural realm via the dream, required a change of perception. Charles Hinton's 1888 publication, *A New Era of Thought* details ways in which his readers might train themselves to be able to perceive higher dimensions, which were, importantly, not without their supernatural overtones, and was:

> An attempt, in the most elementary and simple domain, to pass from the lower to the higher. In pursuing it the mind passes from one kind of intuition to a higher one, and with that transition the horizon of thought is altered. It becomes clear

23 Margaret Wertheim writes, 'First explored by writers, artists and mystically inclined philosophers, this seemingly fantastical concept would eventually give rise to an extraordinary new scientific vision of reality, one in which space itself would come to be seen as the ultimate substrate of all existence. Here, we are not just talking about the extra dimension of time, but also about extra spatial dimensions.' *The Pearly Gates of Cyberspace: A History of Space from Dante to the Internet* (Sydney: Doubleday, 1999), p. 191.

24 A. T. Schofield, *Another World*, 1888 (London: Swan Sonnenschein, 1905) pp. 81-6.

that there is a physical existence transcending the ordinary physical existence; and one becomes inclined to think that the right direction to look is, not away from matter to spiritual existences but towards the discovery of conceptions of higher matter, and thereby of those material existences whose definite relations to us are apprehended as spiritual intuitions.[25]

Similarly, Newcombe, in his article entitled 'The Philosophy of Hyper-Space', writes:

There is a region of mathematical thought which might be called the fairyland of geometry. The geometer here disports himself in a way which, to the non-mathematical thinker, suggests the wild flight of an unbridled imagination rather than the sober sequence of mathematical demonstration. Imaginative he certainly does become, if we apply this term to every conception which lies outside of our human experience. Yet the results of the hypotheses introduced into this imaginary universe are traced out with all the rigor of geometric demonstration. It is quite fitting that one who finds the infinity of space in which our universe is situated too narrow for his use should, in his imaginative power, outdo the ordinary writer of fairy tales, when he evokes a universe sufficiently extended for his purposes.[26]

This association of hyperspace with fairytales and supernatural space is no coincidence, but instead reflects the ways that the new hyperspace philosophies adopted a kind of space, and a way of conceiving of it, that echoed previous literary and popular scientific constructions of both Somnial Space and the supernatural realm. All were spaces that existed simultaneously beyond and within the natural world, overlapping with it in invisible and mysterious ways. Most importantly, all could also be accessed via alternative states of mind. The conflation of these ideas was beautifully represented in a map of 'the borderland' by Frederick Myers, which charted not only conscious and subconscious mental spaces, but also their intersections with supernatural space, and hyperspatial connections across time and matter.[27]

The growing sense that supernatural space could now be charted

25 Charles Hinton, *A New Era of Thought* (London: Swan Sonnenschein, 1888), p. xiv.

26 S. Newcomb, 'The Philosophy of Hyperspace,' Science (1898), p. 1.

27 *Borderland: A Quarterly Review and Index, Volume 3*, contains the article "Mr. Myers on the Subliminal Self" pp 44-49, with a map on page 47.

and mapped via concepts of higher-dimensional space and their psychological correlations was an important conceptual development that had a profound effect on literature. Whereas authors from Coleridge to Kingsley had utilized the space of the dream to access the supernatural world, in the wake of hyperspace theories, the later works of Carroll and MacDonald—*Alice through the Looking-Glass* in 1872 and *Lilith* in 1895—employ hyperspace philosophy to represent the supernatural world as part of a single, consistent universe. This universe was directly accessed as higher dimensions of ordinary space, and as such, they prefigure the subsequent literary developments of a completely removed secondary world that would occur in the fantasies of Morris, and later, the Inklings.

While *Looking-Glass* was published before the advent of hyperspace theories, as a mathematician, Carroll was acutely aware of the developing trends toward non-Euclidean geometry, and would most certainly have been aware of the development of these theories into early models of hyperspace, as well as their adoption by the spiritualist imagination as examples of transcendental, spiritual space. L.D. Henderson suggests that Carroll's 'exploration of mirror images and symmetry in *Through the Looking-Glass* [...] with their four-dimensional implications, stands as comment on contemporary English fascination with higher dimensions,'[28] and Elizabeth Throesch argues that they were taken up as models of hyperspace in the intellectual and popular climate that followed. Indeed, for Throesch, 'That Carroll was concerned with, or at least aware of, the dimensional analogy is further demonstrated by the fact that he owned a first-edition copy of Abbott's *Flatland*', a novel that 'was published after the *Alice* books,' but which 'Carroll may have been interested in [...] because his Flatlanders [...] are products of the same interpretive impulse that rules the inhabitants of Wonderland and the Looking-Glass World'.[29]

Looking-Glass takes as its mode of entry into 'the other world' not the liminal space of the dream but the distorting, space-altering properties of a mirror, through which Alice passes into the inverted space of Looking-glass world beyond. Alice's journey into this world is first occasioned by her curiosity and her difficulty in imagining

---

28   Linda Dalrymple Henderson, *The Fourth Dimension and Non-Euclidean Geometry in Modern Art* (Princeton: Princeton University Press, 1983), p. 22.

29   Elizabeth Throesch, 'Nonsense in the Fourth Dimension of Literature: Hyperspace Philosophy, the "New" Mathematics, and the Alice Books' (Iowa City: University of Iowa Press, 2009), p. 43.

what such an inverted, distorted space would look like. As she steps through the liminal plane of the mirror, she finds that it is a space in which to move forwards one must move backwards, to observe objects one must look away from them, and the faster one runs the more they remain in the same place. The world, 'if this is the world at all,' says Alice, is described with physical reality: an expansive network of fields and woods, divided by brooks and hedges, that resembles a giant chess board.[30] A more corporeal landscape than that of *Alice*, its elements take on magical properties, and the construction of the Looking-Glass world as a kind of higher-dimensional space allows Carroll to relate it to the developing appropriations of such spaces to explain supernatural phenomena. According to Gardner, 'Carroll was interested in psychic phenomena and automatic writing,'[31] a fact that casts interesting light on the scene in *Looking-Glass* when the White King is dumbfounded by his pencil that is writing as if with a will of its own, apparently unable to see that it is really Alice holding it.[32] 'Automatic writing, as it was called, was a major aspect of the spiritualist craze in the nineteenth century. A disembodied spirit was believed to seize the hand of a psychic [...] and produce messages from the Great Beyond.'[33] The fact that Alice has emerged from the 'great beyond'—the other side of the mirror, makes her a ghostly figure that echoes the spiritualist application of higher dimensions to explain automatic writing and similar psychic phenomena.

Yet, the discourse of the dream and its ability to destabilize fundamental notions of reality, space and existence has not disappeared altogether. While Alice's initial dream of Wonderland is familiar, in *Looking-Glass*, the Red King now dreams of her, and Tweedledee asks:

> 'If he left off dreaming about you, where do you suppose you'd be?'
>
> 'Where I am now, of course,' said Alice.
>
> 'Not you!' Tweedledee retorted contemptuously. 'You'd be nowhere. Why you're only a sort of thing in his dream!'
>
> 'If that there King was to wake,' added Tweedledum, 'you'd

---

30 Lewis Carroll, *Through the Looking-Glass* in M. Gardner (ed.), *The Annotated Alice: The Definitive Edition* (New York: W. W. Norton and Co., 2000), p. 163.

31 Gardner, *Annotated Alice*, p. xv.

32 Carroll, *Looking-Glass*, p. 147.

33 Gardner, *Annotated Alice*, p. 147.

go out—bang!—just like a candle! [...] You know very well you're not real.'[34]

This inversion masterfully destabilizes the base assumptions upon which prevailing laws of nature and reality were established. Alice, as the protagonist and our common referent in the natural world, through which we experience the strangeness of the inverted space behind the looking-glass, has now become a figment of someone's imagination, and thus has been charged with only existing in space while the dream continues. In a neat inversion of our expectations of reality, the Red King and his world only exist while Alice dreams of them, and yet, within this dream space, Alice herself is only a figment of the Red King's dream, and thus her experience of space and reality are confined to his dreamworld. The question for the reader becomes one of spatial reference—is Alice perceiving the Red King in the space of her own dream, which is itself an imaginary space within the space of her everyday world, or is she currently walking through the space of the Red King's dream, and thus existing within the space of another consciousness? If dream worlds are not real—is it Alice or the Red King that bear reality in the natural world? Beyond this, is the natural world merely a version of someone's dream-space?[35] The implications for further extending and enfolding the various layers of dream space and experience here is never-ending—a chaotic, ever-repeating fractal that plays on Carroll's ideas of madness as a liminal space between the natural and dream worlds characterized by 'an inability to distinguish which is the waking and which the sleeping life,'[36] and its deeper contemporary associations with the overlapping spaces of dreams and the supernatural. Carroll perpetuates this confusion to the end of the story, in which the question of whose dream it really was is left as the final question of the book, as the Red King continues to sleep and Carroll asks, 'Life, what is it but a dream?'[37]

Appearing in 1895, *Lilith* was originally subtitled 'A Tale of the Seventh Dimension' and, likely drawing upon Abbott's *Flatland*, MacDonald employs hyperspace theories to create a multilayered world that, like Carroll's texts, completely destabilizes boundaries

---

34 Carroll, *Looking-Glass*, p. 189.

35 Prickett suggests this interesting configuration may relate to theological notions that the material world only exists in the mind of God, a notion that finds a parallel in Hindu mythology (*Victorian Fantasy*, p. 141).

36 Lewis Carroll cited in Gardner, *Annotated Alice*, p. 67.

37 Carroll, *Looking-Glass*, p. 273.

between natural and supernatural, and sleeping and waking. According to Jeffrey Bilbro, 'MacDonald's use of dimensions [...] has remained underappreciated,'[38] which is a shame, given the crucial position the novel occupies between earlier dream fantasies and the later secondary-world fantasies of Morris and the Inklings. Unlike the earlier dreamlike transition of *Phantastes*, in an intertextual reference to Carroll's *Looking-Glass*, as well as an indication of altered perception, a mirror is the liminal medium through which Vane passes into 'the region of the seven dimensions'[39]—a space that, as Greville MacDonald notes, correlates with 'the much debated *fourth dimension*—that concept of existence which, being spiritual, is not indeed independent of the concrete, but contains and controls the concrete three dimensions in creative manifestation'.[40] After an 'upward' journey through a winding and climbing series of liminal thresholds—doorways, passageways, stairs—each one representing a crossing into layered 'beyond' spaces, Vane discovers the mirror, only to observe 'that it reflected neither the chamber nor my own person'. On moving closer, he stumbles over 'the frame of the mirror' and finds himself in 'a wild country, broken and heathy'.[41] A fully realized geographical landscape, this space is nevertheless overlaid upon the natural world. The Raven informs Vane that, 'you have not yet left your house, neither has your house left you. At the same time it cannot contain you, or you inhabit it!': 'That tree stands on the hearth of your kitchen, and grows nearly straight up its chimney.'[42] This world is 'so much another that most of its physical, and many of its mental laws are different from those of this world. As for moral laws, they must everywhere be fundamentally the same'.[43]

The importance of the space of the mind and its relationship of overlap with the supernatural realm is suggested by Vane's reference to the central 'garret spaces' in which he discovers the mirror as 'The

---

38 Jeffrey Bilbro, '"Yet more spacious Space": Higher-Dimensional Imagination from *Flatland* to *Lilith*.' *North Wind* (2009), p. 11.

39 George MacDonald, *Lilith* (Los Angeles: Indo-European, 2012), p. 17.

40 Greville MacDonald, *George MacDonald and His Wife* (London: 1924), p. 549.

41 MacDonald, *Lilith*, p. 6.

42 Ibid., p. 17.

43 Ibid., p. 38. See Prickett's *Victorian Fantasy* for a discussion of MacDonald's moral laws (particularly p. 182).

brooding brain of the building [...] full of mysterious dwellers.'[44] These 'mysterious dwellers' of higher dimensions are associated by the household staff with ghosts and supernatural beings, in accordance with the spiritualist interpretations of hyperspace. Indeed, Vane's discovery of 'the region of the seven dimensions' is first occasioned when he investigates the ghostly 'apparition' of Mr. Raven, who appears and disappears within the house: 'There were some who believed he was not dead; but both he and the old woman held it easier to believe that a dead man might revisit the world he had left, than that one who went on living for hundreds of years should be a man at all.'[45] Likewise, the land of seven dimensions itself is associated with the supernatural realm of the afterlife. When Vane enters it, he asks, 'Could it be that I was dead [...] and did not know it? Was I in what we used to call the world beyond the grave?'[46] It is an association of hyperspace with the supernatural afterlife that is repeated throughout the narrative in characteristic liminal symbolism: on a wide heath, Vane 'stood in the burial-ground of the universe; its compass the unenclosed heath, its wall the gray horizon, low and starless!' where he is 'assailed by a cold that seemed almost a material presence, and I struggled across the threshold as if from the clutches of an icy death'.[47]

So intertwined are these natural and supernatural spaces that the magic in *Lilith* is not limited to the alternative dimensions, but, by means of liminal portals, occurs in the primary world as well.[48] Importantly, this interweaving of the natural and supernatural worlds creates a single higher-dimensional, and thus, in MacDonald's worldview, a single supernatural world. As Prickett suggests, like the liminal books and ancient manuscripts that form such prominent symbols in the text, as Vane journeys through hyperspace, his 'task is not to inhabit one world or the other, but rather constantly straddle the two and to insist (despite appearances) on their ultimate congruity'.[49] Likewise, Vane's inability to distinguish between the dreaming and waking worlds by the end of the tale recalls Carroll's similarly destabilizing constructions in *Looking-Glass*. Importantly, it

---

44 Ibid., p. 11.

45 Ibid., p. 4.

46 Ibid., p. 10.

47 Ibid., pp. 24-5.

48 Robert A. Collins, 'Liminality in *Lilith*' in L. H. Harriman (ed.), *Lilith in a New Light* (Jefferson: McFarland, 2008), p. 9.

49 Prickett, *Victorian Fantasy*, p. 202.

is through this ambiguous representation of dreaming space and the 'real' world, in addition to the intermingling of dimensional space and the natural and supernatural worlds, that MacDonald's universe begins to approximate a fully realized secondary world fantasy.

It is through this construction of an imaginative secondary world, and the reflective distance that it provides it readers, that *Lilith* heralds the emergence of the modern fantasy genre—an intellectual and aesthetic development that would be consolidated that same year in the first secondary world fantasies of William Morris, and later drawn upon heavily by fantasists such as Tolkien and C.S. Lewis. Indeed, Lewis especially openly acknowledged his heavy influence by MacDonald, and we may take it as no coincidence that Lewis's later use of higher dimensions in his mid-twentieth-century fantasies echoes MacDonald's nineteenth-century creations. Like Carroll, Lewis was also reported to have 'read and enjoyed' Abbott's *Flatland*,[50] which only serves to reinforce the importance of the literary connection between Victorian ideas of hyperspace and the development of modern secondary world fantasy in both its nineteenth-century inventors such as Carroll and MacDonald, and its twentieth-century inheritors, the Inklings.

---

50 David L. Neuhouser, 'C. S. Lewis, George MacDonald, and Mathematics', *Wingfold* (1995, p. 24.

BIBLIOGRAPHY

Abbott, Edwin A., *Flatland: A Romance of Many Dimensions by a Square* (1884) 5th ed., New York: Barnes and Noble, 1963.

Bilbro, Jeffrey L., '"Yet more spacious Space": Higher-Dimensional Imagination from *Flatland to Lilith*', *North Wind* 28 (2009), pp. 1-12.

Carroll, Lewis, *Alice in Wonderland* and *Through the Looking-Glass. The Annotated Alice: The Definitive Edition.* Ed. M. Gardner, New York: W. W. Norton and Co., 2000.

Carter, Lin, 'Introduction', in W. Morris, *The Well at the World's End*, Vol. 1, London: Pan/Ballantine, 1971, pp. i-x.

Coleridge, Samuel T., *The Notebooks of Samuel Taylor Coleridge*, Ed. K. Coburn. 4 vols., London: Routledge and Kegan Paul, 1957.

Collins, Robert A., 'Liminality in *Lilith*', in Lucas H. Harriman (ed.), *Lilith in a New Light*, Jefferson: McFarland, 2008, pp. 7-14.

Gardner, Martin, *The Annotated Alice: The Definitive Edition*, New York: Norton, 2000.

Henderson, Linda D., *The Fourth Dimension and Non-Euclidean Geometry in Modern Art*, Princeton: Princeton UP, 1983.

Hinton, Charles H., *A New Era of Thought*, London: Swan Sonnenschein, 1888.

Hunt, Peter and Lenz, Millicent (eds), *Alternative Worlds in Fantasy Fiction*, London: Continuum, 2001.

Kaplan, Fred, *Dickens and Mesmerism: The Hidden Springs of Fiction*, Princeton: Princeton University Press, 1975.

Kingsley, Charles, *The Water-Babies: A Fairy Tale for a Land Baby* (1863), Hertfordshire: Wordsworth Classics, 1994.

MacDonald, George, *Lilith* (1895), Los Angeles: Indo-European, 2012.

MacDonald, George, *Phantastes: A Faerie Romance for Men*

and Women (1858), in Works of Fancy and Imagination, Vols. 5 and 6, London: Strahan, 1871.

MacDonald, George, *George MacDonald and His Wife*, London: 1924.

Manlove, Colin, 'The Circle of the Imagination: George MacDonald's *Phantastes* and *Lilith*', *Studies in Scottish Literature* 17.1 (1982), pp. 55-80.

Mendelson, Michael, 'George MacDonald's *Lilith* and the Conventions of Ascent', *Studies in Scottish Literature* 20.1 (1985), pp. 197-218.

Neuhouser, David L., 'C. S. Lewis, George MacDonald, and Mathematics', *Wingfold* 9 (1995), pp. 17-28.

Newcomb, S., 'The Philosophy of Hyperspace', *Science* ns 7.158 (1898), pp. 1-7.

Prickett, Stephen, *Victorian Fantasy*, Bloomington: Indiana UP, 1975.

Schofield, Alfred T., *Another World* (1888), London: Swan Sonnenschein, 1905.

Stead, William Thomas, editor. 'Mr. Myers on the Subliminal Self,' *Borderland: A Quarterly Review and Index, Volume 3.1*, pp 44-49.

Stevenson, Robert L., *The Essays of Robert Louis Stevenson, A Selection*, London: MacDonald, 1950.

Throesch, Elizabeth, 'Nonsense in the Fourth Dimension of Literature: Hyperspace Philosophy, the "New" Mathematics, and the *Alice* Books', in Cristopher Hollingsworth (ed.), *Alice Beyond Wonderland: Essays for the Twenty-first Century*, Iowa City: U of Iowa P, 2009, pp. 37-52.

Wertheim, Margaret, *The Pearly Gates of Cyberspace: A History of Space from Dante to the Internet*, Sydney: Doubleday, 1999.

Genre Problems:
Andrew Lang and J.R.R. Tolkien
on (Fairy) Stories and (Literary) Belief

Sharin Schroeder

J.R.R. Tolkien's 'On Fairy-stories', which owed its genesis to the 1939 Andrew Lang lecture at the University of St. Andrews, is an essay about belief, both primary and secondary. In the essay, Tolkien attempts to set right the misunderstandings held by many nineteenth-century writers, including Andrew Lang, about the type of faith early creators of fantasy had in their own marvelous stories. While Lang thought that early fantasy creators must have believed in the possibility of the marvels they recounted, Tolkien demurred. However, a closer analysis of the two men's work shows that the distinction between primary and secondary belief, though real and important, has never been simple to make. Every individual, when dealing with the unseen, must decide precisely where the barrier between the religious and the fantastic lies, and there is no way to prove one has decided the distinction correctly.

Distinguishing poetic from religious faith is complicated by the fact that mythopoeic fantasy writers have often used the fantastic to work through religious questions. Most admirers of writers who have made this attempt, writers such as George MacDonald, C.S. Lewis, Margaret Oliphant, John Milton, or even Mary Shelley, would agree that one of the strengths of the fantastic as a genre is the way it allows for speculative theology. However, the overlap can also lead to genre confusion and conflation.

Both Lang and Tolkien have been criticized for not making the distinction between Faërie and religion clear enough. Tolkien, in 'On Fairy-stories', blames Lang for confusing literary belief with actual belief.[1] Tom Shippey, in *Road to Middle-earth*, sees the same confusion, at least rhetorically, in 'On Fairy-stories' because Tolkien '[r]epeatedly [...] plays the trick of pretending that fairies are real [...] This comes perilously close to whimsy, the pretence that something not true is true to create an air of comic innocence'.[2] Shippey identifies

---

1   J.R.R Tolkien, *Tolkien on Fairy-Stories: Expanded Edition with Commentary and Notes*, (London: HarperCollins, 2008), p. 52.

2   Tom Shippey, *The Road to Middle-earth* (Boston: Houghton Mifflin, 2003), p. 49.

a reticence to speak directly, claiming that there is a 'strong circularity' in the essay, 'as if Tolkien were hovering around some central point on which he dared not or could not land'.[3]

Since the 2008 publication of *Tolkien On Fairy-stories*, which includes Tolkien's notes and drafts, it has become apparent that Tolkien's treatment of Faërie was not whimsical but rather an effort to work through the distinctions among magic, theology, and literature.[4] In Manuscript B, Tolkien claims, '*Miracle and magic* are not so easy to distinguish from one another. They have in fact only become distinguished by Christian theology'.[5] The drafts also show, however, that Shippey is correct that Tolkien was hovering around an unnamed central point. Shippey, indeed, had identified what that point was: '[Tolkien] came closest to it [...] when he brushed past the edges of single words, especially *spell* and *evangelium* [...] for the Old English translation of Greek *evangelion*, "good news", was *gód spell*, "the good story".'[6] In other words, in 'On Fairy-stories', Tolkien was seeking the precise link between a good spell, a good story, and the gospel. In the published version, and more particularly in his drafts, Tolkien's defense of the fairy story is tied up with a genre question: how does one reconcile the fairy story, a literary genre containing wonderful

---

3 Ibid., p. 50.

4 Verlyn Flieger writes that Tolkien's 'repeated use of the word 'perilous' is the marker of how seriously Tolkien took the concept' (Smith, p. 60). Tolkien leaves the possibility of elvish existence open in 'On Fairy-stories', but he does not do so in a whimsical way: 'if elves are true, and really exist independently of our tales about them, then this also is certainly true: elves are not primarily concerned with us, nor we with them. Our fates are sundered, and our paths seldom meet' (p. 32). It seems that Tolkien's occasional treatment of the fairy as potentially real may be related to his distaste for authors who do not take their fantastic creations seriously enough and instead explain them away: 'since the fairy-story deals with marvels, it cannot tolerate any frame or machinery suggesting that the whole thing is a figment or illusion' (p. 35). For more on Tolkien and belief in fairies, see the following pages in *Tolkien On Fairy-stories*: 188, 233–235, 252, 254, 257, 260–61, 293–95.

5 Tolkien, 'On Fairy-stories', p. 252. Tolkien's discussion of Miracle, Magic, Marvel, and Mechanism and their distinction from Faërie is particularly interesting (ibid., pp. 252–57). It appears that Tolkien is not criticizing magic and miracle for being too similar but rather, in this writing, attempting to continue in the nicety of the theological distinctions that separate them.

6 Shippey, *The Road to Middle-earth*, p. 51.

events, with the Christian faith, whose gospel story also contains wonderful events, but whose miracles are put forward as meant to be believed with a faith not merely poetic?

When Tolkien's essay is read in light of Lang's work on fairy tales and religion, it becomes evident that he is responding to particularly nineteenth-century genre concerns: what from supernatural-invoking texts ought to be read as true and historical? Lang, with research interests in Homeric criticism, fairy tales and folklore, and the burgeoning fields of anthropology and the science of religion, was well versed in the controversies in these fields. Yet Tolkien, with the benefit of hindsight, undertook to correct some of Lang's views. As with *Beowulf* in 'Beowulf: The Monsters and the Critics', in 'On Fairy-stories', Tolkien recovered literature for literary criticism rather than mere anthropological or historical treatment. He criticized Lang for identifying the fairy story genre as particularly belonging to children, and, more importantly, for misunderstanding the difference between primary and secondary belief—for thinking some of the writers actually believed their tales.

By differentiating between primary and secondary belief, Tolkien improved upon Lang's understanding of early literature and religion and contributed to the better understanding of literature that invokes the fantastic. Addressing Lang's writings was important because they had been influential in solidifying positions about the writers and audience of the fairy story, thereby setting up how later romances and fairy stories would be reviewed by critics.[7] However, Tolkien's readings of Lang were only partially correct. Like many before him, Tolkien relied on some of Lang's most famous but least careful occasional writing to make his points; Tolkien did not always consider how this very quotable Lang had changed his mind over time, nor did he consider Lang's motivations and how his written words often differed from his actual beliefs and desires.

---

7   Indeed, though Tolkien did not know it yet, Lang's writings on the romance and his reviews of H. Rider Haggard's work, though Lang was all in favor of both, helped create the discourse for negative critical responses to *The Lord of the Rings*. Some critics refused to believe The Lord of the Rings was written for adults; others supposed Tolkien believed in his fantastic characters in the primary sense. See Richardson's review of *The Two Towers*, 'New Novels' (1955), Wilson's 'Oo, Those Awful Orcs' (1956), and Gueroult's BBC interview with Tolkien (1965). I discuss Lang and *The Lord of the Rings* reviews in more detail in 'She-who-must-not-be-ignored: Gender and Genre in *The Lord of the Rings* and the *Victorian Boys' Book*'.

Finding the true, definitive Lang and the true, definitive Tolkien is, of course impossible, and any account of the two men's work must balance the desire for accurate life histories with the desire for accurate reception history. After all, whatever Lang's true motivations were, it was the public's understanding of Lang's ideas, not Lang's actual ideas, that had the lasting influence on how critics read the genres of the romance and the fairy story.[8] However, understanding the evolution of Lang's positions sheds light on how nineteenth-century religious questions affected later readings of the fairy story. Not only do I seek to explain why Tolkien's insistence on the separation between religious and literary belief was necessary, I also wish to establish how the aspects of Lang's thought that Tolkien missed or misunderstood should affect critical readings of sacred and secular genre confusion. Both Lang and Tolkien were using the literary to understand the theological, and, although Tolkien's understanding of *eucatastrophe* allowed him to come to a more satisfying conclusion than Lang did, in fact, Lang's and Tolkien's reaction to the fairy story was often similar because they were starting from similar questions about the relationship between the fairy story and religious faith. Lang and Tolkien's writings and oral statements also demonstrate that, however carefully theological writing and literary criticism might try to distinguish primary and secondary belief, the two types of beliefs do shape one another in fascinating ways.

CONTEXTUALIZING ANDREW LANG (1844–1912)

The first task of the critic who wishes to understand how Victorian critics such as Lang affected Tolkien is to try to put Lang's work in its historical context. To do so, readers need to look back to the cultural environment into which Lang was born and educated, when his earliest ideas on literature—especially fairy story—and religion were formed. In the nineteenth-century many critics were redrawing genre categories, lumping together marvel-containing writings that had previously been considered separately. Since the 1820s, English

---

8   Nathan Hensley makes a strong case that 'the Andrew Lang effect' is more important than Lang's actual writing, that Lang 'emerges not so much as a figure worth recovering [...] but as what Latour calls a 'mediator': an agent of connection that serves to link various sectors of its network in active, shaping ways' (par. 5). While I focus on recovering Lang proper as a key to understanding this genre question, I agree with Hensley that Lang's key role was that of mediator and that the impact of literary networks should be an object of study in itself.

proponents of German higher criticism had argued that scholars should apply the same methods of interpretation to the Old Testament as to the *Iliad*, and the big debate over *Essays and Reviews* in the 1860s was whether clergymen were allowed to use these historical critical methods to critique the Bible just as they would critique any other ancient book.[9]

Lang was well aware of these debates as a student in St. Andrews and Glasgow. The 1863 handwritten *St. Leonard's Magazine* (by St. Andrews students) contains a satirical poem on the booksellers and Benjamin Jowett, one of the *Essays and Reviews* writers, that is probably by Lang. Lang contributed most of the articles to this periodical even in 1863, when he was writing as a foreign correspondent from Glasgow. The poem, signed 'Longhop', mocks the publisher Elder as execrating the Broad Church, Kingsley, Stanley and Jowett: 'If one is worse than all the rest / I am prepared to show it / To be that Heretic emblest / The Greek Professor Jowett' (lines 5-8). In the poem, this bookseller claims that these men should be taken up both by the Free Church and the Index Expurgatorious, 'But until then the book I'll sell'.[10]

Lang won the University of Glasgow's Snell scholarship to Oxford, and by 1864 he was enrolled in the college where Jowett taught (and would become Master in 1870) and where Matthew Arnold was Professor of Poetry.[11] Oxford in the 1860s and 1870s was a hotbed for discussions about the relationship between literary criticism and religious belief, and Lang, first as a student at Balliol and then as a fellow at Merton (1868-1874), would have been following

---

9 For more on how higher criticism affected Victorian critics' understandings of the genres of the Bible and the *Iliad*, see McKelvy p. 135, Turner pp. 142-46, and Schroeder pp. 323-25.

10 Andrew Lang, 'The Lay of the Bookselling Elder', St. Leonard's Magazine (28 Nov. 1863), p. 17. This manuscript magazine (ms30142a-c) is housed in the University of St. Andrews Special Collections. I am grateful to the librarians in this archive and the University of St. Andrews Special Collections' Visiting Scholar Scheme for making it possible for me to read this and other Lang manuscripts.

11 Lang's admiration of the former is evident from his eulogy of Jowett in the 14 October 1893 *Illustrated London News* ('The Master of Balliol'). Lang also greatly admired Arnold's poetry, though he admits that as an undergraduate he did not attend Arnold's lectures, 'which were not compulsory' (Roger Lancelyn Green, *Andrew Lang: A Critical Biography* (Leicester: Edmund Ward, 1946), p. 34).

the controversies.

In the 1870s, the new disciplines of anthropology and folklore continued the practice of genre conflation. At Oxford in 1872 Lang read *Primitive Culture* by E. B. Tylor, whose interest in totems and savage survivals greatly interested Lang.[12] Tylor, Edward Clodd, and Lang himself examined ceremonies, myths, and fairy tales across cultures, looking for survivals of humans' former religious beliefs and cultural taboos in extant stories and contemporary religious practices.[13] Lang's first foray into this field, 'Mythology and Fairy Tales', was published in 1873 in the *Fortnightly Review*, when Lang still held his fellowship, but by 1874 Lang had resigned his fellowship at Merton and begun making his way independently as a journalist, author and scholar.[14]

Once he had established himself as a journalist, Lang became an extremely prolific, but also fairly divisive, writer. According to Roger Lancelyn Green, Lang wrote approximately three hundred volumes, 'even excluding the great amount of Lang's work that is lost to us in the anonymous files of forgotten daily newspapers'.[15] Nathan Hensley notes that 'placing a final number on Lang's far-flung and multiply distributed texts [...] is all but impossible' (par. 12). Such quantities of writing, so much of it ephemeral, has led to a peculiar reception history.

Lang's ubiquity in the nineteenth-century press led as much to Lang's misunderstanding as to his understanding. Lang has been

---

12   Green, Andrew Lang, p. 69.

13   One of the most controversial instances of such study happened two decades later, in 1896, when Clodd, as president of the Folk-lore Society, 'undertook a painstaking scrutiny of the "savage" origins of certain Christian sacraments and points of doctrine according to Tylorian methods' (Marjorie Wheeler-Barclay, *The Science of Religion in Britain* (Charlottesville: University of Charlottesville Press, 2010), p. 136. Numerous members, including William Gladstone, resigned after this address was published.

14   In early 1877, a decade before the height of Lang's fame, Lang reviewed George MacDonald's *Thomas Wingfold, Curate* in the same *Fortnightly Review* where he had written 'Mythology and Fairy Tales'. The review was negative but respectful, and it showed an admiration for MacDonald's other work. For more on this review and similarities between Lang and MacDonald's works, see John Patrick Pazdziora's 'How the Fairies were not Invited to Court' in *Rethinking George MacDonald: Contexts and Contemporaries*' (Glasgow: Scottish Literature International, 2013).

15   Green, *Andrew Lang: A Critical Biography*, p. x.

criticized (then and now) because he had a disproportionate amount of power, but publishing in so many places also hurt him. Readers and critics simply could not follow all of Lang's interdisciplinary (or pre-disciplinary) research as it appeared in multiple formats, and Lang was frequently misrepresented and misreported. Lang's facile use of language made him highly quotable, and distortions of his out-of-context quotations were gripping and convenient strawmen for controversialists. Yet his light approach to serious topics could also unintentionally offend. His colloquial language and amusing anecdotes could fool listeners and readers into a misplaced confidence of comprehension, with the result that his real motivations and erudition remained hidden.

After Lang's death, such misunderstandings increased. Since Lang wrote so much, since his most-read writing appeared in newspapers, and since he strongly discouraged a posthumous biography—requesting that his letters be destroyed—much of Lang's work simply disappeared. As Marysa Demoor notes, 'only the most trenchant, or the most indelible lines from his critical endeavour survived. Taken out of context, these often distorted posterity's image of Lang as a critic.'[16] Thus Lang—while he may be, as Nathan Hensley writes, 'the vanished mediator of the late-Victorian mediascape'—is also quite a slippery critic with whom to engage (par. 1).

LANG'S IMPACT ON TOLKIEN

In 1939, Tolkien made a valiant attempt to engage Lang. Criticism shows that Tolkien read a significant amount of Lang's fairy-story-related writings for his St. Andrews lecture and published revision, including Lang's first article on the subject, 'Mythology and Fairy Tales'; the 1889 introduction to the large-paper edition of *The Blue Fairy Book*; Lang's introduction to *Grimm's Household Tales*; and the prefaces to all twelve fairy books. Many of Tolkien's own key fairy tale examples come directly from these writings, such as those of 'Bertha Broadfoot' and 'The Frog-King' and 'The Black Bull of Norroway'. Tolkien also at least knew of one of Lang's more esoteric discoveries, the Revd Kirk's 'Mysterious Commonwealth of Elves and Fairies', and it is possible he may have read Lang's lengthy introduction to Perrault.[17] Additionally, Tolkien had access to the best secondary

---

16 Marysa Demoor, ed., *Dear Stevenson: Letters from Andrew Lang to Robert Louis Stevenson* (Leuven: Uitgeverij Peeters, 1990), p. 22.

17 Tolkien, 'On Fairy-stories', pp. 260, 298-99. The evidence for Tolkien's

source on Lang even before it was published. In 1943, while revising his St. Andrews lecture for publication, Tolkien was an examiner (along with D. Nichol Smith) of Roger Lancelyn Green's B.Litt. thesis. Revised and published as *Andrew Lang: A Critical Biography* in 1946, it has not yet been superseded. Green's thesis would have exposed Tolkien to additional quotations from works by Lang.[18]

Yet despite Tolkien's concerted endeavors, 'On Fairy-stories' does not represent Lang's definitive views on fairy story. Perhaps it was not meant to: Tolkien intentionally removed many references to Lang in the published version in order to give the essay a more universal appeal. While Tolkien's portrayal of Lang in the references that remain is not wildly off-base, it homogenizes Lang in a way that does not represent the dynamic nature of Lang's thinking. Lang's opinions were liable to shift when his ceaseless curiosity revealed new data: while some of positions, such as his admiration of romance and his views on poetry, remained fairly clear and constant, he was open to amending or replacing fact-based theories if investigations or conversations were convincing.[19] Lang was working in newly emerging disciplines whose rules were unwritten and whose boundaries had not yet been set. Lang gloried in persuading and in being persuaded, and, unlike Tolkien, he did not hesitate to write or even publish before his mind was made up.

One of Lang's chief roles was that of catalyst. W.P. Ker wrote of 'those sudden letters that came, showering sparks into the centre of a controversy'.[20] George Stuart Gordon, in his 1927 Andrew Lang

---

reading of Lang's introduction to Perrault is slim; Tolkien does not mention the work specifically in his 'On Fairy-stories' drafts. However, Tolkien repeatedly refers to Perrault in his essay, and many of the tales in *The Blue Fairy Book* are Perrault's. Green mentions the essay in his biography (and presumably in his thesis) alongside *Myth, Ritual and Religion*, Lang's introductions to Grimm, Cupid and Psyche, and Kirk's *Secret Commonwealth of Elves, Fauns and Fairies* as 'Lang's most enduring contribution to the study of folklore' (Green, *Andrew Lang*, p. 70).

18   Tolkien did not pass Green's thesis in 1943, but sent it back for revisions, working with Green weekly during Michaelmas Term in 1943, because he 'wanted to know more about the fairies!' (Scull and Hammond I.262). See also I.258 and II.352. Green passed in March of 1944.

19   A letter to anthropologist E. B. Tylor is typical: Lang frames his objection to some specifics about a solar myth hypothesis by saying 'I don't believe' and then adding, in parentheses, 'at present' (f. 130b).

20   W.P. Ker, 'Andrew Lang, D. Litt' (London: Oxford University Press, 1913), p .9.

lecture, claimed that Lang's lack of a standard book (to which scholars could refer for Lang's absolute positions) was not actually a weakness. 'When a study is in the making, as so many of Lang's were, a Big Book, a Standard Book, as we call it, is more likely to be a hindrance than a help. Large Standard Books, however impressive and even useful they may be, tend inevitably to arrest movement'.[21] Lang's evolving opinions spurred on other authors and led to greater understanding of the subject at hand.

For Tolkien, too, Lang's writing had a catalyst effect. As is well known, the fairy books that bear Lang's name were the companions of Tolkien's childhood, and it was through the *Red Fairy Book* that he made his first acquaintance with Sigurd and Fáfnir: 'best of all [was] the nameless North of Sigurd of the Völsungs, and the prince of all dragons'.[22] Lang's account of his own motivation in marketing new editions of these old tales, as given in his introduction to a book on folklore by Marian Rolfe Cox, was that he desired to provide children with good reading material: 'I confess that I still have a child-like love of a fairy-story for its own sake; and I have done my best to circulate Fairy Books among children'.[23]

Tolkien notes several times in his letters that it was partly due to Lang and his collaborators that Tolkien had originally believed the fairy story to be a children's genre, but studying Lang's writings more thoroughly led Tolkien to change his mind. In 1961, Tolkien explained to his aunt Jane Neave that at the time of his writing *The Hobbit*, 'I had not freed myself from the contemporary delusions about "fairy-stories" and children':

> I had to think about it, however, before I gave an "Andrew Lang" lecture at St. Andrews on Fairy-stories; and I must say I think the result was entirely beneficial to *The Lord of the Rings*, which was a practical demonstration of the views that I expressed. It was not written "for children", or for any kind of person in particular, but for itself. (If any parts or elements in it appear 'childish', it is because I am childish, and like that kind of thing myself now.[24]

21 George Gordon, 'Andrew Lang' (London: Oxford University Press, 1928), p. 13.

22 Hart, Rachel, 'Tolkien, St. Andrews, and Dragons' (Waco: Baylor University Press, 2007), p. 8; Tolkien, 'On Fairy-stories', p. 55.

23 Andrew Lang, 'Introduction', *Cinderella: Three Hundred and Forty-five Variants* by Marian Rolfe Cox (London: The Folk-lore Society, 1893), p. xi.

24 J.R.R. Tolkien, *The Letters of J.R.R. Tolkien* (Boston: Houghton Miffin,

As is clear here, Tolkien's main problem with Lang was the branding of the fairy books for children, but, as can be seen from Tolkien's admission in this letter and from Lang's confession of his 'child-like love of a fairy-story for its own sake', both Lang and Tolkien liked certain things in a story that other readers might brand as 'childish' but which were the 'kind of thing' they liked *now* and were keen to defend.

Tolkien does praise Lang in 'On Fairy-stories'. He acknowledges Lang's triumphant victory over philologist Max Müller's 'disease of language' theory (though Lang's name has dropped out of the published draft).[25] Tolkien also notes his and Lang's mutual dislike 'of flower-fairies and fluttering sprites with antennae', and he cites Christopher Dawson's *Progress and Religion* as demonstrating Lang's lasting impact on the study of religion's interaction with mythology.[26] He claims that, as fairy-story collections go, '[i]n English none probably rival either the popularity or the inclusiveness, or the general merits of the twelve books of twelve colours which we owe to Andrew Lang and to his wife'.[27] However, while Tolkien elevates Lang's anthologies above most such endeavors, which are 'attics and lumber-rooms [by nature] a jumble of different dates, purposes, and tastes', Lang's collections still only receive 'rummage-sale' status: 'Someone with a duster and a fair eye for things that retain some value has been round the attics and the box-rooms'.[28] Lang and his wife have found stories that are worth telling, but, to Tolkien, the tales still exude the feeling of being unwanted by the adults and thus 'made into and

---

1981), p. 310. See also Tolkien's draft to Walter Allen (p. 297).

25   Tolkien, 'On Fairy-stories', pp. 41, 221.

26   Tolkien writes, 'Andrew Lang said, and is by some still commended for saying, that mythology and religion (in the strict sense of that word) are two distinct things that have become inextricably entangled, though mythology is in itself almost devoid of religious significance' ('On Fairy-stories', p. 44). Tolkien footnotes Dawson as the example, and in his second footnote, paraphrases Dawson without precise citation when noting that hasty anthropological surveys too often find only the 'wilder tales' rather than a people's true religion (Dawson, pp. 73-77; Andrew Lang, *Perrault's Popular Tales* (Oxford: The Clarendon Press, 1888), p. xciv). Tolkien also shows he agrees with Dawson and Lang on religion and mythology's entanglement. See 'On Fairy-stories', p. 44, also pp.182-83, 200.

27   Tolkien, 'On Fairy-stories', p. 33.

28   Ibid., p. 51.

presented as books for children'.[29]

Tolkien saw Lang's collections as 'partly a by-product of his adult researches in mythology and folklore', and Tolkien ascribes many of Lang's errors of literary criticism to that research. Both Lang and Müller seemed under the impression that the strange events in fairy stories ought to have appeared plausible occurrences to their original tellers.[30] In 'On Fairy-stories' Tolkien more sensibly argues for the distinction between primary and secondary belief, cautioning folklorists and anthropologists to remember that 'they are dealing with items whose primary object was story building, and whose primary reason for survival was the same'.[31] 'It is of little avail to consider totemism' or to ask whether the legend of Iphigeneia's sacrifice in the Iliad '[came] down from a time when human-sacrifice was commonly practiced'.[32]

However, although Lang's appreciation of stories as stories may have sometimes been sidetracked by his interest in an anthropological point (as Tolkien perhaps was distracted from time to time by a philological one), both men's interest in fairy story was primarily literary. They agreed that the main audience for fairy tales was not the folklorist or the scholar: these were tales, not research mines. Both men objected to what Tolkien would call that 'misleading shorthand' by which 'students of folk-lore' express themselves when comparing tales.[33] In Lang's introduction to Marian Rolfe Cox's *Cinderella: Three Hundred and Forty-five Variants of Cinderella, Catskin, and Cap O'Rushes*, he notes that his first reaction to 'her learned and elaborate work' was horror at 'these skeletons of the tale. It was as if one had

---

29 Ibid., p. 51.

30 See Lang's 'Mythology and Fairy Tales' where Lang uses totemism to answer Müller's question as to how 'The Frog King' could have ever been invented (pp. 625–26). Tolkien points out the fallacy of asking this question at all: 'the point of the story lies not in thinking frogs possible mates, but in the necessity of keeping promises (even those with intolerable consequences)' ('On Fairy-stories', p. 74).

31 Tolkien, 'On Fairy-stories', p. 80.

32 Ibid., pp. 74, 80.

33 Ibid., p. 38. Lang writes, 'If I have ever hinted that tales are only valuable as materials of anthropology, instead of being the oldest novels, full of grace and charm, may the Folk-lore Congress hand me over to the secular arm' [...] 'I cannot, like Mr. Jacobs, "hope" for a day when, "instead of having to read the tale", we shall be content with a technical summary of its incidents! Having to read the tale!' (Lang, 'Introduction', *Cinderella*, pp. xxi-ii).

a glimpse into the place where Hop o' my Thumb's Giant kept the bones of his little victims. Dry bones of child-like and charming tales are these, a place of many skulls'.[34]

Lang and Tolkien also agreed that the child reader is often a better judge of stories than the adult. In the aborted preface to George MacDonald's 'The Golden Key', Tolkien explains, when discussing the wrongheadedness of labeling the fairy story as 'specially suitable for children' that the label, though incorrect, 'is actually a compliment to "fairy tales", since real children are generally good judges of tales as tales'.[35] Lang makes a similar judgment on children's good literary taste in his *Morning Post* article 'Homer and the Books of Samuel', where Lang remarks that 'The Old Testament [...] is almost never

---

34 Lang, 'Introduction', Cinderella,. p. vii.

35 Tolkien, *Smith*, p. 73. Tolkien's relationship to MacDonald is complex. In 'On Fairy-stories' he praises 'The Golden Key' and gives *Lilith* qualified praise (p. 44). He also mentions MacDonald in several parts of Manuscript B, though some of these are struck through. In one crossed-out section, Tolkien writes 'For me at any rate fairy-stories are especially associated with Scotland: not through any special knowledge [...] but simply by reason of the names of Andrew Lang and George MacDonald. To them in different ways I owe the books which most affected the background of my imagination since childhood' (p. 207). In another crossed-out section of Manuscript B, Tolkien writes that he gave his children fairy-story books that he liked himself 'such as *The Princess and the Goblin*' (p. 231). Later in the manuscript, Tolkien writes 'George MacDonald, in that mixture of German and Scottish flavours (which makes him so inevitably attractive to myself), has depicted what will always be to me the classic goblin. By that standard I judge all goblins, old or new' (p. 250). Attentive readers will find similarities in the goblins' capture of Curdie in *The Princess and the Goblin* and the goblins' capture of the dwarves in *The Hobbit*. Later in life, however, Tolkien was less complimentary to MacDonald. After agreeing to write a preface to 'The Golden Key', Tolkien found himself disliking it on the reread. He wrote to Clyde Kilby, 'I found that a highly selective memory had retained only a few impressions of things that moved me, and re-reading G. M. critically filled me with distaste' (Tolkien, *Smith*, p. 69). He never finished the preface: 'If I had gone on I should only have written a severely critical or 'anti' essay on G. M.—unnecessary, and a pity since G. M. has performed great services for other minds—such as Jack's. [...] It is better anyway to preach by example than by criticism of others. But *Smith* remains as it were "an anti-G.M. Tract"' (p. 70). See also the interview with Henry Resnik, where Tolkien calls George MacDonald 'a horrible old grandmother' before correcting himself, noting that a grandmother is 'a very fin[e] woman figure, of course, really' (p. 5).

read (except by small boys) for human pleasure' (f. 41). Lang sides with a recent reviewer who wrote, 'Higher critics [...] are the last men in the world to read a poem for its literary value.' 'Of course they are', Lang concurs, 'a schoolboy does it, but critics don't and can't'.

For Tolkien, however, children are not only good readers of tales but are also, or at least should be encouraged to be, good critics. He objects to Lang's assumption that children are the natural audience for fairy stories *because* they are more likely to believe them, highlighting that children too have secondary belief. Furthermore, Tolkien criticizes Lang's casual equation of the actual physical child who will read his collected fairy stories and the metaphorical 'child' that Lang claims would have created them.

Lang writes in his preface to the large-paper edition of *The Blue Fairy Book* that the stories represent 'the young age of man true to his early loves, and have his unblunted edge of belief, a fresh appetite for marvels'.[36] Tolkien disagrees:

> I fear that Lang's words, stripped of sentiment, can only imply that the teller of marvelous tales to children, must, or may, or at any rate does trade on their credulity, on the lack of experience which makes it less easy for children to distinguish fact from fiction in particular cases, though the distinction in itself is fundamental to the sane human mind, and to fairy-stories.[37]

While Tolkien believes that children are concerned with knowing whether the stories they are told are true, he maintains that the question is not an indication of children's easy credulity but rather an indication of their early attempts to become literary critics. Children want to be able to distinguish among genres:

> [Children's] question is hardly evidence of "unblunted belief", or even of the desire for it. Most often it proceeds from the child's desire to know which kind of literature he is faced with. Children's knowledge of the world is often so small that they cannot judge, off-hand and without help, between the fantastic, the strange (that is rare or remote facts), the nonsensical, and the merely "grown-up" [...] But they recognize the different classes, and may like all of them at times. Of course the borders between them are often fluctuating or confused; but

---

36   Andrew Lang, 'Introduction', *The Blue Fairy Book* (London: Longmans, Green & Co.), p. xi.

37   Tolkien, 'On Fairy-stories', p. 52.

that is not only true for children.[38]

Tolkien does a better job than Lang in describing the type of belief that a reader has and desires when reading a fairy story, a secondary belief that keeps readers inside the story rather than undesirably pulling them out of it. However, this point on which Tolkien founds his argument, though a fair representation of Lang's words, does not call attention to Lang's actually contradictory views on the subject of fairy stories and belief.

While in 'On Fairy-stories' Tolkien has made Lang notorious for trading on the easy credulity of children, at times Lang claims that children are not credulous at all. In his preface to *The Green Fairy Book* (1892), Lang first equates children with the original fairy tale writers, whom he claims were 'much like children in their minds', loved stories, and really believed in witches and magic rings. He also equates the ability to write a good fairy story with the ability to 'believe enough in their own stories'. However, despite Lang's equation of children with these early and credulous hearers and authors, in this same preface he inconsistently informs children that they actually don't believe— that they are not credulous like the supposed original crafters of fairy tales. Lang writes, 'probably you who read the tales know very well how much is true and how much is only make-believe, and I never yet heard of a child who killed a very tall man merely because Jack killed the giants, or who was unkind to his stepmother, if he had one, because, in fairy tales, the stepmother is often disagreeable'.[39]

Tolkien notes that Lang's imagined child-readers don't match up either with Tolkien's experiences with children or his memories of his own childhood.[40] Nor however, fascinatingly, do Lang's classifications of children match up with Lang's childhood. He writes in the preface to *The Plain Princess* that, 'It is not so easy to know what children themselves really like', for children seem to like reading about rather unsavory characters: giants, dragons, wicked stepmothers, ogres, and cannibals. 'This appears to be the taste of children in general. When

---

38 Tolkien, 'On Fairy-stories', p. 53-4.

39 Andrew Lang, 'Preface', *The Green Fairy Book*, p. 10. Lang had used almost identical language, not about children, in his 1888 'Literary Anodynes', where he stated, 'Judges are notorious novel-readers; yet I never heard that they fled from their wedded wives to woo strange maidens because such things are done in romance' ('Literary Anodynes', *The New Princeton Review* (Sep. 1888), p. 147).

40 Tolkien, 'On Fairy-stories', p. 54.

one says "children," [...] one mainly means little girls, for they are fond of reading; whereas little boys, if they will allow me to say so, care for nothing but machinery, and wheels, and oil that is not sweet-scented, and telephones, about which they are quite awfully learned'.[41]

After making these sweeping generalizations, Lang then notes that he himself never fit the stereotypes he has just laid out:

> When I was a little boy, it is to be supposed that I was a little muff: for I read every fairy tale that I could lay my hands on, and knew all the fairies in *A Midsummer Night's Dream*, and all the ghosts in Sir Walter Scott, and I hated machinery of every description. These tastes and distastes I have never overcome.[42]

Lang admits that his tastes have not changed with his adulthood, but his assumptions about others' tastes lead him to believe that he is singular. He relies on assumed knowledge about children as a class, but in actuality he was very much like Tolkien, who also hated machinery and who found the 'notion that motor-cars are more "alive" than, say, centaurs or dragons [...] curious; that they are more "real" than, say, horses is pathetically absurd'.[43] In fact, when Tolkien takes issue with Lang's statements, he is arguing less against Lang than against commonplaces Lang never chose to question. Lang's fairy books for children were reifying the Victorian association of fairy books with children rather than creating it.

Interpreting Lang Today

It becomes especially difficult today for the critic to know exactly how to read Lang's comments associating the fairy story with the child. Tolkien certainly read them as negative, and they were indeed often self-deprecatory, but although Lang called a taste for the romance and the fairy-story childlike, he always believed in these genres' value.

This fact still requires careful parsing. In *Tolkien On Fairy-stories*, Verlyn Flieger and Douglas Anderson maintain that 'Lang's Darwinian assumption that fairy-stories were leftovers from the childhood of human development led to the corollary assumption that the tales were therefore leftover fare for human children, who would

---

41 Andrew Lang, 'Introduction', *The Plain Princess and Other Stories* (London: Longmans, Green, and Co., 1905), p. vii.

42 Ibid., p. 334. While it is uncertain whether Tolkien read this preface, he certainly read this quotation, as it appears in Roger Lancelyn Green's thesis.

43 Tolkien, 'On Fairy-stories', p. 71.

in the course of time, like the human race in general, mature into adulthood and put away childish things'.[44] Flieger and Anderson are certainly correct that an assumption that fairy tales were for children led some to the idea that it was a genre to put away by adulthood, but it is worthwhile to note that this was not Lang's own position.

In 'Realism and Romance' (1887), Lang's most-often-cited defense of genres which highlight action and marvels, Lang protests against those who call his love of romance savage and juvenile:

> Are we to be told that we love the "Odyssey" because the barbaric element has not died out of our blood, and because we have a childish love of marvels, miracles, man-eating giants, women who never die, "murders grim and great," and Homer's other materials? Very well. "Public opinion," in Boston, may condemn us, but we will get all the fun we can out of the ancestral barbarism of our natures. I only wish we had more of it.[45]

In Lang's essay, it is those who dislike the romance who claim it involves 'a childish love of marvels, miracles, man-eating giants'; this criticism comes from the outside, not from Lang. Lang not only makes the case that genres do not improve over time, he also continues his imagined critics' metaphor of progress from manhood to old age.

> The Coming Man may be bald, toothless, highly "cultured," and addicted to tales of introspective analysis. I don't envy him when he has got rid of that relic of the ape, his hair; those relics of the age of combat, his teeth and nails; that survival of barbarism, his delight in the last battles of Odysseus, Laertes' son.[46]

Thus by 1887, two years before the publication of *The Blue Fairy Book*, Lang has shown that he no longer believes progress to be uniformly positive. Instead, with his praise of the fairy story and the romance, Lang was positioning himself against critics, real and imagined, who used the terms *child*, *childlike*, and *childish* in a negative sense. Such posturing, however, was dangerous; Lang's tone frequently angered critics who were determined to secure the novel's

---

44   Verlyn Flieger and Douglas Anderson, *Tolkien On Fairy-stories: Expanded Edition with Commentary and Notes* (London: HarperCollins, 2008), p. 22.

45   Andrew Lang, 'Realism and Romance', *The Contemporary Review* (Nov. 1887), p. 689.

46   Ibid., p. 689.

place in high rather than popular culture. Marysa Demoor accurately claims that Lang 'could have prevented [the] largely posthumous fall from grace' that resulted from his consistent championship of the romance: 'If he had had the inclination, Lang could have created an aesthetic of the romance and so have lent his own viewpoint and the genre more seriousness, intellectualizing the apparently plebian adventure story'.[47] Instead, Lang's tone is at times lightly bantering, at times careless, at times self-deprecatory and apologetic. As Lang's writings drew the battle lines and consolidated critical opinion about fairy story and romance, advocates of these genres have been on the defensive ever since.

These critical opinions of Lang's also have religious implications. In fact, Lang's work from the 1870s to the 1890s shows a clear shift regarding the possibility of progress in either art or religion. Lang was studying myths and fairy tales alongside early religions in the hope that these tales would illuminate forgotten or little understood religious practices. In the early 1870s he had accepted the idea of progress in both literature (from fairy tale to mythology) and faith (from 'lower' religion to 'higher'). In 'Mythology and Fairy Tales' (1873), Lang successfully argues that mythology developed out of fairy tales rather than dwindling into them (as both Walter Scott and Müller believed) and that solar myths and corrupted and forgotten language could not explain the preposterous or even barbaric events in fairy tales.

It seems that at this time Lang also saw in this progress (from a shorter fairy story to a greater myth) a key to understanding the origin and development of religion. Lang claimed that an anthropological understanding of myths and stories could teach the truth about the development of people's 'religious imagination', which he then believed, with Tylor, to have been proven to have universally gone through a stage of Fetishism: 'Faith will thus be manifest as a continual and rational progress, from the worship of the objects nearest sense, to the adoration of the bodiless forces that strike the loftier imagination, and thence to the higher polytheisms'.[48]

By the late 1880s, when he wrote 'Realism and Romance' and *Myth, Ritual and Religion* (1887), gave the Gifford Lectures on Natural Religion (1889-90), and began to publish the fairy books (1889), Lang's understanding of progress had changed. He no longer believed that progress in literature was good or even possible. By 1889

---

47 Demoor, *Dear Stevenson*, p. 21.

48 Lang, 'Mythology and Fairy Tales', p. 620.

he had also abandoned his belief in faith as a continual and rational progress. In his lecture 'Religion and Progress' at Dundee, Lang not only declines to explain the origin of religion, as he believed no givers of explanations had any 'practical historical acquaintance with anything concerning the matter', he also moves away from earlier remarks he had made associating religion with progress, saying instead, 'When [he] went into and considered the beliefs of various races about a Deity, he confessed his opinions underwent a certain change, and he himself had found that he was gradually veering round to the opinions of Max Müller, which was not his intention when he started the subject. (Laughter and applause)'.[49] Lang could no longer maintain that religion advanced as society advanced, or that 'as a race grew wiser, and secured better clothes and better homes and better food, his ideas about a Deity would become purer, loftier, and nobler'.[50] Instead, highly developed societies often had less than noble ideas about God while what Lang considered to be among the most savage of societies had many laudable religious ideas: 'if [the audience] looked into the belief of an all Father, of the permanence of the human life, of after punishment, &c., there was very little to choose between the lowest savage and the most advanced philosopher of the day'.[51]

By 1898, in *The Making of Religion*, 'after more than twenty years of labour in the cause of a science of cultural evolution', Lang would renounce in print Tylor's theory that religion evolved from primitive animism, instead controversially claiming that 'the earliest and most natural belief of primitive man was in a single God the Creator, the righteous Maker and Judge of men, and that degradation rather than evolution had followed in the wake of the earliest stages of civilization'.[52] In other words, Lang no longer believed that religion

49 Green, *Andrew Lang*, p. 3.

50 Ibid., p. 3.

51 Ibid., p. 3. In *Myth, Ritual and Religion* (1887) Lang examines ethnographic data that supported the idea that several 'tribes of Australians, Bushmen, and Andamanese were said to believe in moral, anthropomorphic creator gods who were older and in some instances more powerful than the mass of spirits and lesser gods who figured most prominently in the ritual observances of these peoples' (Wheeler-Barclay, *The Science of Religion*, p. 129). See Wheeler-Barclay's chapter on 'Andrew Lang: The Antipositivist Critique', for a thorough examination of these controversies.

52 Wheeler-Barclay, *The Science of Religion*, p. 104; Green, Andrew Lang, p. 73. Lang's conception of early society's belief in an all Father creator-

followed the same path of development as fairy-stories. These latter were built up, sometimes becoming myths, while religious beliefs, in Lang's opinion, often became wilder and less pure.

Lang is difficult to understand, however, because not only was he continuously publishing new theories and revising old ones, his care in thinking through his new theories and applying them uniformly varied. Though never intentionally dishonest, Lang, in his graceful prose, relied on quick quips and well-phrased metaphors, and he sometimes exchanged accuracy for elegance, thereby undermining his point. At the Dundee lecture, for instance, Lang proclaims his disbelief in progress by using a metaphor of progress: 'The science of religion was [...] in its infancy, and perhaps could never reach maturity.' Although he has just exploded the idea that progress and religion walk hand in hand, he cannot move away from the metaphor of progress, infancy, and growth. Although Lang might come to a new conclusion in one area of his studies, and although Lang had personal evidence that one of his long-held ideas might not be correct, he left some inconsistent ideas unquestioned. When Tolkien responds negatively to Lang's apparent views of children in the fairy-book prefaces, he is responding to Lang at his most hasty and inconsistent.[53]

The very preface to the 1892 *Green Fairy Book*, whose readers' credulity, Tolkien complains, Lang traded upon, demonstrates another point of comparison between the two authors. Despite Lang and Tolkien's fondness for the burlesque of the fairy-story (*Prince Prigio* and *Farmer Giles of Ham* would both fit into that genre), Lang and Tolkien both agree that the fairy-story genre has been damaged by careless and cynical handling. Lang writes, 'There are not many people now, perhaps there are none, who can write really good fairy

---

God is, of course, the variant of religion that Tolkien chose for his Middle-earth: 'God is the supreme, the creator' (Gueroult interview). Some might say such a choice is obvious, given Tolkien's Catholic background. However, as Trevor Hart notes in 'Tolkien, Creation, and Creativity', the *Silmarillion* is not a simple retelling of Genesis, and Tolkien, with certain limits, 'felt free to call into existence imaginary worlds of sorts that varied greatly in their particulars (even their religious particulars) from the actual world he knew' (Trevor Hart, 'Tolkien, Creation, and Creativity' (Waco: Baylor University Press, 2000), p. 43).

53 It is ironic that Lang's fairy book prefaces, which he claimed more than once were not read (see the prefaces to the Crimson and the Orange fairy books), have been among the most lasting of his work, circulated as they were in popular books for children that have remained in print.

tales, because they do not believe enough in their own stories, and because they want to be wittier than it has pleased Heaven to make them'.[54]

If by 'believing enough in their own stories' Lang means really believing 'that witches could turn people into beasts, that beasts could speak, that magic rings could make their owners invisible, and all the other wonders in the stories', the sort of belief that Lang discusses earlier in his *Green Fairy Book* preface, Tolkien would disagree, but it seems that in this part of the preface Lang may actually be mourning the fact that so few among the Victorians can take the fairy story seriously. Instead the 'fairies try to be funny, and fail; or they try to preach, and succeed'.[55] Lang and Tolkien seem to agree that 'one thing must not be made fun of, the magic itself. That must in that story be taken seriously, neither laughed at nor explained away.'[56]

So, yes, in the main, Tolkien's criticisms of Lang on fairy stories and children were correct, but they are also in part a misunderstanding. When Tolkien criticizes Lang for believing that children are the natural audience for fairy stories rather than adults, this is in part because Tolkien himself loves the fairy story and does not enjoy being thought juvenile for his taste. But Lang also enjoys the fairy story. Lang, however, accounts for that love by believing it is the remnant of his savagery and childlikeness; he, unlike Tolkien, is not insulted by being associated with either what Lang calls 'the savage' or with the boy.

It is, in fact, Lang's consistent self-deprecatory tone about the topics Lang most cared about that led to the disparagement of the genres that Lang actually loved, and in which his taste was not terribly different from that of the Inklings. Green, in 'The Mystery of Andrew Lang', notes the affinity between descriptions of Lang's motivations and Lewis's description of joy, 'that unsatisfied desire which is itself more desirable than any other satisfaction'.[57]

---

54   Lang, *Green Fairy Book*, p. xi.

55   Andrew Lang, 'Preface', *The Lilac Fairy Book*, p. viii.

56   Tolkien, 'On Fairy-stories', p. 33.

57   Green, 'The Mystery of Andrew Lang', pp.12-13; C.S. Lewis, *Surprised by Joy* (Orlando: Harcourt, 1955), p. 17-18. Green here quotes Andrew Lang's statement of 1888 that 'only the impossible can satisfy human aspiration' and cites Desmond MacCarthy that Lang was 'a poet who, all his life, had been homesick for he knew not what, but supposed he had often found it in old loyalties and that 'romance'—boyish, historical, sentimental—which in all

Similarly, Lang's opinions about religion, though certainly less orthodox and less public than Tolkien's, were closer to Tolkien's than might be supposed. Unlike Tolkien, Lang did not accept divine revelation as an axiom. However, while both men's studies in religion, folklore, and fairy-tale overlapped and informed one another, each would, at times, react against scholars who conflated sacred and secular genres overmuch and thereby touched a hidden nerve.

Lang kept his most serious feelings private, only occasionally touching upon them in an article or a private letter, such as his review of 'Theological Romances', including Mary Augusta Ward's *Robert Elsemere*, or in his letter to Edward Clodd about the latter's life of Christ. In the review of Ward's landmark novel of religious doubt, Lang objects to Elsmere's proclamation that

> "*miracles do not happen!*" [...] This is enough for him, but no argument can possibly make it enough for everybody. [...] in spite of the opinions of Mrs. Ward's Squire and of Mr. Langham, and of the ingenious David Hume, and Mr. Thomas Paine (who really knew as much about the matter as the rest of them), many perfectly sane persons are unconvinced of the negative [...] What was good enough for Pascal is to me not incredible, and people in this mood will not easily be converted to the negatives of Mr. Elsmere.[58]

This serious side of Lang was not visible to Tolkien, but it is

---

his criticism he defended with such witty acrimony'.

58 Lang, 'Theological Romances', p. 820. A few lines later, however, Lang backs away from making a firm statement as to his own religious views: '*Elsemere* is much exercised with the miracle of the Resurrection of our Lord, which he abandons as incredible. To speak of such topics', Lang writes, 'above all in the review of a novel, is, in the last degree, distasteful to me. But I can readily suppose that, as to this matter, Belief has not uttered her last words nor published her latest argument' (pp. 820-21). For a similar hint into Lang's religious views, see a letter Lang wrote in 1880 to Edward Clodd in thanks for the copy of Clodd's *Jesus of Nazareth*: 'I have not yet recovered your new address and am constrained to thank you through Paul [Clodd's publisher] for Jesus. This sounds not such a very wrong thing to do. [...] For plentiful ignorance I cannot criticize you except that I miss the Resurrection in your biography. This is, or ought to be, a burning question, but alas! il y a fagots et fagots but none for the heretic. Perhaps the more Christian plan would be to convert you, but it is longer and more uncertain and less amusing to a faithful people. With many thanks all the same, though I do not fancy we can agree on the subject' (Edward Clodd, *Memories* (New York: G. Putnam's Sons, 1916), pp. 214).

beginning to be better understood. Both men's religious beliefs in the primary world would affect how they responded to the secondary world of fairy and romance.

The (Im)possibility of Genre Crossing

Even though Tolkien saw potential perils at the intersections of the 'narrow road', the 'braid, braid road', and the 'bonny road [...] to fair Elfland', because Tolkien's actual religious beliefs were more hopeful than Lang's, he was able to formulate a more optimistic approach to genre crossing and genre overlap than Lang did.[59] For Lang, the happy ending in the fairy story cannot take place in real life. For Tolkien, on the other hand, the fairy-story serves as pattern and reminder of the one fairy-story he believed really happened: 'The Resurrection is the eucatastrophe of the story of the Incarnation. This story begins and ends in joy'.[60]

Lang was ultimately hindered in his ability to argue for the romance by his inability to see in it transformative staying power. In his 1888 article 'Literary Anodynes' for the *New Princeton Review*, Lang argues for merely temporary escapism, comparing romance reading to opium smoking, with 'none of the ill effects'; he thinks such escapism as natural as 'the timely tendency to sleep at night'.[61] The fairy-story takes one away from real life to a place where things are better—though only for a time.

Lang's tone in this article is light and should therefore be interpreted with care; like all of Lang's articles it represents a static moment in Lang's ever-developing views.[62] However, 'Literary

---

59 Tolkien, 'On Fairy-stories', pp. 28-29.

60 Ibid., p. 31.

61 Lang, 'Literary Anodynes', p. 147. Lang compares reading an analytical or naturalistic novel, on the other hand, to 'the wearing, voluntarily, of an iron chain studded with spikes' (ibid., p. 149).

62 'Literary Anodynes', and indignant responses to it, laid the groundwork for the unsympathetic critical views of romance that Lewis and Tolkien would later contest. In *Cosmopolitan*, Hjalmar Hjorth Boyesen pounced on Lang's desire for his fiction to be a temporary escape: 'Instead of arousing and energizing the intellectual powers, the novel is to lull them asleep' (*19*; Oct. 1895, p. 691). Boyesen saw Lang's taste for the romance over the analytical realistic novel as 'evidence of intellectual immaturity [...] If a critic finds such stuff admirable, it is because he is yet in the juvenile state, when character yet lies largely beyond his ken and more brute incident has to take its place' (ibid., pp. 691, 692). Boyesen takes the position of Lewis's unnamed critics in

Anodynes' shows that in some ways Tolkien had more belief in the fairy story than Lang did. Though Lang's prefaces would later claim that good fairy tale authors believe their own tales, 'Literary Anodynes' appears not to have belief enough. Because Lang had no faith in the lastingly transformative nature of reading fantasy, he could never quite make the escape of the prisoner permanent. Reacting to *Robert Elsemere*, Lang says, 'Let me forget that 'miracles do not happen'; carry me where they do happen'. [63]

While for Tolkien, the fairy story was the highest form of art because it admitted a promise of the joy of the gospel, for Lang, the happy ending was good in fairy story, but it was suspect in real life. In his 1889 introduction of *The Blue Fairy Book*, Lang quotes from 'The Black Bull of Norroway', as Tolkien would near the end of 'On Fairy-stories':

> Seven lang years I served for thee,
> The glassy hill I clamb for thee,
> The bluidy shirt I wrang for thee,
> And wilt thou not wauken and turn to me?

Lang continues, 'They will not waken and turn to us, our lost loves, our lost chances, not for all our services, all our singing, not for all our waiting seven or twice seven long years. But, in the fairy tale, he heard, and he turned to her'.[64] Lang, too, recognizes the eucatastrophe and consolation of this fairy story's ending, but it does not cross over into his actual life, and he quickly moves on from his commentary to another point.

When Tolkien cites the same lines from this ending to the fairy story, 'He heard and turned to her', it is the moment of joy in the essay, and an introduction to his epilogue in which, through the gospel story, Tolkien claims that fairy tales do come true: the Gospels 'contain many marvels—peculiarly artistic, beautiful, and moving: 'mythical' in their perfect, self-contained significance, and among the marvels is the greatest and most complete conceivable eucatastrophe'.[65] Thus, although primary belief in a marvel-containing story is certainly not

---

'On Three Ways of Writing for Children' who are 'now less likely to [praise Lewis] for his perennial youth' (as late-Victorian writers like Stevenson and Conan Doyle were praised—often by Lang) 'than [to scorn and pity him] for arrested development' (ibid., p. 34).

63 Lang, 'Literary Anodynes', p. 147.

64 Lang, *Blue Fairy Book*, p. xiii.

65 Tolkien, 'On Fairy-stories', pp. 78.

required of an author or a reader, neither should marvels in themselves preclude the possibility of a reader's primary belief.

For Tolkien, the reader's emotional reaction to eucatastrophe is similar, whether the person is reading fantastic stories meant to be fictional or miraculous stories purported to be true. In a 1944 letter to his son Christopher, Tolkien writes of another apparently true eucatastrophe, describing a reported miracle at Lourdes that he believes to be 'fully attested *fact*':

> at the story of the little boy [...] with its apparent sad ending and then its sudden unhoped-for happy ending, I was deeply moved and had that peculiar emotion we all have—though not often. It is quite unlike any other sensation. And all of a sudden I realized what it was: the very thing that I have been trying to write about and explain—in that fairy-story essay that I so much wish you had read that I think I shall send it to you. For it I coined the word "eucatastrophe": the sudden happy turn in a story which pierces you with a joy that brings tears.[66]

Though Tolkien does not believe the marvels he describes in *The Lord of the Rings* in the primary sense, he does believe that marvels of a different kind are possible. Perhaps it is this that allows *Faërie* its transcendent and transformative power for him. Still, when faced with marvel-containing genres, Tolkien believes that the reader, in Lang's words, 'probably [...] know[s] very well how much is true and how much is only make-believe'.[67] Tolkien, in 'On Fairy-stories', wishes to make this point more clearly than Lang had in his sometimes contradictory statements.

However, despite all of Tolkien's efforts to separate primary and secondary belief and to distinguish his views from Lang's portrayal of gullible authors and occasionally credulous, childlike listeners, the question of primary belief would still come up. In 1965, in a quick-paced and sometimes non-sequitur-filled BBC interview, Denys Gueroult suspected Tolkien of believing in the reality of his own fantastic creations.

In the interview, Gueroult at first seems struck by the lack of religion in Middle-earth, and he insists that Tolkien explain religion's role in his fantasy. 'Where is God in *The Lord of the Rings?*' he asks point-blank. 'Mentioned once or twice', Tolkien answers somewhat facetiously. Gueroult presses Tolkien. He notes that when the men

66 Tolkien, *Letters*, p. 100.

67 Lang, *Green Fairy Book*, p. x.

go into battle, they call on Galadriel, or their native country, their weapons, or their king, 'I would have expected them to call on their gods [...] have they no gods as such? I would have thought that a story of this sort was almost dependent upon an intense belief in some theocratic division, some hierarchy.' Tolkien's answer, given on the fly, is certainly less carefully thought out than his workings and re-workings of points literary and theological in 'On Fairy-stories'. However, it fascinatingly demonstrates that even after Tolkien's efforts to separate primary and secondary belief in 'On Fairy-stories', the two types of belief still continue, like the mythology and religion Tolkien discusses in 'On Fairy-stories', to 'become entangled'.[68] Tolkien states,

> The man of the twentieth century must of course see, well, whether he believes in them or not, you must have gods in a story of this kind, but he can't make himself believe in Thor and Odin, Aphrodite, Zeus, and that kind of thing [...] I couldn't possibly construct a mythology which had Olympus or Asgaard in it, on the terms in which the people who worshipped those gods believed. God is the supreme, the creator.

Tolkien here stands near the border between primary and secondary belief. He claims that a twentieth-century reader, in order to have secondary belief in Tolkien's tale, requires a secondary world in which the characters believe in gods of some kind. Given Gueroult's first question and his incredulity about the apparent lack of religion in Middle-earth, such a claim seems fair. However, according to Tolkien, the twentieth-century reader's secondary belief could apparently only go so far, and gods such as those of Olympus and Asgaard would distract readers rather than keeping them in the story. Most probably, such gods would have served as a distraction; as C.S. Lewis notes in 'On Science Fiction', one of the strengths of the fantastic as a genre is its ability to work through problems that exist in historical time without forcing the author to include 'all manner of archaeological details which would spoil his book if they were done perfunctorily and perhaps distract our interest if they were done well'.[69] However, it also seems clear that it is 'the man of the twentieth century['s]' inability to *believe* in these gods that clinches the argument. Tolkien himself 'can't make himself believe in Thor and Odin, Aphrodite, Zeus, and that kind of thing'. Thus far Tolkien's primary belief has affected his

---

68   Tolkien, 'On Fairy-stories', pp. 44.

69   C.S. Lewis, 'On Science Fiction' (Orlando, FL: Harcourt, 1982), p. 55.

fantastic tale.

Gueroult, however, goes further and wonders what Tolkien can believe. Lang had posited primary belief to the early creators of fantasy; Gueroult wonders if the modern fantasy writer, Tolkien, might also believe in his own created characters: 'Do you in fact believe, yourself, not in the context of this book, but believe in the Eldar or in some form of governing spirit?' At this point (after a brief correction by Tolkien that *Valar* is the word Gueroult wants, not *Eldar*), there is a painful five seconds of silence, the longest in the interview. Tolkien is not the one to break that silence; Gueroult must change his question: 'Are you in fact a theist?' On safer ground, Tolkien immediately jumps in, 'Oh, I'm a Roman Catholic, devout Roman Catholic, but I don't know about angelology, yes I should, almost certainly, I mean, yes, certainly.'

BIBLIOGRAPHY

Boyesen, Hjalmar Hjorth, 'Novels of Romances and Stories of Real Life', *Cosmopolitan* 19 (Oct. 1895): 689-93. Print.

Clodd, Edward, *Memories*, New York: G. Putnam's Sons, 1916, *HathiTrust*, Web. 4 June 2013.

Dawson, Christopher, *Progress and Religion: An Historical Inquiry* (1929), Washington, D.C.: The Catholic University of America Press, 2001. Print.

Demoor, Marysa, ed., *Dear Stevenson: Letters from Andrew Lang to Robert Louis Stevenson with Five Letters from Stevenson to Lang*, Leuven: Uitgeverij Peeters, 1990. Print.

Flieger, Verlyn, ed., *Smith of Wootton Major: Extended Edition*, J.R.R. Tolkien, London: HarperCollins, 2005. Print.

Flieger, Verlyn and Douglas Anderson, eds., *Tolkien On Fairy-stories: Expanded Edition with Commentary and Notes*, London: HarperCollins, 2008. Print.

Gordon, George, 'Andrew Lang: Being the Andrew Lang Lecture Delivered Before the University of St. Andrews, 1 December 1927', London: Oxford University Press/ Humphrey Milford, 1928. Print.

Green, Roger Lancelyn, *Andrew Lang: A Critical Biography*, Leicester: Edmund Ward, 1946. Print.

Green, Roger Lancelyn, 'The Mystery of Andrew Lang', The 1968 Andrew Lang lecture, University of St. Andrews Special Collections. MS 30463.

Guéroult, Denys, 'J. R. R. Tolkien', Interview with J. R. R. Tolkien. 20 Jan. 1965, *The Spoken Word: British Writers*. BBC, 2008. CD.

Hart, Rachel, 'Tolkien, St. Andrews, and Dragons', *Tree of Tales: Tolkien, Literature, and Theology*, Ed. Trevor A. Hart and Ivan Khovacs, Waco: Baylor University Press, 2007: 1-11. Print.

Hart, Trevor, 'Tolkien, Creation, and Creativity'. *Tree of Tales: Tolkien, Literature, and Theology*. Ed. Trevor Hart and Ivan Khovacs. Waco: Baylor University Press,

2000: 39-53. Print.

Hensley, Nathan, 'What is a Network? (And Who is Andrew Lang?)' *Romanticism and Victorianism on the Net* 64 (Oct. 2013): n. pag. *Érudit*. Web. 15 Oct. 2014.

Ker, W. P., 'Andrew Lang, D. Litt', *Commemorative Addresses on Andrew Lang by W. P. Ker and on Arthur Woolgar Verrall* by J.W. MacKail, Royal Society of Literature: The Academic Committee, London: Henry Frowde, Oxford University Press, 1913: 8-19. Print.

Lang, Andrew, 'Homer and the Books of Samuel', *The Morning Post* N.d.: n. pag. [f. 41]. Newspaper Cutting in *Walker's Century Scrap & Newscutting Book*, MS38546. The Andrew Lang Collection, St. Andrews University, Scotland. Print.

Lang, Andrew, Introduction, *The Blue Fairy Book* [Large Paper Edition], London: Longmans, Green and Co., 1889. Xi-xxii. Print.

Lang, Andrew, Introduction, *Cinderella: Three Hundred and Forty-five Variants of Cinderella, Catskin, and Cap O'Rushes, Abstracted and Tabulated, with a Discussion of Mediæval Analogues, and Notes*, By Marian Roalfe Cox, London: The Folk-lore Society (David Nutt), 1893. *HathiTrust*. Web. 1 June 2013.

Lang, Andrew, Introduction, *Perrault's Popular Tales*, Ed. Andrew Lang, Oxford: The Clarendon Press, 1888. vii-cxv. *HathiTrust*. Web. 8 May 2013. Print.

Lang, Andrew, Introduction, *The Plain Princess and Other Stories*, By Irene Maunder, London: Longmans, Green, and Co., 1905. vii-x. Print.

Lang, Andrew, [Signed Longhop], 'The Lay of the Bookselling Elder', *St. Leonard's Magazine* 4.2 (28 Nov. 1863): f. 31. MS30130-30142. Andrew Lang Collection, St. Andrews University Special Collections, St. Andrews. Print.

Lang, Andrew, Letter to E. B. Tylor. 1883. Letters, etc. to Sir Edward Burnett Tylor, Professor of Anthropology, Oxford, and others, with other papers; 1861-1906. Add MS 50254. ff. 130-31. The British Library. London.

Lang, Andrew, 'Literary Anodynes'. *The New Princeton Review* 63.5 (Sep. 1888): 145-53. Internet Archive, Web. 14 Nov. 2014.

Lang, Andrew, 'The Master of Balliol'. *The Illustrated London News* 14 Oct. 1893: 479. *The Illustrated London News Archive*, Web. 21 Aug. 2014.

Lang, Andrew, 'Mythology and Fairy Tales'. *Fortnightly Review* 13 (May, 1873): 618-31. *British Periodicals*, Web. 31 Jan. 2013.

Lang, Andrew, Preface, *The Green Fairy Book*, London: Longmans, Green and Co., 1892. Print. New York: Dover, 1965. ix-xi. Print.

Lang, Andrew, Preface, *The Crimson Fairy Book*, 1903, New York: Dover, 1967. v-vi. Print.

Lang, Andrew, Preface, *The Lilac Fairy Book*, 1910, New York: Dover, 1968. v-ix. Print.

Lang, Andrew, Preface, *The Orange Fairy Book*, 1906, New York: Dover, 1968. v-vii. Print.

Lang, Andrew, 'Realism and Romance', *The Contemporary Review* 52 (Nov. 1887): 683-693, *British Periodicals*, Web. 31 Jan. 2013.

Lang, Andrew, 'Theological Romances', *The Contemporary Review* 53 (June 1888): 814-824, *British Periodicals*, Web. 31 Jan. 2013.

Lewis, C. S., 'On Science Fiction', *On Stories and Other Essays on Literature* (1966), Orlando, FL: Harcourt, 1982. 55-68. Print.

Lewis, C. S., 'On Three Ways of Writing for Children', *On Stories and Other Essays on Literature* (1966), Orlando: Harcourt, 1982. 31-43. Print.

Lewis, C. S., *Surprised by Joy*, Orlando: Harcourt, 1955. Print.

McKelvy, William, *The English Cult of Literature: Devoted Readers*, 1774-1880, Charlottesville: University of Virginia Press, 2007. Print.

'Mr. Andrew Lang on Religion and Progress', *Dundee Courier and Argus* 16 Mar. 1889: 3. British Newspapers,. Web. 7 Oct. 2014.

Pazdziora, John Patrick, 'How the Fairies were not Invited to Court, *Rethinking George MacDonald: Contexts and Contemporaries*', Ed. Christopher MacLachlan, John Patrick Pazdziora and Ginger Stelle, Glasgow: Scottish Literature International, 2013. 254-72. Print.

Resnik, Henry, 'An Interview with Tolkien', *Niekas* 18 (Spring 1967): 37-47. Print.

Richardson, Maurice, 'New Novels', *Rev. of The Two Towers*, by J. R. R. Tolkien, *New Statesman and Nation* 48 (18 Dec. 1954): 835-36. Print.

Schroeder, Sharin, 'The *Iliad* and the Articles: Francis William Newman's *Reply* to Matthew Arnold', *Nineteenth-Century Prose* 39.1/2 (2012): 323-52. Print.

Schroeder, Sharin, 'She-who-must-not-be-ignored: Gender and Genre in *The Lord of the Rings* and the Victorian Boys' Book', *Perilous and Fair: Women in J.R.R. Tolkien's Work and Life*. Ed. Janet Brennan Croft and Leslie Donovan. Altadena, CA: Mythopoeic Press, 2015. 70-96. Print.

Scull, Christina, and Wayne G. Hammond, *The J. R. R. Tolkien Companion and Guide*, 2 vols., Boston: Houghton Mifflin, 2006. Print.

Shippey, Tom, *The Road to Middle-earth*, Rev. ed., Boston: Houghton Mifflin, 2003. Print.

Tolkien, J.R.R., 'Beowulf: The Monsters and the Critics', *The Monsters and the Critics and Other Essays*, Ed. Christopher Tolkien, London: HarperCollins, 1983. 5-48. Print.

Tolkien, J.R.R., *The Letters of J.R.R. Tolkien*, Ed. Humphrey Carpenter, Boston: Houghton Mifflin, 1981. Print.

Tolkien, J.R.R., *Tolkien on Fairy-Stories: Expanded Edition with Commentary and Notes*, Ed. Verlyn Flieger & Douglas A. Anderson, London: HarperCollins, 2008. Print.

Tolkien, J.R.R., *Smith of Wootton Major: Extended Edition*, Ed. Verlyn Flieger, London: HarperCollins, 2005. Print.

Turner, Frank, *The Greek Heritage in Victorian Britain*, Yale: Yale University Press, 1981. Print.

Wheeler-Barclay, Marjorie, *The Science of Religion in Britain*, 1860-1915, Charlottesville: University of Virginia Press, 2010. Print.

Wilson, Edmund, 'Oo, Those Awful Orcs!' *Nation* 182 (1956): 312-14. Print.

St. George and Jack the Giant-Killer: As 'Wise as Women Are'? Gender, Science, and Religious Faith in George MacDonald's *Thomas Wingfold, Curate* and C.S. Lewis's *Out of the Silent Planet* and *That Hideous Strength*.

Monika B. Hilder

George MacDonald, the Victorian grandfather of fantasy literature and valiant defender of the gospel of Christ might be thought of as another Saint George—the patron saint of both mythopoeic literature and of Christian spirituality. Like the legendary knight who slew the dragon, MacDonald is an iconic figure who, with what Rolland Hein calls 'his Scottish indignation',[1] battled the dragons of his day—both the secular dragons of Victorian materialism and rationalism, and the religious dragons of the spiritually impoverished Christian establishments. Hein asserts, 'MacDonald was a gadfly in his own day, as he continues to be in ours'.[2] Perhaps we might regard his literary and spiritual heir, Oxford and Cambridge professor and Inklings author Clive Staples Lewis, as a similar goad—a culture critic.

Certainly MacDonald's legacy as a troubler of the prevailing ideas of his time is one that Lewis heartily embraced. Like MacDonald whom he called his 'master', Lewis engaged the culture with the purpose to defeat the dragons of atheism and ignorance.[3] And Jack, as Lewis called himself, did so with a compelling originality and jolly vigour that brought him fame. Austin Farrer, for example, described Lewis as the 'bonny fighter' of the Oxford Socratic Club, and A.D. Nuttall hailed Lewis as 'Jack the Giant-Killer' for having fought and slain one giant of the intelligentsia: the giant of subjectivism.[4]

---

1   Rolland Hein, *Creation in Christ: Unspoken Sermons*, George MacDonald (Vancouver: Regent College, 2004), p. 9.

2   Ibid., p. 7.

3   C.S. Lewis, *George MacDonald: An Anthology* (London: Fount, 1990), p. 33.

4   Austin Farrer, 'The Christian Apologist' New York: Harcourt, Brace & World, 1966), p. 25; A.D. Nuttall, 'Jack the Giant-Killer' (Seven: An Anglo-American Literary Review, 1984), p. 84.

Undoubtedly these two men were outstanding thinkers and writers and their impact increases. Given their influence, however, one might wonder, which Victorian and Edwardian cultural biases, if any, perhaps compromise their relevance today? Quickly asked, if not rudely, since MacDonald and Lewis are 'dead, white, male poets,' are they not products of centuries of Western chauvinism, and therefore also perpetuate forms of blindness that we had better recognize than ignore?

In Lewis studies of late the most controversial question is that of gender. Was he a theoretical misogynist, as Owen Barfield claimed?[5] Was he a sexist who at best softened with age? Or have we not yet understood this aspect of Lewis?

MacDonald, on the other hand, fares a good deal better on the question of gender. Indeed, MacDonald appears as a rare visionary: his heroines are exemplary moral leaders and, remarkably, he portrays the 'feminine' nature of the divine alongside that of the 'masculine'.[6] To run to God, he writes, means not only to run toward one's heavenly Father but to also run 'Motherward' to the 'heaven that's heavenliest'.[7]

But regardless of where we land on the controversial question of gender in these authors, perhaps we might classify or even ignore this question as one of historical context? To put it very plainly, 'MacDonald and Lewis probably were sexist, perhaps one more than the other, or equally so, but so what? That was then; we know better now. We are overcoming the oppression of sexism. How does thinking about their probably antiquated views of gender help us to grapple with forces that threaten humanity itself? To the worship of scientism that has given us, in M.D. Aeschliman's words, "a culture of nihilistic consumerism, pornography, and violence"?[8] Before we conclude that the question of sexism in earlier authors, however important, is anachronistic, let us consider another one of Barfield's

---

5   R.L. Green and W. Hooper, *C. S. Lewis: A Biography* (London: William Collins, 1974), pp. 213-14.

6   I use quotations around 'feminine' and 'masculine' in order to emphasize the metaphor. This is in keeping with Lewis's reference to himself as an 'old woman' (Letters 3: p. 521) and his line, '...a "man's man" or a "woman's woman"' (Ibid., p. 158).

7   George MacDonald, *Diary of An Old Soul* (Minneapolis: Augsburg 1975), p. 225.

8   M.D. Aeschliman, 'Modernity' (Grand Rapids: Zondervan, 1998), p. 283.

observations. Barfield spoke of Lewis's consistent 'presence of mind' so that 'somehow what he thought about everything was secretly present in what he said about anything'.[9] Barfield described the organic unity of Lewis's thinking in moral terms: '...I never remember a time when the *moral* aspect of any question under discussion was not the one which principally engaged his attention'.[10] If Barfield was right, then Lewis's views on gender are part of his moral vision. And, given his affinity with MacDonald, we should rethink what it was that both men believed about gender. Further, would the father of English Romanticism, William Wordsworth, whom both authors esteemed, have praised them for being, in his words in *The Prelude* (1850), as 'wise as women are'?[11] If so, how might the so-called 'female wisdom' of MacDonald and Lewis prove intrinsic to their views on the pursuit of science and on the related question of religious faith?

To begin to answer these questions, I would like to pose two more. First, is a person heroic because she is active and self-reliant? Second, is a person heroic because he is passive and dependent? If our answer to the first question is 'yes', a hero is active and self-reliant, then we have identified ourselves with the predominant Western heroic paradigm: the classical one of Greece and Rome. But if our answer to the first question is 'no', activity and self-reliance are not necessarily heroic, and if our answer to the second question is even a tentative 'yes', that a hero might sometimes be passive and dependent, then we have placed ourselves in the path of the lesser known and lesser understood Western heroic paradigm: the spiritual one of Judeo-Christianity.

A bit more on these paradigms. The classical hero is characterized by values such as self-sufficient reason, activity, conquest, and pride. The wrath of Achilles, the deception of Odysseus, the despair of Aeneas, the martial valour of all heroes in establishing worldly power—these qualities undergird our typical idea of the hero as active and self-reliant. Milton identified the classical hero as satanic: in *Paradise Lost* (1667) the fallen angel declares, 'To reign is worth ambition though in Hell:/ Better to reign in Hell, than serve in

---

9   Owen Barfield, *Owen Barfield on C.S. Lewis* (Middletown: Wesleyan University Press), 1989, p. 122.

10   Ibid., pp. 5, 122.

11   William Wordsworth, 'The Prelude', (Boston: Houghton Mifflin, 1850), 12.156.

Heav'n'.[12] And MacDonald described self-reliant heroism this way: 'For the one principle of hell is—"I am my own. I am my own king and my own subject. I am the centre [...] My own glory is, and ought to be, my chief care; my ambition [...] My pleasure [...] My right [...] To do my own will [...] is to be free, is to live." '[13]

On the other hand, biblical spiritual heroism is characterized by values such as an imagination that is open to faith, passivity, submission, and humility—qualities that influence our sympathies with the underdog who overcomes unlikely odds through the transcendent strength of meekness. So David, too young to wear adult battle gear or use conventional weapons, trusts that the battle is the Lord's and slays the giant Goliath. So Mary submits herself to God and becomes the exalted mother of Jesus. So God becomes a human zygote on a journey that takes him to the ultimate humiliation of dying on the cross for the redemption of humanity. In *Paradise Regained* (1671) Milton described Christ's victory over classical heroism thus: 'By Humiliation and strong Sufferance:/ His weakness shall o'ercome Satanic strength'.[14] And Lewis described dependent heroism this way: 'Obedience is the road to freedom, humility the road to pleasure, unity the road to personality'.[15] In a 1959 letter Lewis challenged the ethos of self-sufficiency: 'Everything I need is in my soul? The Heck it is!'[16] Vital for our question of chauvinism is the manner in which these oppositional heroic qualities have been gendered. Activity, autonomy, and pride are associated with the 'masculine'; passivity, dependence, and humility are associated with the 'feminine'. Significantly, the predominance of the 'masculine' classical hero over the 'feminine' spiritual hero speaks to a cultural chauvinism that runs far deeper than literal sexism. Because we have privileged the classical hero, we typically see with chauvinist lenses—and often are unaware of doing so.

We can be too literal-minded about these things: 'men are from Mars and women are from Venus'. It does seem to me that earlier thinkers were much more fluent in regarding gender-as-

12 John Milton, *Paradise Lost* (Indianapolis: Odyssey), 1976, 1.262–3.

13 George MacDonald, 'Kingship' in *Unspoken Sermons III* (Whitehorn: Johannesen, 2004), p. 495.

14 John Milton, 'Paradise Regained' (Indianapolis: Odyssey, 1976), 1.161.

15 C.S. Lewis, 'Membership' (Grand Rapids: Eerdmans, 1977), p. 36.

16 C.S. Lewis, *The Collected Letters of C.S. Lewis, Volume III* (New York: HarperCollins, 2007), p. 1039.

metaphor, thereby viewing all of these heroic characteristics as human characteristics that apply to both sexes. That is why both Wordsworth and Friedrich Nietzsche could point to gender metaphor with ease. Cultural chauvinism was no news to them: Wordsworth because he rejected it; Nietzsche because he embraced it.

Thus, in *The Prelude* (which MacDonald named as 'the best of [Wordsworth's] poems') the poet described his heroic ideal as one who is filled with a 'spiritual Love' that he hailed as 'female softness'.[17] The ethical hero must have a 'heart [...] tender as a nursing mother's heart'.[18] This is everything that Nietzsche loathed. For Nietzsche identifies and at once derides Christian submission as 'feminine' and instead applauds the 'masculine' egotism of the Superman.[19]

It is worthwhile to pause on a phrase that Lewis once whimsically applied to himself: the 'old woman' of Oxford'.[20] What? The boisterous argumentative Lewis, 'the best-read man of his generation' according to William Empson[21] an 'old woman' in the eyes of many of his peers? But as one who stood apart from his atheistic *avant garde* colleagues, a misfit in Oxford, the gender metaphor is accurate. However 'tough' Lewis's 'masculine clubbability' may have been, to cite Bayley, we miss much if we do not recognize the way in which Lewis, like MacDonald, fought cultural sexism without fail.[22]

Is self-reliant reason good? Is faith irrational? Does science in and of itself challenge religious faith? Does religious faith reject science? When might science lead to the abolition of humanity? How might a mythic imagination lead to the restoration of humanity? These are questions that MacDonald and Lewis explore. Both authors are clear on how not science, but scientism—the deification of science in disregard of moral and religious questions—is a form of the myth of progress that ultimately leads to our annihilation. Informed by what

17 George MacDonald, 'The Imagination: Its Functions and Its Culture' (Whitehorn: Johannesen), p. 262; Wordsworth, 'The Prelude', 14.188-231.

18 MacDonald, 'The Imagination: Its Functions and Its Culture', pp. 227-8.

19 Friedrich Nietzsche, *Beyond Good and Evil* (Oxford: Oxford University Press, 1998), pp. 44, 47, 56-7.

20 C.S. Lewis, *Letters*, p. 521.

21 James T. Como, 'Introduction', *Remembering C. S. Lewis* (San Francisco: Ignatius, 2005), p. 35.

22 Peter Bayley, 'From Master to Colleague' (San Francisco: Ignatius, 2005), p. 176.

Wordsworth called 'female softness', MacDonald and Lewis reject scientism.

In the novel *Thomas Wingfold, Curate*, MacDonald critiques scientism through the progressive young barrister, George Bascombe. Bascombe is the quintessence of a nineteenth-century British version of the classical 'masculine' hero. He is 'tall and handsome as an Apollo and strong as the young Hercules' with the matching self-satisfaction one would expect of a physically healthy, educated, and self-reliant male of the middle-class who is destined to rise in society.[23] Moreover, his pride, the reader is told, does not even seem offensive.[24] What self-respecting Victorian would not, at least at first, consider Bascombe to be 'the right sort of fellow'? Certainly, Bascombe advocates the very beliefs that many Victorians held in high esteem: rationalism; faith in progress to ever-greater physical and moral heights; personal material prosperity; and the renunciation of all objections to the above. In Bascombe, MacDonald holds a mirror to society, and asks, 'Is the classical hero truly the desirable one?'

Bascombe represents those atheists who have deified empirical reason, thereby making a religion out of science. He regards himself as a realist, a grown man, who wishes to 'sweep away all illusions' from the many children of the world.[25] He views the Christian hope of victory over death as 'rubbish' and applauds instead having the 'courage to face the facts of existence' which, in his view, mean that the dying man must be regarded as soon becoming 'only an unpleasant mass of chemicals'.[26] He sings a song about his own life as a 'fearless flame' in the face of final extinction with a vigour that would do George Bernard Shaw proud.[27] This self-appointed prophet is convinced that his 'mission' is 'to destroy the beliefs of everybody else'.[28]

The anti-'feminine' nature of Bascombe's heroism is also clear in his use of gendered language. When the tormented youth Leopold asks, what he would do if he were guilty of murder, it takes the barrister only a moment's reflection before he answers with breezy self-assurance: '...I would be a man, and bear it—not a weakling, and

---

23 George MacDonald, *Thomas Wingfold, Curate* (Whitehorn: Johannesen, 2002), p. 12.

24 Ibid., p. 12.

25 Ibid., p. 17.

26 Ibid., pp. 25, 462.

27 Ibid., p. 18.

28 Ibid., pp. 33, 31.

let it crush me. No, by Jove! it shouldn't crush *me*!'.[29] And he derides the curate's growing Christian faith in terms of 'believ[ing] all his grandmother told him!'[30]

In Bascombe, MacDonald makes clear that a commitment to philosophical materialism has dire implications. The very sanctity of life is threatened by the barrister's social Darwinism and related anti-Semitism. He would have all physically and mentally challenged infants killed and disallow such adults to marry and have children.[31] Thus, when Bascombe encounters the misshapen dwarfs, Joseph Polwarth and his niece Rachel, this 'high priest of social morality' boldly pronounces his 'doctrine of [eugenics]'.[32] 'It is shameful!' he says in righteous anger. 'Such creatures have no right to existence [...] Monsters ought not to live'.[33] With similar aggression Bascombe illustrates how eugenics is linked to anti-Semitism. The barrister understands that his views stand in direct opposition to the legacy of the Jewish faith inherent in Christianity whereby each individual human soul is of infinite value. He declares to Helen, 'To go whining after an old Jew fable in these days of progress! [...] This matter has to do with the well-being of the race; and we *must* think of others, however your Jew-gospel, in the genuine spirit of the Hebrew of all time, would set everybody to the saving of his own wind-bubble of a soul'.[34] For Bascombe, the soul, the 'feminine' Psyche in relation to the 'masculine' divine, does not exist, but only the classical 'masculine' strength of mind and body. Therefore, only the politically correct deserve to live. And so the Jew, the Christian, and the physically and mentally challenged are all people who would need to be eliminated—a progressivism that a mere half century later came to fruition in Hitler's Third Reich.

MacDonald also portrays how scientism proves irrational. Bascombe, who prides himself as a clear, unprejudiced thinker, is only pseudo-rational.[35] He parrots popular theories and demands of empirical reason what she cannot answer: whether or not God exists.

29 Ibid., p. 321.

30 Ibid., p. 153.

31 Ibid., p. 46-7.

32 Ibid., pp. 315, 246.

33 Ibid., pp. 45-6.

34 Ibid., p. 241.

35 Ibid., p. 33.

He believes that an apparently chaotic, meaningless universe would have produced meaning—in particular, the rationality of his own thinking. This champion of the new age increasingly repels some of his peers.

Helen Lingard, initially, is Bascombe's 'disciple'.[36] She admires what she thinks of as George's masculine strength, and likewise despises the weakness of her brother Poldi.[37] But Helen comes to identify her utilitarian prudence as a hellish selfishness akin to murder.[38] Out of what the narrator uncritically calls her 'woman's weakness for the side attacked', she clings to the idea that the welfare of the individual is tied to the greater good.[39] Love for her suffering brother is the crucible whereby her sleeping soul awakens.

Likewise, the curate Thomas Wingfold comes alive. He is a foil to George Bascombe. Next to the barrister's Greek godlike appearance, Wingfold looks like a 'nobody'.[40] Beside the barrister's self-assurance, he appears 'weak' and openly uncertain about his own beliefs.[41] Like Ransom in Lewis's *Out of the Silent Planet*, the minister is an ethical man who struggles to make sense of the conflicting claims of scientism and Christian faith. And as with Ransom, Wingfold's budding identity as a spiritual hero is tied to his 'feminine' receptivity.

The curate's softening is evident in his sensitivity to nature. Contemplating the night sky causes him to 'feel [that] there ought to be more—as if the night knew something he did not; and he yielded himself to its invasion'.[42] (The psychosexual imagery of the curate submitting to 'invasion' is echoed in Lewis's writings, including *That Hideous Strength*.) As Wingfold strives to learn more about Jesus and to obey Him, he senses that 'he ha[s] been visited and upheld by a power whose presence and even influence escaped his consciousness'.[43] He recognizes the inadequacy of empirical reason before the great metaphysical questions and begins 'to feel after God'.[44] He embraces

---

36 Ibid., p. 33.

37 Ibid., p. 49.

38 Ibid., pp. 245-6, 372, 478.

39 Ibid., p. 17.

40 Ibid., p. 13.

41 Ibid., pp. 13, 52.

42 Ibid., p. 21.

43 Ibid., p. 59.

44 Ibid., p. 281.

obedience to Christ as the only power that can set humanity free.[45] Unlike the Superman Bascombe, the minister exhibits meekness, declaring the need to 'hide [one's self] in God, as the child would hide from the dark in the folds of his mother's mantle'.[46] Unlike the apostle of eugenics, Wingfold embraces the dying murderer, Leopold, and the suffering dwarf, Joseph Polwarth, as eternal souls, brothers on the common journey toward the only possible true home, 'the home of God's heart'.[47]

In the deformed dwarfs, Joseph and Rachel, MacDonald in particular illustrates how 'feminine' weakness can lead to spiritual strength. Rachel radiates a 'satisfaction' that does not arise from the self, and Joseph exhibits a 'spiritual tenderness' that enables him to be 'like a father in Christ' to others.[48] Whereas Helen's aunt Mrs Ramshorn derides him as 'the little object', the dwarf is in fact a spiritual giant.[49]

Significantly, Joseph's spirituality enables him to argue against scientism. In doing so, Polwarth does not claim that human intellect can prove the existence of God. Instead, he points to the *un*scientific manner in which science is sometimes elevated to a religion, pointing out too how in these instances the Christian origins of scientific investigation are denied.[50]

As MacDonald has said of imaginative inquiry and its relation to science and religion, 'To inquire into what God has made is the main function of the imagination. It [...] refuses to regard science as the sole interpreter of nature, or the laws of science as the only region of discovery'.[51] Empiricism, a narrow form of reason, is inadequate, and therefore, when elevated to the exclusion of emotion, ethics, and religious imagination, is most dangerous. MacDonald denounces the amoral pursuit of science in these words: 'Alas for the science that will sacrifice the law of righteousness.... It is the old story: the greed of

---

45 Ibid., p. 498.

46 Ibid., p. 429.

47 Ibid., p. 424.

48 Ibid., pp. 68, 170, 460.

49 Ibid., p. 433.

50 Ibid., p. 87.

51 George MacDonald, 'The Imagination: Its Functions and Its Culture' (Whitehorn: Johannesen, 1996), p. 2.

knowing casts out righteousness, and mercy, and faith'.[52]

The legacy of George MacDonald's Christian spirituality and critique of scientism is plain in C.S. Lewis's thinking. He stated, 'Christian theology can fit in science, art, morality, and the sub-Christian religions. The scientific point of view cannot fit in any of these things, not even science itself'.[53] Like MacDonald who insisted that 'the roots of science' are hidden in 'the unseen',[54] Lewis reasoned, 'even to think and act in the natural world we have to assume something beyond it [...] In order to think we must claim for our own reasoning a validity which is not credible if our own thought is merely a function of our brain, and our brains a by-product of irrational physical processes [...] The concept of nature itself is one we have reached only tacitly by claiming a sort of *super*-natural status for ourselves.'[55] He concluded, '...Nature herself as a whole is *not* natural [...] the universe is one great miracle'.[56] In his space trilogy, Lewis illustrates the terrible consequences of scientism.

In the first two novels of the trilogy, *Out of the Silent Planet* and *Perelandra*, the physicist Dr. Weston is Lewis's classical champion of the new age—he is the so-called strong man, a self-declared 'wise, new man'.[57] Big, bold, and brilliant, this scientist is the loud 'larger than life' charismatic leader who towers above the rest of humanity. As his name implies, Weston represents the height of Western humanism, or rather its demise in the Nietzschean Superman. In his words, 'The world leaps forward through great men and greatness always transcends mere moralism'.[58] He is the prototype of what Lewis described in *The Abolition of Man*—a trained intellect without moral conscience. In other words, Weston is another Lucifer.

Weston is an imperialist. He dismisses all non-scientific

---

52 George MacDonald, 'The Hope of the Universe' (Whitehorn: Johannesen, 2000), p. 219.

53 C.S. Lewis, 'Is Theology Poetry?' (London: Geoffrey Bles , 1962), p. 165.

54 George MacDonald, 'Wordsworth's Poetry' (Whitehorn: Johannesen, 1996), p. 58.

55 C.S. Lewis, 'Miracles' (Grand Rapids: Eerdmans, 1976), p. 27.

56 Ibid., p. 36.

57 C.S. Lewis, *Out of the Silent Planet* (London: Pan, 1974), p. 162.

58 C.S. Lewis, *Perelandra* (New York: Scribner), p. 82.

education as 'trash'.[59] He believes it is humanity's 'right' to colonize other planets.[60] He sees himself as the gifted man of 'destiny' who will secure immortality for humanity as a species, of what the narrator calls 'the sweet poison of the false infinite'.[61] Like MacDonald's Bascombe, Dr. Weston illustrates the legacy of eugenics. The physicist believes that his hired labourer, the intellectually inferior Harry, is sub-human and therefore disposable.[62] Weston is a Darwinist committed to a principle of 'Life' which he explains in terms of natural selection: he dismisses the idea of the value of the individual as an antiquated and intolerable barrier to progress.[63] This principle of 'Life', he declares, 'is greater than any system of morality; her claims are absolute'.[64] For Weston science means power, even ruthless destruction—a worldview which Lewis's protagonist, Dr. Ransom, denounces as raging insanity.[65] And in a moral universe, classical power proves doomed. In *Out of the Silent Planet* Weston is reduced to foolishness and anguish; in *Perelandra* he loses his soul.

The third novel, *That Hideous Strength*, draws the strongest reactions from readers. Critics spurn the novel as sexist for its esteem of marriage and motherhood over education and career. Fans praise the fantasy for its prophetic value for the 21st century. Here Lewis's use of gender metaphor is acute. The story centers on a 'scientist conspiracy' that George Orwell noted as 'realisable', and Christian matrimony is the battleground.[66] So the politics of sex—what the protagonist Jane Studdock does with her mind/body—has everything to do with what Lewis is saying about scientism.

That Hideous Strength is a tale of two cities, the demonically-inspired Belbury of the N.I.C.E. (the not-so-nice National Institute of Co-ordinated Experiments), and the order of Christian faith in the community of St. Anne's. N.I.C.E. is the progressive version of 'masculine' classical heroism. St. Anne's is a model of 'feminine'

---

59 Lewis, *Out of the Silent Planet*, p. 29.

60 Ibid., p. 157.

61 Ibid., p. 82; Lewis, *Perelandra*, pp.158-9,70.

62 Lewis, *Out of the Silent Planet*, p. 20.

63 Lewis, *Perelandra*, pp. 28-9.

64 Lewis, *Out of the Silent Planet*, p. 158.

65 Ibid., p. 29.

66 C.S. Lewis, *That Hideous Strength: A Modern Fairy-Tale for Grown-Ups* (New York: Scribner, 2003), p. 2.

spirituality. The outcome of their conflict will determine the future of humanity: whether we are to become technocratic super-beings who descend into brutality or, instead, remain mortals meant for eternal glory.

Chauvinism is intrinsic to N.I.C.E. Their symbol is 'a muscular male nude grasping a thunderbolt'.[67] Like MacDonald's Bascombe, N.I.C.E. members mock opposition to their new world order as weakly 'feminine'. Lord Feverstone, the former Dick Devine in *Out of the Silent Planet* who is no longer human, having lost his soul, but has 'fine, male energy', declares ethical opposition to biochemical conditioning, sterilization, and liquidation, as belonging to 'all the old women of both sexes'.[68] Fairy Hardcastle's contempt for Jane as 'little wifie', like Filostrato's aversion to sexual intercourse and birth, reveals their war on marriage—a most logical war, because technocracy rejects organic life and because family bonds threaten the totalitarian idea of man as a political animal.[69]

Misogyny is key to N.I.C.E.'s worship of intellectual power. As mind is traditionally associated with the 'masculine', and the body is traditionally associated with the 'feminine', N.I.C.E. commits the ultimate sexism. The mind is everything; the body, nothing. In their occult-inspired pursuit of the technocratic superman, Belbury views Mother Nature as outdated garbage. N.I.C.E. attempts to colonize the body, and so humanity. The parallels with NAZI Germany as well as with our contemporary veneration of technological advancement, especially the dream of transhumanism where the mind is to be immortal and the body abandoned, are striking.

Belbury's doom illustrates Lewis's conviction that epistemological chauvinists commit intellectual and spiritual suicide. As rationalists, their intelligence disintegrates. As abusers of Nature, they reap death. To deny the 'feminine' soul is to first sink into caricature, then to grow wraith-like, bound for hell.

Lewis's answer to this abolition of humanity is the 'feminine' community of St. Anne's. As in name,[70] this group embodies spiritual

---

67 Ibid., p. 212.

68 Ibid., pp. 41, 47.

69 Ibid., p. 169.

70 The name St. Anne's is an allusion to the Catholic tradition in which the mother of the Virgin Mary is St. Anne. See, for instance, Thomas Howard's discussion in 'The Triumphant Vindication of the Body' (Grand Rapids: Eerdmans, 1998), p. 141.

motherhood. Its ethos is one of domesticity, interdependence, and hospitality. Unlike the N.I.C.E. conspiracy, St. Anne's has no political power, makes no economic plans, and does not coerce membership or enforce uniformity of belief. It is a welcoming company of diverse friends, most of them Christian but not all, who are committed to moral truth, given to philosophical discussion, alive to practical matters, work for the common good, and passionately love nature. Whereas Belbury illustrates deception leading to destruction, St. Anne's illustrates clarity leading to healing and restoration. Whereas Belbury is technocratic, St. Anne's illustrates the unity of spirit-mind-body.

St. Anne's is a spiritual beacon illuminating the darkness that threatens to swallow England and the entire world. While Belbury seeks to eradicate organic life, St. Anne's is pregnant with its celebration. With its fruit trees, vegetable garden, greenhouses, barn, stable, and pigsty—a teeming whole—the walled garden of St. Anne's is associated with the female body. Members of the community are diverse, including people from all walks of life and also animals of all species and sizes. Respect, care, and charity—not 'the survival of the fittest'—characterizes this company. St. Anne's represents Logres, the true England in sync with the moral order of the universe. St. Anne's represents the Church, the kingdom of God, and is supported by the ruling angels of the heavenly spheres. St. Anne's is the unlikely David against Goliath, a St. George against the dragon: victorious through divine decree.

This is not to say that the 'good guys' of St. Anne's are innocents immune from the lures of classical heroism. Jane's pride is her besetting sin. Her husband Mark lusts for power and prestige. Dr. Dimble asks himself if there is not an entire Belbury inside him.[71] However, what distinguishes them is their choice to surrender ego, to become vessels of the good—in effect, God-bearers, like Mary the mother of Christ. Instead of worshipping the autonomous self, members of St. Anne's become pregnant with God.

Likewise, Ransom learns to obey and becomes a leader. Willing to wait for spiritual direction, what Charles Williams called the 'passion of patience' (1938: 35), Ransom becomes a channel for heavenly energy. This transformation from 'masculine' independence to 'feminine' surrender is particularly striking when it occurs in Merlin. In conventional terms, the ancient druid is the most masculine figure

---

71 Lewis, *That Hideous Strength*, p. 221.

of the company: formidable in size and magic, his self-reliance is great. But once Merlin grasps that his own might will fail against the Hideous Strength, he becomes passive to the celestial beings. Merlin is opened; the cosmic powers pass into him, and he is no longer his own man. Only as the passive recipient does he become the agent of divine justice upon Belbury's crimes.

Of all the members of St. Anne's, Jane becomes the icon of the community's ethos of submission. At first, though married, she is determined to preserve her independence and privileges academic achievement over potential motherhood. She is a chauvinist in her devotion to intellect at the expense of family life. But Jane has inherited visionary powers, another form of conception that she resents, and her dreams ultimately force her to choose between Belbury and St. Anne's. Once Jane chooses St. Anne's, she starts to let go of rationalism, open herself to community, and soon her 'world [is] unmade'.[72] Jane discovers this truth: in yielding ego to God, healing begins. At last she is strong enough to 'descen[d] the ladder of humility' in her marriage: Jane chooses in 'obedience' what the classical hero must shun—children, pain, and death—and does so in order that love and therefore life might prevail. In embracing what the narrator calls 'the sweet humiliations of organic life', Jane practices the agency of patience and becomes a saviour-figure to her forlorn husband.[73] Love overrules personal power; true power is informed by love. Jane is an image of what all spiritual heroes must become: God-bearers, 'feminine' in relation to the 'masculine' divine.

Jane's husband Mark too grows heroic. A morally weak man after self-importance, Mark is in danger of losing his life and very soul. What saves him is his love for his wife and attraction to her moral resolve. Mark starts to long for a true marriage as never before and in this frame of mind comes to a crossroads. When N.I.C.E. psychologist, Dr. Frost, tries to re-condition Mark by requiring that he abuse a nearly life size crucifix, it is the very helplessness of the image of Christ that stops him.[74] When put to the test of whether to choose evil or weakness, Mark chooses weakness. Although not a Christian, he aligns himself with the moral courage of Christ, and therefore potential martyrdom. From this point on Mark is acutely aware of his unworthiness of Jane. The humiliation of Christ awakens humility

---

72 Lewis, *That Hideous Strength*, p. 221.

73 Ibid., pp. 380, 322.

74 Ibid., pp. 332.

in him; he repents of his arrogant insensitivity and wishes to open himself to Jane. (I don't know of another example in contemporary English literature that so overtly criticizes male chauvinism as Lewis does in the evolution of Mark Studdock from egocentric to loving husband.)

Together Jane and Mark obey Venus. Their mutual submission—Jane's submission to God and then to her husband and childbearing, Mark's submission to the idea of God and then in humility to his wife—is a cameo image of the victory of organic life over technocracy. Scientism is sexist, but true matrimony overcomes scientism.

Thus, St. George MacDonald and Jack Lewis the Giant-Killer might be thought of not as outdated bigots but as countercultural prophets. With 'feminine wisdom' they level a serious challenge at cultural chauvinism. They ask: will we, like typical 'masculine' classical heroes, continue to embrace scientistic ideology, or will we instead, with what Wordsworth called 'meekness' and 'humble faith', seek to dwell within the only 'lasting grandeur' that exists—'pervading love'?[75] For MacDonald and Lewis the stakes cannot be higher—death or life—both in this present world and for eternity.

---

75 Wordsworth, 'The Prelude', 13.27-28; 14.169.

BIBLIOGRAPHY

Aeschliman, M.D., 'Modernity', in Jeffrey D. Schultz and John G. West Jr. (eds.), *The C. S. Lewis Readers' Encyclopedia*, Grand Rapids: Zondervan (1998), 282-3. Print.

Barfield, Owen, in G.B. Tennyson (ed.), *Owen Barfield on C. S. Lewis*, Middletown, CT: Wesleyan University Press, 1989. Print.

Bayley, Peter, 'From Master to Colleague', in James T. Como (ed.), *Remembering C. S. Lewis: Recollections of Those Who Knew Him*, San Francisco: Ignatius (1979/2005) 164-76. Print.

Como, James T., 'Introduction', in James T. Como (ed.), *Remembering C. S. Lewis: Recollections of Those Who Knew Him*, San Francisco: Ignatius (2005), 33–51. Print.

Farrer, Austin, 'The Christian Apologist', in Jocelyn Gibb (ed.), *Light on C. S. Lewis*, New York: Harcourt, Brace & World (1966), 23–43. Print.

Green, R. L. and W. Hooper, *C. S. Lewis: A Biography*, London: William Collins, 1974.

Hein, Rolland, 'Introduction', in Rolland Hein (ed.), *Creation in Christ: Unspoken Sermons, George MacDonald*, Vancouver BC: Regent College (1976/2004), 7–12. Print.

Howard, Thomas, 'The Triumphant Vindication of the Body', in David Mills (ed.), *The Pilgrim's Guide: C. S. Lewis and the Art of Witness*, Grand Rapids: Eerdmans (1998), 133–44. Print.

Lewis, C.S., *Out of the Silent Planet*. London: Pan., 1938/1974. Print.

Lewis, C.S., 'Miracles', in W. Hooper (ed.), *God in the Dock: Essays on Theology and Ethics*, Grand Rapids, Eerdmans 1942/1976, 25–37. Print.

Lewis, C.S., *Perelandra*, New York: Scribner, 1943/2003. Print.

Lewis, C.S., 'Is Theology Poetry?', in *They Asked For A Paper: Papers and Addresses*, London: Geoffrey Bles

(1944/1962), 150–165 Print.

Lewis, C.S., *That Hideous Strength: A Modern Fairy-Tale for Grown-Ups*, New York: Scribner, 1945a/2003. Print.

Lewis, C.S., 'Membership', in *The Weight of Glory and other Addresses*, Grand Rapids: Eerdmans (1945b/1977), 30–42. Print.

Lewis, C.S., 'Preface', in C.S. Lewis (ed.), *George MacDonald: An Anthology*, London: Fount (1946/1990), 21–35. Print.

Lewis, C.S., *The Abolition of Man or Reflections on Education with special reference to the teaching of English in the upper forms of schools*. New York: Macmillan, 1947/1975. Print.

Lewis, C.S., in W. Hooper (ed.), *The Collected Letters of C. S. Lewis, Volume III (Narnia, Cambridge, and Joy, 1950–1963)*, New York: HarperCollins, 1950-1963/2007. Print.

MacDonald, George, *Thomas Wingfold, Curate*, Whitehorn: Johannesen, 1876/2002. Print.

MacDonald, George, 'February 27', in *Diary of An Old Soul*, Minneapolis: Augsburg (1880/1975), 25. Print.

MacDonald, George, 'Kingship' in *Unspoken Sermons, Series Three*, Whitehorn, CA: Johannesen (1889/2004), 492–9. Print.

MacDonald, George, 'The Hope of the Universe', in *The Hope of the Gospel and The Miracles of our Lord*, Whitehorn: Johannesen (1892/2000), 190–224. Print.

MacDonald, George, 'The Imagination: Its Functions and Its Culture', in *A Dish of Orts*, Whitehorn: Johannesen (1893a/1996), 1–42. Print.

MacDonald, George, 'A Sketch of Individual Development', in *A Dish of Orts*, Whitehorn: Johannesen (1893b/1996), 43–76. Print.

MacDonald, George, 'Wordsworth's Poetry', in *A Dish of Orts*, Whitehorn: Johannesen (1893c/1996,) 245–263. Print.

Milton, John, *Paradise Lost*. Indianapolis: Odyssey, 1667/1976. Print.

Milton, John, 'Paradise Regained', in Merritt Y. Hughes (ed.), *John Milton: Complete Works and Major Prose*, Indianapolis: Odyssey (1671/1976), 483–530.

Nietzsche, Friedrich, *Beyond Good and Evil*, (trans. and ed., Marion Faber), Oxford: Oxford University Press, 1886/1998. Print.

Nuttall, A.D., 'Jack the Giant-Killer', *Seven: An Anglo-American Literary Review* (1984), 5: 84-100. Print.

Orwell, George, 'The Hideous Strength (1945): THE SCIENTISTS TAKE OVER.' *Manchester Evening News*, August 16, 1945: 2. Reprinted in *The Complete Works of George Orwell*, Ed. Peter Davison, London: Secker and Warburg, Vol. XVII (1998), No. 2720 (first half) (1945), 250-1. Print.

Williams, Charles, 'Mount Badon', in *Taliessin through Logres*, Grand Rapids: Eerdmans (1938/1974), 1974: 34–6. Print.

Wordsworth, William, 'The Prelude', in Jack Stillinger (ed.), *William Wordsworth: Selected Poems and Prefaces*, Boston: Houghton Mifflin (1850), 193–366. Print.

'A Living House':
Everyday Life and Living
and Sacramental Poetics
in George MacDonald and C.S. Lewis

Rebekah Ann Lamb

Towards the close of *Mere Christianity* (1952), C.S. Lewis appeals to a parable of George MacDonald's located in Book XII of *Phantastes: A Faerie Romance For Men and Women* (1858), a parable built on the metaphor of a 'living house'.[1] Lewis appeals to MacDonald, particularly at this moment in *Mere Christianity*, in an effort to consider how suffering and conversion are both part of the transformation of the human person into a temple for the in-dwelling of the Holy Spirit.[2] In other words, Lewis attempts to work through the fraught and difficult task of describing the nature of grace, suffering and faith through a turn to metaphorical thinking.[3] Before

---

1   George MacDonald, *Phantastes: A Faerie Romance for Men and Women* (Massachusetts: Hendrickson Publishers Marketing, LLC., 2010), p. 102.

2   The idea of the human person as a 'temple' or house for the Holy Spirit is, of course, rooted in Scripture and is especially outlined in, among other places, Paul's first letter to the Corinthians (6:19-20). Likewise, in Book One of *The Confessions*, Augustine takes a particularly Pauline approach to his description of his soul as a place in which the Holy Spirit abides. Most translations of this reference in Book One use the word 'house' as the structure Augustine appeals to in order to explore the fallen subject's desire for his or her soul to be transformed into a temple for the Holy Spirit. Crying to God for salvation, Augustine says: '[t]he house of my soul is too small for you to enter: make it more spacious for your coming. It lies in ruins: rebuild it ...' (Augustine, *The Confessions* (New York: New City Press, 1997), p. 160). Alister McGrath notes that, in his letters of 1936, Lewis 'explicitly' discussed having re-read Augustine's *Confessions* and, from then on, developing a special love for it; he would often suggest it to others who sought out his recommendations for spiritual reading (Alister McGrath, *The Intellectual World of C.S. Lewis*, (West Sussex: John Wiley & Sons, Ltd., 2014), p. 25).

3   Referencing *Surprised by Joy* (1955), Malcolm Guite notes that Lewis often recalled how it was stories, 'the cycle[s] of story and legend' that first 'touched his soul and imagination' before he was able to perceive Christ in, and despite, the kind of kitsch that so often accompanied certain forms of religious poetry and more modern Church architecture (Malcolm Guite,

considering the implications of Lewis's use of the metaphor of a 'living house,' it is helpful to first establish the context in which the metaphor originally appears, in *Phantastes*. In Book XII, MacDonald likens the human person, in his or her spiritual, psycho-somatic totality, to a 'living house'. 'The community of the centre of all creation suggests an interradiating connection and dependence of the parts [of creation],' he writes and, as such, he concludes that '[n]o shining belt or gleaming moon, no red and green glory in a self-encircling twin-star, but has a relation with the hidden things of a man's soul, and it may be, with the secret history of his body as well. They are the portions of the living house wherein he abides'.[4] Here, MacDonald understands the 'living house' as a structural representation, an architectural metaphor, for the spiritual relationship between each person and the rest of the created world. That is to say, the house metaphor functions as a nexus point for examining the 'interradiating connection[s]' between the human person, the cosmos, and the Creator on the one hand, and, on the other, the free human response to such 'connection[s].'

References to homes and houses as being architectural metaphors for growth and suffering in the pilgrimage of faith are scattered throughout MacDonald's and Lewis's writings. Specifically, the house metaphor accompanies Lewis's discussion of ethics and grace in *Mere Christianity*; he invokes MacDonald's image of a 'living house' in *Mere Christianity* so as to examine the wrestle between viewing the world as either strictly ordinary and materialist (bordering on the mundane or boring) or as sacramental, as a conduit or vehicle for the outpouring of divine grace.[5] While MacDonald's original use of the metaphor is bound up with his understanding of the sacramental quality inherent not only in creation but also in *relations* of the self, others and nature to God, Lewis's main purpose in invoking the metaphor is to hone in on the

---

Faith, Hope, and Poetry: Theology and the Poetic Imagination (Surrey: Ashgate Publishing Limited, 2010), p. 48).

4   MacDonald, *Phantastes*, pp.101-102.

5   As Lewis recounts in *Surprised by Joy*, from a young age, the 'memory of a memory' of his family's 'Old House' in Belfast, with its small garden where he and his brother played, was one of the sweetest and most haunting: 'everything else,' he says, 'that had ever happened to me was insignificant in comparison' to that experience (C.S. Lewis, *Surprised by Joy* (London: Harcourt, Inc., 1955), p. 16). Lewis reads an Edenic quality into that memory and implies that the whole nature of existence on earth is one of nostalgia for a home beyond our clear remembering but which, nevertheless, has left its irrevocable imprint in each conscience nonetheless.

problem of suffering and ethics in relation to the Christian conception of freedom, in light of redemption. However, as with MacDonald, Lewis does, of course, approach this problem of conversion, and the pain of submission it requires, through a sacramental consciousness. Meaning, as Bernadette Waterman-Ward has discussed it, a world-awareness rooted in the understanding that things are meaningful in and of themselves but, most importantly, are given greater and sacred significance when they are the means by which God, the Creator, 'interacts and inheres in the world he made,' offering grace to people in specific times and places (often through ordinary, even humble, means and events).[6] Lewis's consideration of the sacramental qualities of ordinary life relates to his contemplation of how Christ's imperative, '[b]e ye perfect,' is not 'idealistic gas'[7]; rather, he asserts, by way of the house-as-metaphor, that Christ's calling is both possible, and translatable, in the context of the rhythms of everyday life and living. In other words, Lewis's sacramental vision is more directly, and explicitly, tied to a discourse on virtue and applied ethics. However, his use of the 'living house' metaphor also parallels another parable, or extended narrative based upon the image of the soul-as-house, from MacDonald's reflection on the Book of Revelation in *Unspoken Sermons* (1867); I will discuss this parable shortly.

The house metaphor functions aesthetically and sacramentally in *Phantastes* and, in *Unspoken Sermons*, it represents an explicit exploration of God's pursuit of humanity, a pursuit motivated by love. Whereas, Lewis re-presents MacDonald's image of a 'living house' so as to offer a narrative that tries to express what role purgation has in the growth towards holiness and charity. In his discussion of social mores, and especially of virtue ethics, throughout *Mere Christianity*, Lewis makes the point that the efforts required to be charitable towards one's neighbour constitute a long and arduous process (here, as in so many instances of Lewis's writing, one gets the sense he is speaking from personal experience) and proves the adage that 'the longest way round is the shortest way home'.[8] 'Home,' here, bears many meanings—among them, growth in moral character and

---

6   Bernadette Waterman-Ward, *World as Word: Philosophical Theology in Gerard Manley Hopkins* (Washington, D.C.: Catholic University of America Press, 2002), p. 145.

7   Lewis, C.S., *Mere Christianity* (San Francisco: HarperCollins Publishers, Inc., 1980), p. 205.

8   Ibid., p. 87.

friendship but, ultimately, it signifies either the sanctification of the human soul, while on earth, or else the nature of Heaven itself; Christ, after all, refers to Heaven as his 'Father's house' (John 14:2).[9] Lewis stresses the point that acquiring the habit of *caritas* often involves the uncomfortable fact of being good to people in the midst of messy, everyday and ordinary circumstances. The laborious efforts required to live out *caritas*, the only theological virtue to last in Heaven, in everyday life and living is a constant theme occurring and reoccurring throughout Lewis's writings, in both his theological writings and his novels. A recognition of the wonder of the ordinary and of how Christ, himself, employs humble and commonplace language to explain extraordinary concepts is a foundational one shaping linguistic and poetic consciousness in Lewis's and MacDonald's writings.

In *The Chronicles of Narnia*, for instance, the whole Narnian cosmos is paradoxically both contained within, and utterly independent of, the commonplace furniture of homes and the curiosities or machines of ordinary life and living: a ring, a wardrobe, a painting, a derailed train, all become access points from our world to that of Narnia's. Of course, such a handling of houses and their features as phenomena that reveal both the *extra-ordinary* dimensions of the ordinary and its immense dignity (which, according to Lewis in *Mere Christianity* and elsewhere, *caritas* seeks to affirm) is by no means unique to Lewis. Presentations of the home as an environment for acquiring virtues, *caritas* being chief among them, and as a means for expanding the imagination, appear in the rhetorical structure of parables throughout the Bible, especially in the New Testament; in the implicit moral

---

9   I am grateful to Stephen Prickett for pointing out to me how houses, in Lewis's writing (particularly in *The Great Divorce* (1945), also serve as a framing metaphor for the question of freedom—especially as this question pertains to the last things: heaven, hell, death, and judgment. As we may recall, *The Great Divorce* opens with a bleak description of what could be contemporary, run-down council houses in the UK: '[h]owever far I went I found only dingy lodging houses,' says the narrator as he first enters what he comes to discover is the terrain of Hell (*The Great Divorce*, San Francisco: HarperCollins Publishers, Inc., 1973, p. 1). The narrator's locodescription of Hell is governed by images of a bleak, banal, and wasted cityscape which represents the narrow thinking of self-centered, self-serving souls. While it is beyond the scope of this present discussion to examine the ways in which houses can be ambivalent structures, representing either goodness or sin (depending on the allegorical bent of the narrative Lewis presents), it is important to emphasize that, in general, Lewis does perceive the house as being a positive metaphor.

imperatives governing the nonsense stories in nursery rhymes and riddles; and, in particular, in the further development of the genres of the Gothic and fairy-tale in Germany during the Romantic period and in England, from the eighteenth century in particular, and onwards.[10] However, Lewis's appeal to the home as metaphor for the soul and its freedom is both an act of continuity with literary traditions of the past and a distinctly modern search for a sense of rootedness, for a home or coherent framework, that enables a poetic epistemology which not only suggests but also supports the concept of the world as being both intelligible and beautiful—despite, and even within, the horrific, jarring, banal, and grotesque which Lewis knew all too well before, and especially following, life in the trenches. His renderings of homes and houses are almost always implicated with revealing the dignity of the ordinary; however, his exploration of the fallen and broken is geared towards detailing the unusual, hidden and painful process that is grace working on nature. This process is perhaps most skillfully accomplished in *Till We Have Faces* (1956) where we are meant to learn goodness from Orual, one of the most unappealing yet, paradoxically, sympathetic of all Lewis's characters.

Lewis's appeal to the metaphor of the 'living house' in his chapter, 'Counting the Cost,' in *Mere Christianity*, echoes MacDonald's rhetorical tactic, in *Phantastes*, of employing the image of a house as a way of mapping out the prolific force of grace in the midst of cosmic and everyday life and living relations. More specifically, however (especially given his attunement to the problem of suffering), Lewis

---

10   As we know, discussions of houses were especially popular throughout the Victorian period. Coventry Patmore's "The Angel in the House" (1854) and Dante Gabriel Rossetti's "The House of Life" (1870-1881), which creates a very different kind of house from Patmore's, represent opposite ends of a wide-ranging spectrum in which the house-as-metaphor is used to explore various Victorian socio-political, devotional, and aesthetic interests. Christina Rossetti's "From House to Home" (1862) is a striking example of another instance in which the house-as-metaphor carries specifically spiritual resonances. The poem chronicles the movement from being merely 'housed' in the fallen world's places and spaces—where the pilgrim soul is 'prun[e]d' by God 'with pain' (Christina Rossetti, 'From House to Home', (London: Penguin Books Ltd., 2005), p. 82)—to finding a home, a place of nourishment and rest, in Christ's wounds. Christ, for Rossetti (as well as for MacDonald and Lewis, among others) is the one who transforms mere structures into places of dwelling, into homes. By extension, then, without Christ, every place is hollow and wasted, like the terrain of Hell as described in *The Great Divorce*.

incorporates the concept of purgative pain into his re-presentation of MacDonald's 'living house;' this is particularly seen in the way he explores the mystery of pain in relation to God's desire to make each person into a 'tremendous thing'.[11] That is to say, Lewis strives to discern, and communicate, by way of the-house-as-metaphor (representative, as it so often is in MacDonald, for the human soul), the dynamic interplay between the human person's freedom and the assent of the soul to grace (to the work of God in personal histories). To examine the way in which he both defers to, and re-works, *Phantastes*, it is useful to quote the passage, at length, where Lewis discusses the concept of a 'living house'.

Just before invoking this metaphor, Lewis provides various ways to view the redemptive quality of suffering in our life; he describes it as being a process of growing into holiness. Seeking to bridge the gap between human logic and the mystical dimension of God's salvific action in one's life, Lewis writes that he 'must borrow another parable from George MacDonald' so as to attempt to accomplish his aim since its nature is not suited to the syllogistic patterns he has relied on in other cases, throughout the text, to support discussions of the legitimacy and reasonability of natural law, among other things:[12]

> Imagine yourself as a living house. God comes in to rebuild that house. At first, perhaps you can understand what He is doing. He is getting the drains right and stopping the leaks in the roof and so on: you knew that those jobs needed doing and so you are not surprised. But presently he starts knocking the house about in a way that hurts abominably and does not seem to make sense. What on earth is He up to? The explanation is that He is building quite a different house from the one you thought of—throwing out a new wing here, putting on an extra floor there, running up towers, making courtyards. You thought you were going to be made into a decent little cottage but He is building a palace. He intends to come and live in it Himself [...] If we let Him—for we can prevent Him, if we choose—He will make the feeblest and filthiest of us into a god or goddess, a dazzling, radiant, immortal creature, pulsating all through with such energy and joy and wisdom and love as we cannot now imagine.[13]

Here, Lewis shifts into the language of analogy, intuiting,

---

11 Lewis, *Mere Christianity*, p. 205.

12 Ibid., p. 251.

13 Ibid., pp. 205-6.

I suggest, the difficulties present in offering a strictly rational explanation for the ways grace, God's work in the human person's life, transforms wounds into a means of sanctification. Yet, despite the difficulty of explaining something as mysterious, and philosophically and theologically complex, as suffering and its possible merits, Lewis's discussion of this phenomenon, by way of the house-as-metaphor, helps us discern a homey and ordinary quality to the whole problem. In other words, as part and parcel of everyday life and living, suffering is, in various ways, an inextricable part of our lived experience and, yet, free assent to the law of divine love, which Lewis particularly outlines in *The Four Loves* (1960), enables us to see how ordinary and humble the process of conversion is. Conversion, a turning-toward Christ, for MacDonald and Lewis, is bound up with the language of building and dwelling, both of which are key habits and actions of human beings throughout history. In turn, and by extension, God's renovation of the 'living house,' is the highest form of poesis: it transforms, as Lewis notes, the 'feeblest' of human beings into a 'dazzling, radiant, immortal creature' who is then able to perceive the ordinary as it truly is: extra-ordinary, 'dazzling,' because made by a personal Creator.[14]

The Christian conception of sacramental vision, which views the humble materials and conditions of ordinary lived experiences as the ground for sanctification (once the soul has assented to the initiation of God—a point both MacDonald and Lewis emphasize, thus only alienating Calvinist brands of doctrine from their otherwise more or less ecumenical discourses) is part of what Lewis identified, and valued most, in MacDonald. 'The quality which had enchanted me in [MacDonald's] imaginative works,' Lewis confesses in his Preface for *George MacDonald: An Anthology* (1946), 'turned out to be the quality of the real universe, the divine, magical, terrifying and ecstatic reality in which we all live'.[15] Here, Lewis is speaking of the impact *Phantastes* made on him in his early adulthood, which he called the most 'strange' and yet 'homely and humble' of books, awakening in him a sense of the sacred quality of the imagination as a kind of poetic epiphany which grasps that goodness is not something fundamentally legalistic but, rather, beautiful, even attractive.[16] Interestingly, G.K. Chesterton

---

14 Ibid., p. 206

15 Lewis, 'Preface', *George MacDonald* (San Francisco: HarperCollins, 1973), p. xxxviii.

16 Ibid., pp. xxxviii-xxxix

also attributed the home-like, or 'homely,' quality in MacDonald's writing as being one of the initial introductions to faith (specifically, poetic faith and then, later in life, faith in Christ) that he found both appealing and realistic because it was firmly and unapologetically grounded in the details of ordinary life and living.

Chesterton's interest in the 'homely' quality of MacDonald's writing is especially apparent in his well-known introduction to Greville MacDonald's, *George MacDonald and His Wife* (1924). In this introduction, Chesterton stresses that MacDonald's uniting of ordinary home life to wonder became the key, for him, to realizing what fantasy writing, and especially the genre of the fairy-tale, was all about: that which is 'most realistic, in the exact sense of the phrase the most like life'.[17] In his *Autobiography* (1939), Chesterton further details how MacDonald's 'glamorous mysticism' and 'faith in the Fatherhood of God' awoke in him, during his childhood, his 'first faith'.[18] However, much earlier, Chesterton more expressly associated MacDonald's 'mysticism,' his sacramental vision of the world, to the renderings of house and home that shape much of the organizing structure and settings in *The Princess and the Goblin* (1872). Chesterton particularly identifies *The Princess and the Goblin* as being MacDonald's most realistic piece of fantasy, sharing that, when he read the story as a child, the story's epic as well as commonplace events seemed plausible within, or transferable to, the very spaces, objects, and shapes of his own family home. Chesterton suggests that MacDonald's realism lies in his ability to make one feel that Irene's adventures in her castle are, simultaneously, foreign to the general, lived experiences of children in late-Victorian England and, yet, familiar in that they satisfied childish yearnings for adventure and could easily adapt to the structure of ordinary homes (to staircases, cellars, cupboards and so on). That is to say, for Chesterton, *The Princess and the Goblin* manages to effect the defamiliarization that is so key to the success of poetry and story-telling as an art form and also accomplishes the more difficult task of stirring within the reader the sense that the story is unfolding in one's ordinary life, in one's very house.

In an attempt to express, as an adult, what he *felt* and *instinctively* knew as a child, when first encountering MacDonald, Chesterton turns to the phenomenon of home-dwelling in order to explain what

---

17   G.K. Chesterton, 'Introduction', *George MacDonald and His Wife* (New York, Johnson Reprint Corp, 1971), p. 9.

18   G.K. Chesterton, *Autobiography* (Kent: Fisher Press, 1992), p. 174.

precisely he means by *The Princess and the Goblin* as realist fiction. Given the way Chesterton speaks about, and thinks through, the narrative form and imagery of the story in such a familiar tone, it is worth reviewing what he has to say with regard to proposing, and defending, the rather curious claim that the very trappings and furniture of the story (its seemingly interminable, shifting staircases, the threat of monsters living below one's home, and the phenomenon of the invisible thread, among other things) are a mix of the strange and ordinary. For, in assessing *The Princess and the Goblin* as he does, Chesterton encourages us to shift our categorical thinking about what constitutes fantasy and reality:

> When I say it [*The Princess and the Goblin*] is like life, what I mean is this. It describes a little princess in a castle in the mountains which is perpetually undermined, so to speak, by subterranean demons who sometimes come up through cellars. She climbs up the castle stairways to the nursery or other rooms; but now and again the stairs do not lead to the usual landings, but to a new room she has never seen before, and cannot generally find again [...] When I read it as a child, I felt that the whole thing was happening inside a real human house, not essentially unlike the house I was living in, which also had staircases and rooms and cellars. This is where the fairy-tale differed from many other philosophies. I have always felt a certain insufficiency about the ideal of Progress, even of the best sort which is a Pilgrim's Progress. It hardly suggests how near the best and word things are to us from the first.[19]

The function of imaginative work, and the ethical as well as aesthetic mission (as well as burden and shape) of the fairy-tale is, for Chesterton, the revelation of the paradox that the ordinary is the very ground of growing into the habit of marveling at the world. The house, as metaphor, in fairy tales, in theological reflection, etc., enables, Chesterton argues, an encounter with the wonder of the ordinary. Moreover, in MacDonald's writings, the house functions as a *structure* or unifying principle underscoring his idea that imaginative vision, which includes a sacramental sensibility, constitutes a re-orienting, a re-building of our understanding of the world as a conduit for God's grace. This 'homely' quality that both Lewis and Chesterton identified as central to their awakening to the wonder of being-in-the-world is often built up by MacDonald's use of the concept of house and home in both their literal and theopoetic implications—this is seen

---

19   G.K. Chesterton, 'Introduction', p. 10.

in *Phantastes* in particular, as I have already mentioned, and also in *Unspoken Sermons*, as well as in other passages of MacDonald's work.

In *Phantastes*, MacDonald perceives art as possessing a reparative or redressing power that gives us a sense of home, of rootedness in the world, for it 'rescues nature from the weary and sated regards of our senses, and the degrading injustices of our anxious, every-day life, and, appealing to the imagination [...] reveals nature in some degree as she really is' which, as a result, unveils 'the true import of the wonder-teeming world'.[20] Like MacDonald's understanding of Fairyland itself (of the world born out of, and structured by, imaginative thinking), the house metaphor functions as a way of representing the building up of the human person's relationship with the cosmos and, most significantly, with God. Imaginative work not only cultivates an education in perception, then, but also generates a *habitus*, a way of dwelling in the world that connects the individual to its main constituents: community, cosmos, and Creator. Turning, for example, to *Unspoken Sermons*, we can see how MacDonald perceives his faith as hinging upon the relation between freedom, the assent of the will, and God's desire to court each human heart. Specifically, he employs the architectural metaphor of the house as a means of showing the sacramental nature of the ordinary concepts, structures, and materials of everyday life and living, of underscoring how 'eternal truths [...] in things find shape and show'.[21] Presenting a short parable, rhetorically framed by the house as representative of the human soul, MacDonald seeks to imagine what Christian *psychomachia*, the wrestle of the fallen human person with the law of Love (rooted in the dynamic nature of the Trinitarian God) is like:

> Men full of things would not once partake with God, were he by them all the day. Nor will God force any door to enter in. He may send a tempest about the house; the wind of his admonishment may burst doors and windows, yea, shake the house to its foundations; but not then, not so, will he enter. The door must be opened by the willing hand, ere the foot of Love will cross the threshold. He watches to see the door move from within. Every tempest is but an assault in the siege of love. The terror of God is but the other side of his love; it is love outside the house, that would be inside love that knows the house is no house, only a place, until it enter—no home,

20 MacDonald, *Phantastes*, pp. 114-5

21 George MacDonald, *Unspoken Sermons* (Nuvision Publications LLC., 2007), p. 122.

but a tent, until the Eternal dwell there. Things must be cast out to make room for their souls the eternal truths which in things find shape and show.[22]

Re-presenting a key passage from *Revelation* in which Christ describes his agapic love for humanity by describing himself as one who 'stand[s] at the door, and knock[s],' inviting 'any man [who] hears [his] voice [to] open the door' so that he may 'come in' and 'sup with him' (3:20), MacDonald emphasizes the centrality of an individual's free and open assent to God's presence in his life. Such an emphasis is not only a poetic (that is to say, indirect or mediated) critique of the Calvinistic rejection of human freedom which MacDonald inherited and then separated from. It also suggests that thinking through the tangles and consequences of freedom and suffering, in ordinary life, is implicitly bound up with the struggle with sin on the one hand, and the outright desperation of God, on his part, to use buffets, if necessary, to at least announce his presence for the soul's consideration.

Suffering, then, and the ordinary trials and tribulations of life, which MacDonald associates both with human freedom and God's allowance of such freedom, are conduits for grace. In other words, sufferings and pains can become kinds of sacramentals. Even the difficult or ugly 'things' of life, then, may give 'shape and show' to 'eternal truths;' a point which, as Daniel Gabelman notes, undergirds MacDonald's theopoetic, imaginative sensibility which discerns that the cosmos, and the events of ordinary existence, are 'full of grace,' and function as 'potential messenger[s] of God's love'.[23] Among other things, we can also see, from this parable, that MacDonald views the house as a dwelling place grounded in communal relationship, love, and the free assent to the movement of grace in one's individual life. MacDonald does not perceive the house as a good home until God abides in it. Within the metaphor of the house, the concepts of freedom and acceptance, faith and love, risk and pain are integrated. The two final problems, risk and pain, are justified by MacDonald to the extent that they may be included in God's attempt to loosen the hinges to the door of the soul, as it were. While appealing to the image of the house to stage the soul's resistance to Christ's in-dwelling there, MacDonald references God's willingness to use violence, to show his love (a divine willingness discussed by the metaphysical

---

22 Ibid., p. 122.

23 Daniel Gabelman, *George MacDonald: Divine Carelessness and Fairytale Levity* (Texas: Baylor University Press, 2013), p. 169.

poets, especially by John Donne in his Holy Sonnets, for example) and so as to encourage the resistant or hesitant soul to surrender to the workings of grace and divine love. Such a view of grace as violent is also employed by Lewis in his own re-working of MacDonald's 'living house' metaphor. As seen earlier in our discussion, Lewis says one's soul, one's 'house,' may be knocked about, 'abominably,' so as to be renovated and made expansive enough for God's in-dwelling.[24]

Gabelman notes that MacDonald views filial (or what we could also term a form of agapic) love, specifically between God the Father and God the Son, as being the principle determining Fairyland's shape and purpose; as such, he concludes, '[m]ore so than the quotidian world, fairyland [the realm of the imagination] is a questing realm that arouses a desire for a 'home-centre' in individuals—a harmonious relationship with the entirety of the cosmos'.[25] Gabelman's understanding of the way that imaginative thinking, for MacDonald, ultimately generates a desire for 'home-centr[ing]' helps us bring together the central theme that MacDonald, as well as Lewis, associates with the metaphor of the 'living house' in *Phantastes*. Specifically, the redemptive possibility inherent in suffering (made possible, in the Christian economy of salvation by Christ's suffering, resurrection, and love) opens up our understanding of the possibility of the work of grace in ordinary events. In both MacDonald's and Lewis's writings, the sacramental embraces the high and low, the ordinary and extraordinary. As such, the house being renovated is a fitting, commonplace representation of the spiritual and metaphysical *process* of not only apprehending the transformative consequences of grace in an individual's life but also of acknowledging, and working through, the pain involved in the fallen human being accepting, and welcoming, God's divine desire to renovate and inhabit his or her soul. In both MacDonald's and Lewis's aesthetic programs, then, rhetoric shaped by images and discussions of house-building and home-dwelling, functions as, among other things, a way of reconciling, and then uniting, the commonplace with the radically unique, the physical with the metaphysical, and the grotesque with grace.

---

24 Lewis, *Mere Christianity*, p. 205.

25 Gabelman, *George MacDonald*, p. 172.

BIBLIOGRAPHY

Augustine, *The Confessions*, Trans. Maria Boulding, O.S.B., New York: New City Press, 1997. Print.

Chesterton G.K., 'Introduction', *George MacDonald and His Wife*, Greville MacDonald, New York: Johnson Reprint Corp, 1971. Print.

Chesterton, G.K., *Autobiography*, Kent: Fisher Press, 1992. Print.

Gabelman, Daniel, *George MacDonald: Divine Carelessness and Fairytale Levity*, Waco: Baylor University Press, 2013. Print.

Guite, Malcolm, *Faith, Hope, and Poetry: Theology and the Poetic Imagination*, Surrey: Ashgate Publishing Limited, 2010. Print.

Lewis, C.S., *Mere Christianity*, San Francisco: HarperCollins Publishers, Inc., 1980. Print.

Lewis, C.S., *The Great Divorce*, San Francisco: HarperCollins Publishers, Inc., 1973. Print.

Lewis, C.S., Preface, *George MacDonald: An Anthology*, San Francisco: HarperCollins Publishers, Inc., 1973. Print.

Lewis, C.S., *Surprised by Joy*, London: Harcourt, Inc., 1955. Print.

MacDonald, George, *Phantastes: A Faerie Romance for Men and Women*, Massachusetts: Hendrickson Publishers Marketing, LLC., 2010. Print.

MacDonald, George, *Unspoken Sermons*, Nuvision Publications LLC., 2007. Print.

McGrath, Alister E., *The Intellectual World of C.S. Lewis*, West Sussex: John Wiley & Sons, Ltd., 2014. Print.

O'Connor, Flannery, *Mystery and Manners: Occasional Prose*, Eds. Sally and Robert Fitzgerald, New York: Farrar, Straus and Giroux, 1969. Print.

Rossetti, Christina, 'From House to Home', *Christina Rossetti: The Complete Poems*. Ed. R.W. Crump, London: Penguin Books Ltd., 2005. Print.

Waterman-Ward, Bernadette, *World as Word: Philosophical*

Informing the Inklings

Theology in Gerard Manley Hopkins, Washington, D.C.: Catholic University of America Press, 2002. Print.

Interpretations of Faerie:
A Reading of Susanna Clarke's
Jonathan Strange and Mr. Norrell,
as Informed by George MacDonald

István Szabadi

Who else can interpret England's history to us and in
particular her northern history, her black northern King? Our
common historians cannot.[1]

In the novel *Jonathan Strange and Mr. Norrell* by Susanna Clarke,
it is said that one needs magic to understand reality. The novel centers
around the characters of Gilbert Norrell and Jonathan Strange, two
practicing magicians living in an era in which there are otherwise
only theoretical-historian magicians. These men strive to revive the
English magic that in the past, during the time of the mythical Raven
King, was very much alive and powerful. In order to understand that
magical past, they need magic: magic that amazes and unsettles,
bringing forth that which was previously obscure, uncertain, and
mystical about the past. Magic makes one doubt reality; it makes one
doubt one's own eyes; it makes one doubt whether something really
happened the way one thought it did. As such, magic at first seems an
improper tool to find the Truth about past reality—instead, its presence
suggests that one will end up with more than one truth, explanation,
or interpretation of that reality. This is the central issue around which
this fantasy novel presented as history is situated. The exploration as
portrayed in Susanna Clarke's book has much in common with ideas
expressed in the work of George MacDonald. Such a continuum into
the new century of fantasy literature is to be expected, for Clarke is
quite open about the influence of the MacDonald-indebted Inklings
upon her own work; she states that *The Chronicles of Narnia* were her
childhood favorites, and that a re-reading of *The Lord of the Rings*
prompted her to write her own novel of 'magic and fantasy'. Thus
with this paper I will examine the similarities in how Clarke and
MacDonald treat interpretation and representation in their texts, and
how much Clarke's work is informed by MacDonald's—how much
she appears to owe him.

Crafting his first fantasy novel almost 150 years before

---

1   Susanna Clarke, *Jonathan Strange and Mr. Norrell* (London: Bloomsbury,
2007), p. 91.

Clarke's own, George MacDonald believed that understanding, or interpretation, does not work through a process of finding an already set meaning, but that instead meaning, or sense, is 'made'. This is a central issue in his essays such as 'The Fantastic Imagination' and—although more subtly—in fiction such as *Lilith*. In both this same idea is expressed: the interpretation of a story, of a symbol, of an event or a character must never be restricted to a 'singularity' but be offered as a multiplicity of possible solutions, understandings, interpretations.

Lilith offers, at certain points, almost purely theoretical insights on meaning-making, or interpretation. At one point the pedagogical character Mr. Raven shows the protagonist Mr. Vane a pigeon and calls it a prayer. Vane does not understand, and he questions Mr. Raven using 'rational' discourse: 'How can a pigeon be a prayer? [...] I understand, of course, how it should be a fit symbol or likeness for one; but a live pigeon to come out of a heart! [...] A prayer is a thought, a thing spiritual'[2]. Nevertheless, Mr. Raven assures Vane that it is indeed the case that a pigeon is a prayer, beyond simple 'literary' assimilation in a pejorative sense: 'prayer' is not a singularizing interpretation of 'pigeon,' but both are equally true.

When Mr. Raven is about to read aloud from the *Book of Lilith* (a thoroughly apocryphal book indeed), Vane remarks:

> What follows represents—not what he read, only the impression it made upon me. The poem seemed in a language I had never before heard, which yet I understood perfectly, although I could not write the words, or give their meaning save in poor approximation. These fragments, then, are the shapes which those he read have finally taken in passing again through my brain.[3]

This problem with expression also occurs in *Phantastes: A Faerie Romance For Men and Women*, the first 'fairy romance' of MacDonald; it is characteristic of MacDonald to deal with the issue of such inability. Unable to write down the 'real', his narrators are always conscious of their role as interpreters, and they seem to acknowledge that the 'presence' of the text can never be reacquired. At one point Vane comes up with a very straightforward yet situationally inappropriate question: 'what does it all mean?'[4] When 'miraculous events' happen

---

2   George MacDonald, *Lilith*, in *The Complete Works of George MacDonald* (Douglas Editions (E-book), 2010), p. 15.(chapter 5)

3   Ibid., p. 75.(chapter 29)

4   Ibid., p. 73. (chapter 28)

(such as Vane appearing somewhere quite magically), he does not ask how it happened or why, but about what it means. This evokes the concept of *allegoresis*, a term utilized by Ulrich Körtner, in which a 'random' text (or some action or 'natural' occurrence) is filled with meaning. Mr. Raven replies to Vane: 'A good question! [...] nobody knows what anything is; a man can learn only what a thing means'. There is no 'finding the thing', only interpreting it, consciously, and knowing that it is the only option. Words within the text are also intentionally polysemic; so plainly inserted in the plot they thus indicate how theoretical the voices in *Lilith* can be: ' "I cannot answer you," Mr. Raven replies to a question, in a 'subdued voice.' ' "I almost forget what they mean by DEAD in the old world. If I said a person was dead, my wife would understand one thing, and you would imagine another" '.[5]

The characters of the story pose an ongoing riddle. Who they are is a question often asked—not only by themselves, but also by the reader. An identity, a role, is always an interpretation of an 'individual' (although 'in-dividual' is already a misnomer), who can take as many as he or she wants: each character has numerous names, and not only names but wholly different identities. Mr. Vane rarely (if ever) remembers his own name when pontificating: 'I became at once aware that I could give him no notion of who I was. Indeed, who was I?' Yet this is 'explained' by Mr. Raven: 'No one can say he is himself, until first he knows that he IS, and then what HIMSELF is. In fact, nobody is himself, and himself is nobody. There is more in it than you can see now, but not more than you need to see'.[6]

Mr. Raven talks much about himself, about who he is, but it is never really enough, never a 'whole truth'. He is said to be many things. Early in the tale a local woman supposes that he might be 'the devil himself' because he initiated Vane's forefather, Sir Upward, to mystical knowledge and magical worlds (thus invoking Faust).[7] He appears as a live raven, a simple bird; in fact, a cousin of the Biblical raven of Noah's ark, that one which never came back.[8] The raven is a common mythical figure, always having divine connections

---

5   Ibid., p. 21.(chapter 7)

6   Ibid., p. 10.(chapter 3)

7   Ibid., p. 7. *Sir Upward* is a version of the name of the protagonist of *Phantastes*, MacDonald's first, much earlier, fairy romance —only there the Greek form is given for the character's name: Anodos.

8   MacDonald, *Lilith*, p. 17.

in different mythological systems: in Celtic mythology ravens are essentially linked to death and warfare, but thus they also have divine power, as war deities like Mórrígan (a fairy goddess linked with the Otherworld) and Badb (a war fury whose name means 'hoodie crow'[9]) take on the form of ravens. These are evoked by MacDonald's raven, but so too are the mythical ravens involved in rebirth and the afterlife.[10] Also evoked is Nordic mythology Odin, chief god of the pantheon, who is associated with ravens that accompany and bring news to him.

Yet *Lilith*'s Mr. Raven is additionally a human being: ' "Look at me," he said, "and tell me who I am." As he spoke, he turned his back, and instantly I knew him. He was no longer a raven, but a man above the middle height with a stoop, very thin, and wearing a long black tailcoat. Again he turned, and I saw him a raven'.[11] The 'human' Mr. Raven, again, does not have a clear identity. He was a librarian in Vane's house, but also he is a sexton of a churchyard, the keeper of the cemetery. The two are closely linked: 'It is much the same profession. Except you are a true sexton, books are but dead bodies to you, and a library nothing but a catacomb!'[12] The term *corpus* refers both to a body (i.e. *corpse*) and a collection of texts. A library is again a symbol of plural interpretations where numerous books present as many representations of reality. The cemetery of Mr. Raven is no simple burial ground either but a chamber where the dead 'sleep', and thus Mr. Raven is very much a Hades figure, which could evoke again a somewhat satanic character. He is suggested as Death, incarnate and real.[13] However, it is also possible to interpret God-like features: as a raven, he digs up worms from the soil, tosses them up in the air, and they fly away, becoming a kind of butterfly. This activity can be understood theologically to mean that he is administering at the rebirth or resurrection or transfiguration of entities being born again, being accepted into heaven.[14] Even though all of these identities are equally valid, the most prevailing, most definite, and most shocking is that Mr. Raven is revealed to be Adam, the first man ever. This

9   Crow and raven are normally mutually interchangeable (Patricia Monaghan, *The Encyclopedia of Celtic Mythology and Folklore* (New York: Facts On File, 2004), p. 391.)

10 Monaghan, *The Encyclopedia of Celtic Mythology and Folklore*, pp. 391-92.

11 MacDonald, *Lilith*, p. 10.(chapter 3)

12 Ibid., p. 18.(chapter 6)

13 Ibid., p. 81.

14 Ibid., p. 13.(chapter 4)

Adamic identity is, however, not simply as a human being, but much rather as *Adam Kadmon*, the 'original man', a spiritual being, more than human, the essence and culmination of creation.[15] This *Adam Kadmon* becomes the first earthly human being only after the Fall. It is obvious from the mythical superhuman qualities of Mr. Raven that he has become the possessor of that Kadmon-identity again. The reason is given quite 'simply': he is again in the grace of God: 'I too have repented, and am blessed.'[16]

According to the story, and also to Judaic mythology, Adam had two wives: Lilith and Eve. In *Lilith*, Eve is still the wife of Adam, but of course, she is referred to as Mrs Raven at first. Her interpretations-identities also include Persephone, queen of the underworld, wife of Hades-Adam-Raven. She has God-like attributes as well, being part of MacDonald's tradition of creating female God-figures, 'the wise woman' who is ancient yet beautiful; she appears, for example, in *Phantastes*, *The Princess and the Goblin*, 'The Golden Key'—and 'The Wise Woman'. She is described as having such eyes that contain the 'whole night-heaven',[17] and together with Mr. Raven they form a God-couple, which could lead to a pagan, non-Christian interpretation. Yet she says the following: 'You know, husband [...], we can give only to him that asks',[18] which resonates with Jesus' saying: 'Ask and it will be given to you' (Matthew 7:7).

The character Lilith, on the other hand, is described as a demon figure—though it is important here to have a proper understanding of what is meant by this term. Mr. Raven-Adam says that Lilith was the first wife God gave him: an angelic being who 'counted it slavery to be one with [him]', and thus left Adam and 'ensnared the heart of the great Shadow, that he became her slave, wrought her will, and made her queen of Hell'.[19] This Lilith, outside of the text, is part of Judaic mythology, being indeed the first wife of Adam who objected being subdued to Adam and fled. Even when being threatened with the death of her demon children, she still declined patriarchal marriage, and took revenge on human male babies.[20] Her figure as such has no

15   Nandor Várkonyi, *Az elveszett paradicsom* (Budapest: Széphalom, 1994), p. 229.

16   MacDonald, *Lilith*, p. 78.(chapter 29)

17   Ibid., p. 17. (chapter 6)

18   Ibid., p.18. chapter 6)

19   Ibid., p. 77.(chapter 29)

20   Sandra M. Gilbert and Susan Gubar, *The Madwoman in the Attic: The*

Scriptural background; there is only one Biblical occurrence of the word, in the book of Isaiah (34:14), and its translation is very diverse. The Latin Vulgate version uses *lamia*, from the proper name of Lamia, a figure from Greek mythology who is a child-eating demon. This reference is alluded to in MacDonald's story: Lilith tries to hunt down a company of children, as well as her own children. The King James Version of the Bible uses 'screech owl', the New International Version has 'night creatures' (plural), but there are also Bibles with 'Lilith' (a simple transcription), 'night bird', 'night monster', the Hungarian versions use 'witch', and there is even the word 'vampire' used for translation. This latter choice is again reflected in the novel *Lilith*: she is literally a vampire who drinks the blood of Vane, when he himself offers it.[21] At one point in the plot Lilith is in a state that leaves Vane undecided as to whether she is dead or alive. She is cold but can be warmed; she looks like a skeleton despite her beautiful long hair.[22] Vane decides to try to revive her, but even when he succeeds it is not obvious that she had not been dead previously. This is one more matter of interpretation. Lilith is also a shape shifter: she can turn into an animal, a spotted leopardess. Just like Eve or Adam, she has numerous identities—interpretations; especially as a shape shifter, transformation means taking on new identities. Mr. Raven theorizes upon the concept: an individual has many selves—beast, bird, fish, serpent, tree, crystal, 'and I don't know how many selves more—all to get into harmony'.[23]

The book even allows different interpretations of what happens to Lilith in the end. A Christian understanding would certainly be that Lilith repents, after she has been convinced to do so, and thus is redeemed—but at first she denies being in need of repentance. It is a basic truth of Christian faith that 'everyone who sins is a slave to sin' (John 8:34) and belongs to the devil in whom 'there is no truth' (John 8:44). Those who belong to him cannot see the truth (John 8:47), thus, in this sense, it is indeed a liberation Lilith goes through when she finally realizes her mistakes and her condition. At first, however, she claims otherwise: 'I will do as my Self pleases—as my Self desires'. Even though she is countered—'You will do as the

Woman Writer and the Nineteenth-Century Literary Imagination (New Haven: Yale University Press, 2000), p. 35.

21 MacDonald, *Lilith*, pp. 59; 63.(chapter 19)

22 Ibid., p. 51.(chapter 18)

23 Ibid., p. 18.(chapter 6)

Shadow, overshadowing your Self inclines you'—she insists: 'I will do what I will to do [...] No one ever made me. I defy that Power to unmake me from a free woman! You are his slave, and I defy you! You may be able to torture me—I do not know, but you shall not compel me to anything against my will!'[24] Thus the text also allows a reading that Lilith is simply forced into submission.

The almost excessive attention the novel *Lilith* pays to the multiple interpretations of figures and objects culminates in its final chapters. After a sort of victory, Vane is finally 'put to sleep' in the chamber of the Ravens, which means that he now will sleep, dream, become perfect and awake to resurrection and eternity. Although by now in the text eternal life seems the goal of the plot, it is exactly at this point that there is a twist: it is not easy to tell what happens in the final chapters, because every description given is necessarily a character's interpretation. All that can be said is that it seems that Vane is woken up from his dream to some unpredicted state of things, but here he meets *a* Mr. Raven who says that Vane is only dreaming. He then awakes again to find that something like resurrection is about to take place (but this is again only an interpretation), and he enters a city and a castle—only to return to his own house in 'reality'. In a totally baffling conclusion the narrator writes:

> Can it be that that last waking also was in the dream? that I
> am still in the chamber of death, asleep and dreaming, not yet
> ripe enough to wake? Or can it be that I did not go to sleep
> outright and heartily, and so have come awake too soon? If
> that waking was itself but a dream, surely it was a dream of a
> better waking yet to come, and I have not been the sport of a
> false vision! Such a dream must have yet lovelier truth at the
> heart of its dreaming![25]

In the penultimate sentence of the novel Vane makes a remark that settles the inevitability of the process of interpretation and the equality of interpretations: 'I wait; *asleep* or *awake*, I wait.'[26]

Throughout *Lilith*, problems with perception, with experiencing reality, characterize the journey of Vane in the parallel universe: 'A single thing would sometimes seem to be and mean many things, with an uncertain identity at the heart of them, which kept constantly

---

24 Ibid., p. 102.(chapter 39)

25 Ibid., p. 126.(chapter 47)

26 Ibid., p. 126.(chapter 47)

altering their look.'[27] Mr. Raven once says, answering Vane's enquiry of their whereabouts: 'You have not yet left your house, neither has your house left you. At the same time it cannot contain you, or you inhabit it!'—they are 'in the region of the seven dimensions'. Vane also elaborates on this: 'I was in a world, or call it a state of things, an economy of conditions, an idea of existence, so little correspondent with the ways and modes of this world—which we are apt to think the only world.'[28] This physical anomaly is embodied by the *'Book of Lilith,'* which exists simultaneously both in Vane's library and in Mr. Raven's: 'Ah, the two worlds! so strangely are they one, And yet so measurelessly wide apart!'[29] Mr. Raven also claims that both Vane's house and the 'fairyland' meadow in which he and Vane stand actually occupy the same space, only Vane does not see it. Mr. Raven tries to describe the state of things:

> 'That tree stands on the hearth of your kitchen, and grows nearly straight up its chimney'
>
> '[…] Then, if I walk to the other side of that tree, I shall walk through the kitchen fire?'
>
> 'Certainly. You would first, however, walk through the lady at the piano in the breakfast-room. That rosebush is close by her. You would give her a terrible start! […] Those great long heads of wild hyacinth are inside the piano, among the strings of it, and give that peculiar sweetness to her playing! […] Ten minutes ago you did not see [the tree], and now you do not know where it stands!'[30]

When Vane is first 'thrown back into reality' he asks himself: 'Had I come to myself out of a vision?—or lost myself by going back to one?   Which was the real—what I now saw, or what I had just ceased to see? Could both be real, interpenetrating yet unmingling?'[31] (This is also the question his forefather, the protagonist in *Phantastes* asked.) It is quite uncertain if at the end of his story he is indeed home or still partakes in a vision, a dream. The worlds here in these books are understood in different ways, and it is suggested that interpreting them as real or visionary is not crucial for their importance; they are

---

27   Ibid., p. 27.(chapter 9)

28   Ibid., p. 9. (chapter 3)

29   Ibid., p. 77.(chapter 29)

30   Ibid., p. 13.(chapter 4)

31   Ibid., p. 22.(chapter 7)

equal in their plurality.

The same attitude that characterizes MacDonald's treatment of multiple identities and interpretations, governs Clarke's novel and her dealing with the problems of history, of possible historical accounts or representations. Clarke's text—'disguised', so to speak, as a historical novel—belongs to a similar literary grouping. In 'History as Fantasy: Estranging the Past in *Jonathan Strange and Mr. Norrell*' Daniel Baker identifies Clarke's novel as a pastiche of 19th-century style, but his definition points to a somewhat different genre: 'It mimics, reproducing all that is familiar about its predecessor, while appropriating, subverting and transforming these 'familiarities' to create something different, something new; it is both representation, appropriation, transformation and commentary on past forms and their continual relationship with contemporary modes.'[32] Linda Hutcheon in *Poetics of Postmodernism* gives name to this genre, calling it historiographic metafiction.[33] *Jonathan Strange and Mr. Norrell* has characteristics in common with novels analyzed in Hutcheon's book (John Fowles's *A Maggot*; J. Michael Coetzee's *Foe;* and Ian Watson's *Chekhov's Journey*). All of these novels provide an unofficial, alternative account of a certain historical period. There are apocryphal accounts of history in *Jonathan Strange and Mr. Norrell* as well that are similar to those in Norfolk's novel. For instance, the whole of the Napoleonic wars is waged with magical aid: Norrell and Strange both do magic upon the instructions of their government, both in England in the Peninsular War with the Duke of Wellington. The representation of historical figures also contributes to the apocryphal nature of the novel as all those figures are heavily involved in the magical reality: the Duke of Wellington, the mad King George III and Lord Byron all appear in the novel with a first-hand experience of magic. Furthermore, gothic writers (such as William Beckford, Matthew Lewis and Ann Radcliffe) are presented as contributors to magic: there is debate over whether the horrors of their writing could be used in magic to create dreams 'that Mr. Norrell could then pop into Buonaparte's [sic] head'.[34] Sir Walter Scott also appears in

32 Daniel Baker, 'History as Fantasy: Estranging the Past in *Jonathan Strange and Mr. Norrell*', in *Otherness: Essays and Studies* 2.1 (2011), p. 3.

33 Linda Hutcheon, *A Poetics of Postmodernism: History, Theory, Fiction* London: Routledge (1988), p. ix.

34 Clarke, *Jonathan Strange and Mr. Norrell*, p. 311.

the novel to write about Mr. Norrell.[35] However, the novel ventures even further than this; what it offers is the invention and a thorough rewriting of what is represented as an uncanonized, forgotten aspect of public history.

According to Hutcheon's theory, the attention drawn to history is a key characteristic of historiographic metafiction. She finds that 'the presence of the past' is an important concept of postmodernism and thus is a crucial aspect of historiographic metafiction—'history is now, once again, an issue—and a rather problematic one at that.'[36] This surfaces at several points in the novel, most strikingly in its exhaustive rewriting of history. Hutcheon attributes to the genre an attitude of 'critical revisiting, an ironic dialogue with the past' instead of 'a nostalgic return' (Hutcheon 1988: 4). Such revisiting allows the author to give a voice to oppressed, to minoritarian discourses (Hutcheon 1988: 61). Thus by choosing history (and thus with it the problems of and attitudes to history) as a central theme, even as a central plot element of the novel, Clarke conjures the presence of the past: the basic difference between Norrell and Strange is shown in their attitude towards magical history and the past reality of magic, and the controversy of their principles becomes one of the major driving forces of the plot.

Jonathan Strange and Mr. Norrell, as historiographic metafiction, differs significantly from the classical, 19th-century historical novel. György Lukács in *A történelmi regény (The Historical Novel)* examines the characteristics of that genre, and here I would like to point out three characteristics that Hutcheon also discusses in *A Poetics of Postmodernism*. First, Lukács argues that the protagonist, as a historical figure, always embodies and internalizes the nation and the ideology it fights for: '[the hero's] human greatness is based on the fact that her/his personal passion, personal aims coincide with the actual great historical currents and that she/he combines the positive and negative sides of this current'.[37] This is contrasted by the postmodernist historical figure in Hutcheon's theory: 'the protagonists of historiographic metafiction are anything but proper types: they are

---

35   Ibid., p. 363.

36   Linda Hutcheon, *A Poetics of Postmodernism: History, Theory, Fiction* (London: Routledge) 1988, pp. 4, 87.

37   György Lukács, *A történelmi regény* (Budapest: Magvető) 1977, p. 44. My translation.

ex-centrics.'[38] Jonathan Strange and Mr. Norrell both struggle finding their proper place in their own time in addition to their place within the huge magical tradition. They cannot embody a tradition that they cannot—or do not want to—understand. Hutcheon also argues that while historical fiction, according to Lukács, uses historical data and evidence only to increase the verifiability of the novel by assimilating and internalizing it, postmodern fiction 'actually uses historical data' but rarely assimilates them.[39] Such methodology is clearly present in Clarke's novel though the device of including huge amount of bibliographical data and footnoting. The third characteristic of which Lukács writes is concerned with actual historical figures: 'historically significant figures [...] are compositionally supporting characters'[40] but 'in postmodern novels [...] this is hardly the case.'[41] Clarke's novel presents historical figures like the Duke of Wellington as characters that are heavily involved in the plot. Lukács suggests that the author of historical fiction 'lets them [the historical figures] act of their own accord' but in *Jonathan Strange and Mr. Norrell* they do not appear only to 'play themselves', that is, to act the way they did in 'real' history.[42] As I have discussed before, that these characters are apocryphal means that they are significant in the novel.

Hutcheon considers the presence of footnotes an important element of historiographic metafiction, and Clarke's novel uses them extensively. Hutcheon writes that the genre uses 'the paratextual conventions of historiography (especially footnotes) to both inscribe and undermine the authority and objectivity of historical sources and explanations'.[43] The footnotes in *Jonathan Strange and Mr. Norrell* create a small universe, an alternative reality with the multitude of stories told in them, showing that the novel is balancing on the borderline between fiction and history, simulating the truth-manufacturing textual machinery of footnotes in order to offer a number of supernatural anecdotes.

In identifying the genre of *Jonathan Strange and Mr. Norrell*, one realizes that through its generic characteristics Clarke's novel deliberately draws attention to the problems of representing history.

38 Hutcheon, *A Poetics of Postmodernism*, p. 114.

39 Ibid., p. 114.

40 Lukács, *A történelmi regény*, p. 45. My translation.

41 Hutcheon, *A Poetics of Postmodernism*, p. 114.

42 Lukács, *A történelmi regény*, p. 45. My translation.

43 Hutcheon, *A Poetics of Postmodernism*, p. 123.

In *Historical Representation*, F. R. Ankersmit investigates how history is presented to us and discusses how historians intend to reveal past reality.[44] He makes a distinction between two modes of talking about that reality: *description* and *representation*. For Ankersmit description means speaking about reality through a subject-predicate construction. For example, one can describe the earth by saying that 'the earth is globular', a claim the truth or falsity of which can be verified simply by deciding if the subject possesses that property or not. Description is mimesis in terms of language and it takes its own truthfulness for granted.

As opposed to this, Ankersmit's notion of representation suggests a mode in which two things are presented between which relation is metaphorical in nature. For instance, the statement 'the earth is a spaceship' is definitely not true as a description (the earth is not a spaceship) but in a diegetical sense, in the world created by the metaphor, true properties of the earth can be derived from this statement.[45] Hayden White writes that historical representations are by no means identical to scale models—physical models whose accuracy can be evaluated by measurements. It is the alien, distant, or even absent status of the past that prevents historians from achieving this. Their representations are not mimetic copies but 'metaphorical statements' that can be regarded as true or false only in their metaphorical sense.[46]

One representation, one metaphor, alone cannot generate a full rendering of reality: numerous different statements can be true, like for instance 'the earth is a spaceship', 'the earth is a garden'; these statements can coexist without rendering each other false.[47] Hayden White's theory on the process of 'emplotment' is applicable here to Clarke's novel. White argues that 'the events are *made* into a story by suppression or subordination of certain of them and the highlighting of others' and so from 'value-neutral' events it is possible to create an almost infinite number of different kinds of representations.[48] The lack of any single truth results in accumulating and investigating

---

44   F.R. Ankersmit, *Historical Representation* (Stanford: Stanford University Press) 2001, pp. 12-14.

45   Ibid., p. 13

46   White, *Tropics of Discourse* (London: The Johns Hopkins University Press) 1985, p. 81.

47   Ankersmit, *Historical Representation*, p. 14.

48   Hayden White, *Tropics of Discourse*, p. 84.

various truths: '[H]istorical insight is not a matter of a continuous "narrowing down" of previous options, not of an approximation of the truth, but, on the contrary, is an 'explosion' of possible points of view.'[49] The acceptance of parallel true metaphors is the only way to a fuller understanding: '[W]e are relatively helpless if we have only one metaphor. Only if more metaphors are available can a comparison be made and only then can their relative shortcomings and merits be discussed. This may explain why we don't have in history just one more or less authoritative account, accepted by all historians.'[50] In *Jonathan Strange and Mr. Norrell* two magicians differ significantly in their attitude to multiple interpretations: Mr. Norrell strives to obtain every single book which is concerned with magic and magical history. When Strange is trying to buy some magical books, 'the bookseller smiles and bows and says, "Ah sir, you are come too late! I *had* a great many books upon subjects magical and historical. But I sold them all to a very learned gentleman of Yorkshire." It is always Norrell.'[51] Meanwhile, Norrell himself wants to write a comprehensive study of magic (and magical education) so that everyone would know *his* account of the past as the only and definitive version. This account would omit the Raven King and the fairies who embody the kind of magic that is beyond the scope of institutionalization intended by Norrell. Norrell is sure that 'Great Britain's best interests were served by absolute silence on these subjects' (Clarke 2007: 539).

The mechanism of interpretation, of multiple interpretations, is exemplified in Clarke's novel in the scene in which *Vinculus*, the book of the Raven King in human form, is rewritten by the King. The street sorcerer is glad that the 'strange, blue marks', 'the King's letters' written on his skin, have changed, as it indicates that magic is indeed alive and, like every living entity, is subject to constant change. He feels that *a* History is different from *a* Prophecy, in the hierarchical sense mentioned before. However, he does not perceive that on a certain level these are very similar 'texts'. Trying to tell what will happen seems as problematic as telling what has happened. The method both of a Prophecy and a History is based on interpreting signs. When the street sorcerer is questioned, with a demand to tell the meaning of the new text, or even one letter from it, he says: 'It means last Tuesday [...] It means three pigs, one of 'em wearing a

---

49   Ankersmit, *Historical Representation*, p. 16.

50   Ibid., p. 14.

51   Clarke, *Jonathan Strange and Mr. Norrell*, p. 278.

straw hat! It means Sally went a-dancing in the moon's shadow and lost a little rosy purse!'[52] The confusion becomes total if one realizes that even the overall meaning or purpose of the new text is unknown and the possibilities are unlimited. 'Perhaps I am a Receipt-Book! Perhaps I am a Novel! Perhaps I am a Collection of Sermons!'[53] The text can again be a Prophecy, but also again a History. The scope of possible interpretations is rendered infinite.

Creating multiple interpretations, representations, is central to the formation of *Jonathan Strange and Mr. Norrell*. Susanna Clarke's novel reveals the problems of historiography, of the interpretation of the past, and of interpretation itself. This is in accordance with MacDonald's expressions in his essays and in *Lilith*: both authors argue through their texts that a single interpretation—a single, original meaning—is unattainable; a multiplicity of interpretations arise in their writing, yet this does not hinder understanding but rather improves one's chance to grasp more of the 'reality' of the past, or of a story. Considering the work of Clarke through the lens of MacDonald, adds another layer to one's reading of *Jonathan Strange and Mr. Norrell*. It also makes evident that MacDonald was a forerunner of and an influence upon postmodern thinking as expressed by such as Hutcheon, White, and Ankersmit. Thus I have I intended to provide another representation of MacDonald and of Clarke's novel, hoping to enrich our understanding of both.

---

52   Ibid., p. 995.

53   Ibid., p. 994.

BIBLIOGRAPHY

Ankersmit, F. R., *Historical Representation*, Stanford: Stanford University Press, 2001. Print.

Baker, Daniel, 'History as Fantasy: Estranging the Past in Jonathan Strange and Mr. Norrell', in *Otherness: Essays and Studies* 2.1, 2011. Print.

Clarke, Susanna, *Jonathan Strange and Mr. Norrell*, London: Bloomsbury, 2007. Print.

Gilbert, Sandra M. and Gubar, Susan, *The Madwoman in the Attic: The Woman Writer and the Nineteenth-Century Literary Imagination*, New Haven: Yale University Press, 2000. Print.

Hutcheon, Linda, *A Poetics of Postmodernism: History, Theory, Fiction*, London: Routledge, 1988. Print.

Lukács, György, *A történelmi regény*, Budapest: Magvető, 1977. Print.

MacDonald, George, *Lilith*. in *The Complete Works of George MacDonald*, Douglas Editions (E-book), 2010.

Monaghan, Patricia, *The Encyclopedia of Celtic Mythology and Folklore*, New York: Facts On File, 2004. Print.

Várkonyi, Nandor, *Az elveszett paradicsom*, Budapest: Széphalom, 1994. Print.

White, Hayden, *Tropics of Discourse*, London: The Johns Hopkins University Press, 1985. Print.

White, Hayden, *A történelem terhe*, trans. Berényi Gábor et al, Budapest: Osiris, 1997. Print.

CONTRIBUTORS

Stephen Prickett is Regius Professor Emeritus of English Language and Literature, at the University of Glasgow and honorary Professor of English at the University of Kent, Canterbury. He has taught at the University of Sussex, the Australian National University in Canberra (where he had the chair of English), Duke University, North Carolina, and Baylor University, Texas, where he was Margaret Root Brown Professor, and Director of the Armstrong Browning Library. He is a Fellow of the Australian Academy of the Humanities, former Chairman of the U.K. Higher Education Foundation, former President of the European Society for the Study of Literature and Theology, President of the George MacDonald Society, and holds honorary doctorates from the Universities of Artois, (France), and Bucharest (Romania). He has published two novels, nine monographs, ten edited volumes, and over a hundred articles on Romanticism, Victorian Studies and literature and theology. His fourteen-language, *Reader in European Romanticism*, (2010) won the Jean-Pierre Barricelli Prize for the best work in Romantic Studies that year. His most recent publication is *The Edinburgh Companion to the Bible and the Arts* (2014).

Malcolm Guite is a poet and priest, working as Chaplain of Girton College, Cambridge. He also teaches for the Divinity Faculty and for the Cambridge Theological Federation, and lectures widely in England and North America on Theology and Literature. He is the author of *What do Christians Believe?* (2006), *Faith Hope and Poetry* (2010; 2012), *Sounding the Seasons; Seventy Sonnets for the Christian Year* (2012) , *The Singing Bowl : Collected Poems* (2013) , and *The Word in the Wilderness* (2014) . He contributed the chapter on Lewis as a poet to the *Cambridge Companion to C.S. Lewis* (2010). Revd. Dr. Guite works as a librettist for composer Kevin Flanagan and his *Riprap* jazz quartet, and has also worked in collaboration with American composer J.A.C. Redford, and Canadian singer-songwriter Steve Bell. He was the inaugural 'Artist in Residence' at Duke Divinity School, North Carolina, in September 2014, and 'Visionary in Residence' at Biola University, Los Angeles, in March 2015.

Kirstin Jeffrey Johnson is an independent scholar based in the Ottawa Valley, Canada, and director of the Linlathen Lectures. Her doctorate at University of St. Andrews, Scotland, was on the 'Relational & Revelational Nature of MacDonald's Mythopoeic Art'.

She has tutored students in Inklings studies in Oxford, and currently lectures internationally on MacDonald, Tolkien, and Lewis. Dr. Jeffrey Johnson is on the Advisory Board of the Inklings journal *VII: An Anglo-American Literary Review*, a member of the Canadian Inklings Institute, and a regular contributor to *ArtWay* journal. A list of her publications and lectures may be found at kirstinjeffreyjohnson.com, and her book *Storykeeper: The Mythopoeic Making of George MacDonald* is forthcoming. She also wrote the introduction and afterword for the Romanian translation of *The Golden Key* (Aula Magna, 2016), and is one of the MacDonald specialists in Andrew Wall's documentary, *The Fantasy Makers: Tolkien, Lewis, & MacDonald* (2018).

Trevor Hart is Rector of Saint Andrew's Scottish Episcopal Church in St. Andrews, Scotland and Honorary Professor of Divinity in the University of St. Andrews. Before embarking on full-time pastoral ministry he was for thirty years a university teacher, latterly as Professor of Divinity in St. Andrews where, in 1990, he co-founded (with Jeremy Begbie) the Institute for Theology, Imagination and the Arts. Professor Hart has taught and supervised many research students on topics related to Inklings studies, and has lectured and published widely on the relationship between Christian theology, imagination and the arts. His most recent volume is *Making Good: Creation, Creativity and Artistry* (Baylor UP, 2014), and he has recently published an essay on the Inklings in the *Routledge Companion to Literature and Religion*. Further details of Trevor's profile and publications are available at **trevorahart.com**

Daniel Gabelman is Head of English at King's Ely in Cambridgeshire. He completed his doctorate at the University of St. Andrews in 2011 with a thesis focusing on George MacDonald's fairytales, which came out with Baylor University Press in 2013 under the title *George MacDonald: Divine Carelessness and Fairytale Levity*. He has published on other 19th & 20th century literary figures including G. K. Chesterton, C.S. Lewis, Lewis Carroll, J. M. Barrie and Lord Byron as well as on topics such as miracles, fairytale endings, and the relationship between theology and lightness. Currently he is completing a groundbreaking monograph on doodling in the long nineteenth century, investigating previously unstudied marginal sketches in the manuscripts, books and notebooks of artist-writers such as William Thackeray, Edward Lear, William Blake, Max Beerbohm and G. K. Chesterton. He is also one of the MacDonald specialists in

Andrew Wall's documentary, *The Fantasy Makers: Tolkien, Lewis, & MacDonald* (2018).

Jean Webb is Professor of International Children's Literature and Director of the International Forum for Research in Children's Literature at the University of Worcester, UK. She has been an Executive Board member of the Children's Literature Association and a Board Member of the International Research Society for Children's Literature. She has lectured internationally. Her publications are wide ranging and include: Deborah Cogan Thacker and Jean Webb, *Introducing Children's Literature: Romanticism to Postmodernism*, London, Routledge, 2002; Jean Webb [ed] *"A Noble Unrest": Contemporary Essays on the Work of George MacDonald* Cambridge Scholars Press, 2007; 'A.A. Milne's poetic world of childhood in *When We Were Very Young* and *Now We Are Six*' Louise Joy (ed) *Poetry and Childhood* Trentham, 2010; 'Picture Books and Multiple Readings: *When We Lived in Uncle's Hat* by Peter Stamm and Juta Bauer.' Evelyn Arzipe, Maureen Farrell, Julie McAdam (ed) *Picturebooks Beyond the Borders of Art, Narrative and Culture* Routledge, 2013; 'Food: Changing Approaches to Food in the Construction of Childhood in Western Culture' in Yan Wu, Kerry Mallan, Roderick McGillis, (eds.) *(Re)imagining the World: Children's Literature's Response to Changing Times.* Springer 2013 and a new area of research 'Health, Sickness and Literature for Children'. In Maria Nikolajeva and Clementine Beauvais (ed.) *The Edinburgh Companion to Children's Literature* Edinburgh University Press 2017.

Bethany Bear Hebbard earned her PhD from Baylor University in 2012. In her doctoral work, she studied the influence of Samuel Taylor Coleridge on George MacDonald, specifically on their shared vision of literary traditions serving the universal Church. She has published work along these lines in *The Edinburgh Companion to the Bible and the Arts* (2013), and she has also traced the play between imagination and Christian community through the works of John Bunyan, in publications such as *Studies in Philology*. After three years at the University of Mobile in south Alabama, she returned to Texas, where currently she directs a missional apprenticeship program at Community First! Village. She also works alongside her husband Steven, who uses organic farming to create restorative communities for the chronically homeless, refugees, and other marginalized peoples. Like her literary icons—Herbert, Bunyan, Coleridge, MacDonald, Rossetti, and others—she strives to sustain an English literary tradition that inspires a life of spiritual friendship, and that heralds the gospel's good news to the poor.

Kirstin A. Mills specializes in Gothic, Romantic and Victorian Literature, with a particular interest in the relationships between dreams, alternative states of consciousness, optics and vision, space, and the supernatural, and the ways in which these intersect at the borders of literature, psychology and science. Her doctorate at Macquarie University in Sydney, Australia explored the evolution of these ideas across the eighteenth and nineteenth centuries within a context of speculative investigation into the spaces of the supernatural and the sciences of the mind. She has published on the literary and cultural representations of these ideas in Horace Walpole, Mary Shelley and contemporary digital media adaptations, and has several forthcoming book chapters examining aspects of the Gothic in Romantic, Victorian, and twenty-first-century contexts. She is currently preparing a monograph based upon her doctoral thesis. Kirstin teaches English Literature – from Gothic and Children's to Australian and Contemporary Literature – at Macquarie University in Sydney, and is also a practicing artist, illustrator and creative writer. More information about her current research, publications and creative projects can be found at **www.kirstinmills.com**.

Sharin Schroeder is an associate professor of English at Taipei Tech, Taiwan. She has published on Margaret Oliphant, Francis Newman, Rider Haggard, and Andrew Lang; her other research focuses on the impact of nineteenth-century writers upon J.R.R. Tolkien's fantasy and critical works. Relevant book chapters include "'It's Alive!': Tolkien's Monster on the Screen" in *Picturing Tolkien: Essays on Peter Jackson's The Lord of the Rings Film Trilogy* (2011) and "She-who-must-not-be-ignored: Gender and Genre in *The Lord of the Rings* and the Victorian Boys' Book" in *Perilous and Fair: Women in the Works and Life of J.R.R. Tolkien* (2015). She is also the creator of the Andrew Lang Site at www.andrewlang.org. Her archival research here was funded by Taiwan's Ministry of Science and Technology, and by the St. Andrews Special Collections' Visiting Scholar Scheme.

Monika B. Hilder is Professor of English at Trinity Western University, Langley, British Columbia, and co-founder and co-director of Inklings Institute of Canada **www.twu.ca/iic**). She has published a three-volume study of C.S. Lewis and gender: *The Feminine Ethos* in *C.S. Lewis's* Chronicles of Narnia (2012), *The Gender Dance: Ironic Subversion in C.S. Lewis's Cosmic Trilogy* (2013), and *Surprised by the Feminine: A Rereading of C.S. Lewis and Gender* (2013), which examines how gender metaphor in Lewis's writings resists dominant cultural chauvinism with a vision of ethical humanity. She received her doctorate at Simon Fraser University, "Educating the Moral Imagination: The Fantasy Literature of George MacDonald, C.S. Lewis, and Madeleine L'Engle," for which she was awarded the Dean of Graduate Studies Convocation Medal for Academic Excellence. She has also published on George MacDonald, L.M. Montgomery, and Madeleine L'Engle, is a 2011 recipient of the Clyde S. Kilby Research Grant, Marion E. Wade Center, Wheaton College, Illinois, and participated in CBC Radio *IDEAS* documentary, "C.S. Lewis and the Inklings."

Rebekah Lamb recently obtained her doctorate in Victorian Literature, with a specialization in Pre-Raphaelite poetry and art, from the University of Western Ontario (London, Ontario, Canada). She is an Etienne Gilson Post-Doctoral Fellow at the University of St. Michael's College, in the University of Toronto, and an Adjunct Professor of Literature and Humanities Studies at Our Lady Seat of Wisdom College (Barry's Bay, Ottawa Valley, Ontario). She is occasionally a visiting tutor for the Centre for Faith and Culture's Summer School in Oxford, UK. Recently, she has published on Christina Rossetti, Dietrich von Hildebrand, and G.K. Chesterton.

István Szabadi received an MA degree from the Institute of English and American Studies of the University of Debrecen, Hungary in 2012 and completed his PhD studies at the British Studies Programme at the Doctoral School of Literature in 2015 while also studying theology at the Debrecen Reformed Theological University. His proposed dissertation discusses the figure of the sage in MacDonald's fantasies, theology, and self-image. Currently he is working as a translator of literature and theology.

EDITORS

Michael Partridge was born in what he likes to call the East Anglian part of Essex and now lives in Cheshire. In 1995 he created *The Golden Key* web site (**www.george-macdonald.com**), online home to the George MacDonald Society where he is responsible for membership and online presence. A Fellow of the Chartered Insurance Institute, he retired after 40 years in insurance and has recently completed a Graduate Diploma in Theology with the Westminster Theological Centre/ University of Chester with whom he is now continuing his MA studies.

Kirstin Jeffrey Johnson is an independent scholar based in the Ottawa Valley, Canada, and director of the Linlathen Lectures. Her doctorate at University of St. Andrews, Scotland, was on the 'Relational & Revelational Nature of MacDonald's Mythopoeic Art'. She has tutored students in Inklings studies in Oxford, and currently lectures internationally on MacDonald, Tolkien, and Lewis. Dr. Jeffrey Johnson is on the Advisory Board of the Inklings journal *VII: An Anglo-American Literary Review*, a member of the Canadian Inklings Institute, and a regular contributor to *ArtWay* journal. A list of her publications and lectures may be found at **kirstinjeffreyjohnson.com**, and her book *Storykeeper: The Mythopoeic Making of George MacDonald* is forthcoming. She also wrote the introduction and afterword for the Romanian translation of *The Golden Key* (Aula Magna, 2016), and is one of the MacDonald specialists in Andrew Wall's documentary, *The Fantasy Makers: Tolkien, Lewis, & MacDonald* (2018).

THE GEORGE MACDONALD SOCIETY

The importance of George MacDonald's work and influence is increasingly being rediscovered and the George MacDonald Society works to further this interest. Established in 1981, the Society publishes a respected annual journal, North Wind which carries articles related to MacDonald's life and work, reviews of new books, and other publications relevant to MacDonald Studies. A newsletter, Orts is also produced to provide news of events, meetings, lectures and any other information of interest to our members.

For more information visit our web site **www.george-macdonald. com**.

INDEX

consciousness 25, 37, 40, 64, 106, 115, 116, 117, 132, 134, 135, 136-7, 142, 188, 201, 202

Cosmopolitan 170

Cowie, Revd George 34

Cox, Marian Rolfe 157, 159

creativity 2, 24, 41, 50, 60, 63-6, 108

creation, create (human) [see also *sub-creation*] 14, 24, 37, 40, 49, 50, 63-6, 86, 103, 108, 118, 119, 121, 123, 130, 133, 137, 142, 144, 145, 150, 165, 172, 174, 200, 221, 223, 224

creation (Divine act) 23, 24, 40, 64, 65

Creation (*noun*) [see also *Nature*] 23, 40, 50, 51, 96, 101, 107, 200, 217

sub-creation 40, 41, 48, 50

D

Dante 8, 9, 41, 43, 46, 47, 48, 49, 51

Darwin, Charles 35, 100

Darwinism 101, 163, 187, 191

Dawson, Christopher 158

Dearborn, Kerry 17

Demoor, Marysa 155, 165

dimensions 9, 13, 60, 129, 138, 140, 141, 143, 144, 145, 202, 220

Dodgson, Charles [see *Carroll, Lewis*]

Donne, John 210

Dumitrescu, Mihaela 103

dream (dreamscape) 129-145

in *Carroll* 82, 106, 129-145; *in Clarke* 221; *in Lewis* 6, 194; *in MacDonald* 81, 87, 106, 129-145, 219, 220

E

Edgeworth, Maria 73, 74

Edwards, Bruce and Michael 114, 116

Eliot, T.S. 10, 108, 109

empiricism 19, 26, 27, 60, 186-9

Empson, William 185

enchantment 22, 23, 88, 89

Enlightenment 27, 72

Essays and Reviews 153

Evangelical 19, 72

God (Deity) [see also *Jesus*]
24, 58-65, 142, 184,
199, 201, 203

in Barfield 24-5; *in
Coleridge* 19; *in Lang*
166-7; *in Lewis* 9,
193, 194, 195, 204-
5; *in Kingsley* 100; in
MacDonald 23, 24,
25, 32, 34, 58-65, 107,
119, 121, 124, 182,
187, 188-9, 200, 201,
204-6, 207-10, 216,
217; *in Tolkien* 40, 167,
172-3; *as Creator* 23,
24, 40, 58, 65, 100,
107, 119, 166, 167, 173,
200, 201, 204, 205,
208; *existence of* 186-7,
189; *Fatherhood of* 59,
80, 86-7, 107, 166,
182, 202, 206, 210;
grace 199, 200, 201,
203, 204, 205, 207,
209, 210, 217; *I Am* 24;
image of 24, 58-60, 65,
193; *imagination of* 24,
25, 58, 59, 64, 65, 87;
kingdom of 121, 193;
Logos 26, 58; *redemption
by* 23, 204, 218;
revelation of 19, 119,
124; *Spirit* 25, 40, 48,
59, 64, 199; *Trinity* 59,
208

gods 166, 173, 216

Gospel(s) 38, 150, 151, 171,
181, 187

Gothic 131, 132, 136, 203,

221

Green, Roger Lancelyn 153,
154, 156, 163, 166

*Andrew Lang: A Critical
Biography* 153, 154, 156

"The Mystery of
Andrew Lang" 168

Gueroult, Denys 151, 167,
172-4

Guite, Malcolm 17-27, 199

H

Haggard, H. Rider 41, 151

Hart, Trevor 57-66, 167

Hein, Rolland 181

Henderson, L.D. 140

Hensley, Nathan 152, 154,
155

Herrick, Robert 115

Hilder, Monika 181-195

Hinton, Charles 138-9

higher criticism 153, 161

Homer 46, 151, 160, 164

Hunt, Peter 130

human nature 21, 22, 23, 58,
60, 72, 74, 90, 109, 121,
164, 186, 203, 208

Hume, David 27, 169

Hutcheon, Linda 221-3, 226

Hyperspace 129-45, 139

I

image, imagery 58, 62, 71,

OTHER BOOKS OF INTEREST

Phantastes by George MacDonald: Annotated Edition
John Pennington and Roderick McGillis, Editors

Phantastes was a groundbreaking book in 1858 and continues to be a seminal example of great fantasy literature. Its elusive meaning is both alluring and perplexing, inviting readers to experience a range of deep feelings and a sense of profound truth. This annotated edition, by two renowned MacDonald scholars, provides a wealth of information to better understand and enjoy this masterpiece. In addition to the text, there are 184 pages containing an authoritative introduction, life chronology, textual notes, book reviews, and comparative source materials. With 354 footnotes to explain obscure words and literary references, this enhanced edition will benefit any reader and provide a solid foundation for future scholarship.

A good critical edition of George MacDonald's *Phantastes* has long been needed, and now we have it. This fine, comprehensive edition provides an accessible and illuminating introduction to this profound work.

—Colin Manlove, author of *Scotland's Forgotten Treasure: The Visionary Novels of George MacDonald*

C. S. LEWIS

C. S. Lewis: Views From Wake Forest - Essays on C. S. Lewis
Michael Travers, editor

Contains sixteen scholarly presentations from the international C. S. Lewis convention in Wake Forest, NC. Walter Hooper shares his important essay "Editing C. S. Lewis," a chronicle of publishing decisions after Lewis' death in 1963.

"Scholars from a variety of disciplines address a wide range of issues. The happy result is a fresh and expansive view of an author who well deserves this kind of thoughtful attention."
Diana Pavlac Glyer, author of *The Company They Keep*

The Hidden Story of Narnia:
A Book-By-Book Guide to Lewis' Spiritual Themes
Will Vaus

A book of insightful commentary equally suited for teens or adults – Will Vaus points out connections between the *Narnia* books and spiritual/biblical themes, as well as between ideas in the *Narnia* books and C. S. Lewis' other books. Learn what Lewis himself said about the overarching and unifying thematic structure of the Narnia books. That is what this book explores; what C. S. Lewis called "the hidden story" of Narnia. Each chapter includes questions for individual use or small group discussion.

Why I Believe in Narnia:
33 Reviews and Essays on the Life and Work of C. S. Lewis
James Como

Chapters range from reviews of critical books , documentaries and movies to evaluations of Lewis' books to biographical analysis.
"A valuable , wide-ranging collection of essays by one of the best informed and most accute commentators on Lewis' work and ideas."
Peter Schakel, author of *Imagination & the Arts in C. S. Lewis*

C. S. Lewis: His Literary Achievement
Colin Manlove

"This is a positively brilliant book, written with splendor, elegance, profundity and evidencing an enormous amount of learning. This is probably not a book to give a first-time reader of Lewis. But for those who are more broadly read in the Lewis corpus this book is an absolute gold mine of information. The author gives us a magnificent overview of Lewis' many writings, tracing for us thoughts and ideas which recur throughout, and at the same time telling us how each book differs from the others. I think it is not extravagant to call C. S. Lewis: His Literary Achievement a tour de force."

Robert Merchant, *St. Austin Review*, Book Review Editor

In the Footsteps of C. S. Lewis: A Photographic Pilgrimage to the British Isles
Will Vaus

Over the course of thirty years, Will Vaus has journeyed to the British Isles many times to walk in the footsteps of C. S. Lewis. His private photographs of the significant places in Lewis' life have captured the imagination of audiences in the US and UK to whom he has lectured on the Oxford don and his work. This, in turn, prompted the idea of this collection of 78 full-color photographs, interwoven with details about Lewis' life and work. The combination of words and pictures make this a wonderful addition to the library of all Lewis scholars and readers.

Speaking of Jack: A C. S. Lewis Discussion Guide
Will Vaus

C. S. Lewis Societies have been forming around the world since the first one started in New York City in 1969. Will Vaus has started and led three groups himself. *Speaking of Jack* is the result of Vaus' experience in leading those Lewis Societies. Included here are introductions to most of Lewis' books as well as questions designed to stimulate discussion about Lewis' life and work. These materials have been "road-tested" with real groups made up of young and old, some very familiar with Lewis and some newcomers. *Speaking of Jack* may be used in an existing book discussion group, to start a C. S. Lewis Society, or as a guide to your own exploration of Lewis' books.

Light: C. S. Lewis's First and Final Short Story
Charlie W. Starr
Foreword by Walter Hooper

Charlie Starr explores the questions surrounding the "Light" manuscript, a later version of story titled "A Man Born Blind." The insights into this story provide a na ew key to understanding some of Lewis's most profound ideas.

"As literary journalism, both investigative and critical, it is top shelf"
    James Como, author of *Remembering C. S. Lewis*

"Starr shines a new and illuminating light on one of Lewis's most intriguing stories"
    Michael Ward, author of *Planet Narnia*

C. S. Lewis & Philosophy as a Way of Life: His Philosophical Thoughts
Adam Barkman

C. S. Lewis is rarely thought of as a "philosopher" per se despite having both studied and taught philosophy for several years at Oxford. Lewis's long journey to Christianity was essentially philosophical – passing through seven different stages. This 624 page book is an invaluable reference for C. S. Lewis scholars and fans alike

C. S. Lewis' Top Ten: Influential Books and Authors, Volume One
Will Vaus

Based on his books, marginal notes, and personal letters, Will Vaus explores Lewis' reading of the ten books he said shaped his vocational attitude and philosophy of life. Volume One covers the first three authors/books: George MacDonald: *Phantastes*, G.K. Chesterton: *The Everlasting Man*, and Virgil: *The Aneid*. Vaus offers a brief biography of each author with a helpful summary of their books.

"Thorough, comprehensive, and illuminating"
    Rolland Hein, Author of *George MacDonald: Victorian Mythmaker*

C. S. Lewis' Top Ten: Influential Books and Authors, Volume Two
Will Vaus

Volume Two covers the following authors/books: George Herbert: *The Temple*, William Wordsworth: *The Prelude*, Rudopf Otto, *The Idea of the Holy*.

C. S. Lewis' Top Ten: Influential Books and Authors, Volume Three
Will Vaus

Volume Three covers the following authors/books: Boethius: *The Consolation of Philosophy*, James Boswell, *The Life of Samuel Johnson*, Charles Williams: *Descent into Hell*, A.J. Balfour: *Thiesm and Humanism.*

C. S. Lewis Goes to Heaven:
A Reader's Guide to The Great Divorce
David G. Clark

This is the first book devoted solely to this often neglected book and the first to reveal several important secrets Lewis concealed within the story. Lewis felt his imaginary trip to Hell and Heaven was far better than his book *The Screwtape Letters*, which has become a classic. Readers will discover the many literary and biblical influences Lewis utilized in writing his brilliant novel.

C. S. Lewis Goes to Hell
A Companion and Study Guide to The Screwtape Letters
William O'Flaherty

The creator and host of "All About Jack" (a podcast feature of EssentialCSLewis. com) has written a guide to *The Screwtape Letters* suitable for groups or individuals. Features include a topic index of major and minor themes, summaries of each letter, questions for reflection, and over a half-dozen appendices of useful information.

Joy and Poetic Imagination: Understanding C. S. Lewis's "Great War" with Owen Barfield and its Significance for Lewis's Conversion and Writings
Stephen Thorson

Author Stephen Thorson began writing this book over 30 years ago and published parts of it in articles during Barfield's lifetime. Barfield wrote to Thorson in 1983 saying, ""*...you have surveyed the divergence between Lewis and myself very fairly, and truly 'in depth...'*". This book explains the "Great War" between these two friends.

Exploring the Eternal Goodness: Selected Writings of David L. Neuhouser
Joe Ricke and Lisa Ritchie, Editors

In 1997, due to David's perseverance, the Brown Collection of books by and about C. S. Lewis and related authors came to Taylor University and the Lewis and Friends Colloquium began. This book of selected writings reflects his scholarship in math and literature, as well as his musings on beauty and the imagination. The twenty-one tributes are an indication of the many lives he has influenced. This book is meant to acknowledge David L. Neuhouser for his contributions to scholarship and to honor his life of friendship, encouragement, and genuine goodness.

Inklings Forever, Volume X: Proceedings from the 10th Francis White Ewbank Colloquiunm on C. S. Lewis & Friends
Joe Ricke and Rick Hill, Editors

In June 2016, the 10th biennial Frances Ewbank Colloquium on C. S. Lewis and Friends convened at Taylor University with the special theme of "friendship." Many of the essays and creative pieces collected in this book explore the important relationships of Inklings-related authors, as well as the relationships between those authors and other, sometimes rather surprising, "friends." The year 2016 marked the 90th anniversary of the first meeting of C.S. Lewis and J.R.R. Tolkien – a creative friendship of epic proportions

What a feast! It is rare that a book of proceedings captures the energy and spirit of the conference itself: this one does. I recommend it.

> Diana Pavlac Glyer, Professor of English at Azusa Pacific University and author of *The Company They Keep* and *Bandersnatch: C. S. Lewis, J. R. R. Tolkien, and the Creative Collaboration of the Inklings*

Mythopoeic Narnia: Memory, Metaphor, and Metamorphoses in C. S. Lewis's The Chronicles of Narnia
Salwa Khoddam

Dr. Khoddam offers a fresh approach to the *Narnia* books based on an inquiry into Lewis' readings and use of classical and Christian symbols. She explores the literary and intellectual contexts of these stories, the traditional myths and motifs, and places them in the company of the greatest Christian mythopoeic works of Western Literature.

CHRISTIAN LIVING

Keys to Growth: Meditations on the Acts of the Apostles
Will Vaus

Every living thing or person requires certain ingredients in order to grow, and if a thing or person is not growing, it is dying. *The Acts of the Apostles* is a book that is all about growth. Will Vaus has been meditating and preaching on *Acts* for the past 30 years. In this volume, he offers the reader forty-one keys from the entire book of Acts to unlock spiritual growth in everyday life.

Open Before Christmas: Devotional Thoughts For The Holiday Season
Will Vaus

Author Will Vaus seeks to deepen the reader's knowledge of Advent and Christmas leading up to Epiphany. Readers are provided with devotional thoughts for each day that help them to experience this part of the Church Year perhaps in a more spiritually enriching way than ever before.

"Seasoned with inspiring, touching, and sometimes humorous illustrations .... I found his writing immediately engaging and, the more I read, the more I liked it. God has touched my heart by reading Open Before Christmas, and I believe he will touch your heart too."
The Rev. David Beckmann, The C.S. Lewis Society of Chattanooga

God's Love Letter: Reflections on I John
Will Vaus

Various words for "love" appear thirty-five times in the five brief chapters of I John. This book invites you on a journey of reading and reflection: reading this book in the New Testament and reflecting on God's love for us, our love for God, and our love for one another.

Jogging with G.K. Chsterton: 65 Earthshaking Expeditions
Robert Moore-Jumonville

Jogging with G.K. Chesterton is a showcase for the merry mind of Chesterton. But Chesterton's lighthearted wit always runs side-by-side with his weighty wisdom. These 65 "earthshaking expeditions" will keep you smiling and thinking from start to finish. You'll be entertained, challenged, and spiritually uplifted as you take time to breath in the fresh morning air and contemplate the wonders of the world.

"This is a delightfully improbable book in which Chesterton puts us through our spiritual and intellectual exercises."
Joseph Pearce, author of *Wisdom and Innocence: A Life of G.K. Chesterton*

GEORGE MACDONALD

Diary of an Old Soul & The White Page Poems
George MacDonald and Betty Aberlin

The first edition of George MacDonald's book of daily poems included a blank page opposite each page of poems. Readers were invited to write their own reflections on the "white page." MacDonald wrote: "Let your white page be ground, my print be seed, growing to golden ears, that faith and hope may feed." Betty Aberlin responded to MacDonald's invitation with daily poems of her own.

Betty Aberlin's close readings of George MacDonald's verses and her thoughtful responses to them speak clearly of her poetic gifts and spiritual intelligence.
      Luci Shaw, poet

George MacDonald: Literary Heritage and Heirs
Roderick McGillis, editor

This latest collection of 14 essays sets a new standard that will influence MacDonald studies for many more years. George MacDonald experts are increasingly evaluating his entire corpus within the nineteenth century context.

This comprehensive collection represents the best of contemporary scholarship on George MacDonald.
      Rolland Hein, author of *George MacDonald: Victorian Mythmaker*

In the Near Loss of Everything: George MacDonald's Son in America
Dale Wayne Slusser

In the summer of 1887, George MacDonald's son Ronald, newly engaged to artist Louise Blandy, sailed from England to America to teach school. The next summer he returned to England to marry Louise and bring her back to America. On August 27, 1890, Louise died leaving him with an infant daughter. Ronald once described losing a beloved spouse as "the near loss of everything". Dale Wayne Slusser unfolds this poignant story with unpublished letters and photos that give readers a glimpse into the close-knit MacDonald family. Also included is Ronald's essay about his father, *George MacDonald: A Personal Note*, plus a selection from Ronald's 1922 fable, *The Laughing Elf*, about the necessity of both sorrow and joy in life.

A Novel Pulpit: Sermons From George MacDonald's Fiction
David L. Neuhouser
Each of the sermons has an introduction giving some explanation of the setting of the sermon or of the plot, if that is necessary for understanding the sermon. *"MacDonald's novels are both stimulating and thought-provoking. This collection of sermons from ten novels serve to bring out the 'freshness and brilliance' of MacDonald's message." from the author's introduction*

Behind the Back of the North Wind: Essays on George MacDonald's Classic Book
Edited and with Introduction by John Pennington and Roderick McGillis

The unique blend of fairy tale atmosphere and social realism in this novel laid the groundwork for modern fantasy literature. Sixteen essays by various authors are accompanied by an instructive introduction, extensive index, and beautiful illustrations.

Through the Year with George MacDonald: 366 Daily Readings
Rolland Hein, editor

These page-length excerpts from sermons, novels and letters are given an appropriate theme/heading and a complementary Scripture passage for daily reading. An inspiring introduction to the artistic soul and Christian vision of George MacDonald.

Shadows and Chivalry:
C. S. Lewis and George MacDonald on Suffering, Evil, and Death
Jeff McInnis

Shadows and Chivalry studies the influence of George MacDonald, a nineteenth-century Scottish novelist and fantasy writer, upon one of the most influential writers of modern times, C. S. Lewis—the creator of Narnia, literary critic, and best-selling apologist. This study attempts to trace the overall affect of MacDonald's work on Lewis's thought and imagination. Without ever ceasing to be a story of one man's influence upon another, the study also serves as an exploration of each writer's thought on, and literary visions of, good and evil.

Crossing a Great Frontier: Essays on George MacDonald's Phantastest
John Pennington, Editor

"This is the first collection of scholarly essays on George MacDonald's seminal romance Phantastes. Appropriately to the age of its hero Anodos, here we have twenty-one of the best essays written on Phantastes from 1972 onwards, in which straightforward literary analysis works together with contextual, psychological, metaphysical, alchemical and scientific approaches to the elucidation of this moving and elusive work."
  Colin Manlove, author of *Scotland's Forgotten Treasure: The Visionary Novels of*
  George MacDonald

The Downstretched Hand:
Individual Development in MacDonald's Major Fantasies for Children
Lesley Willis Smith

Smith demonstrates that MacDonald is fully aware of the need to integrate the unconscious into the conscious in order to achieve mature individuation. However, for MacDonald, true maturity and fulfillment can only be gained through a relationship with God. By exploring MacDonald's major biblical themes into his own myth, Smith reveals his literary genius and profound understanding of the human psyche. Smith interacts with other leading scholarship and in the context of other works by MacDonald, especially those written during the same time period.

POP CULTURE

To Love Another Person: A Spiritual Journey Through Les Miserables
John Morrison

The powerful story of Jean Valjean's redemption is beloved by readers and theater goers everywhere. In this companion and guide to Victor Hugo's masterpiece, author John Morrison unfolds the spiritual depth and breadth of this classic novel and broadway musical.

Through Common Things: Philosophical Reflections on Popular Culture
Adam Barkman

"Barkman presents us with an amazingly wide-ranging collection of philosophical reflections grounded in the everyday things of popular culture – past and present, eastern and western, factual and fictional. Throughout his encounters with often surprising subject-matter (the value of darkness?), he writes clearly and concisely, moving seamlessly between Aristotle and anime, Lord Buddha and Lord Voldemort.... This is an informative and entertaining book to read!"
      Doug Bloomberg, Professor of Philosophy, Institute for Christian Studies

The Many Faces of Katniss Everdeen: Exploring the Heroine of The Hunger Games
Valerie Estelle Frankel

Katniss is the heroine who's changed the world. Like Harry Potter, she explodes across genres: She is a dystopian heroine, a warrior woman, a reality TV star, a rebellious adolescent. She's surrounded by the figures of Roman history, from Caesar and Cato to Cinna and Coriolanus Snow. She's also traveling the classic heroine's journey. As a child soldier, she faces trauma; as a growing teen, she battles through love triangles and the struggle to be good in a harsh world. This book explores all this and more, while taking a look at the series' symbolism, from food to storytelling, to show how Katniss becomes the greatest power of Panem, the girl on fire.

Myths and Motifs of The Mortal Instruments
Valerie Estelle Frankel

With vampires, fairies, angels, romance, steampunk, and modern New York all in one series of books, Cassandra Clare is exploding onto the scene. This book explores the deeper world of the Shadowhunters. There's something for everyone, as this book reveals unseen lore within the bestselling series.

Virtuous Worlds: The Video Gamer's Guide to Spiritual Truth
John Stanifer

Popular titles like *Halo 3* and *The Legend of Zelda: Twilight Princess* fly off shelves at a mind-blowing rate. John Stanifer, an avid gamer, shows readers specific parallels between Christian faith and the content of their favorite games. Written with wry humor (including a heckler who frequently pokes fun at the author) this book will appeal to gamers and non-gamers alike. Those unfamiliar with video games may be pleasantly surprised to find that many elements in those "virtual worlds" also qualify them as "virtuous worlds."

BIOGRAPHY

Sheldon Vanauken: The Man Who Received "A Severe Mercy"
Will Vaus

In this biography we discover: Vanauken the struggling student, the bon-vivant lover, the sailor who witnessed the bombing of Pearl Harbor, the seeker who returned to faith through C. S. Lewis, the beloved professor of English literature and history, the feminist and anti-war activist who participated in the March on the Pentagon, the bestselling author, and Vanauken the convert to Catholicism. What emerges is the portrait of a man relentlessly in search of beauty, love, and truth, a man who believed that, in the end, he found all three.

"This is a charming biography about a doubly charming man who wrote a triply charming book. It is a great way to meet the man behind A Severe Mercy."

Peter Kreeft, author of *Jacob's Ladder: 10 Steps to Truth*

Remembering Roy Campbell: The Memoirs of his Daughters, Anna and Tess
Introduction by Judith Lütge Coullie, Editor
Preface by Joseph Pearce

Anna and Teresa Campbell were the daughters of the handsome young South African poet and writer, Roy Campbell (1901-1957), and his beautiful English wife, Mary Garman. In their frank and moving memoirs, Anna and Tess recall the extraordinary, and often very difficult, lives they shared with their exceptional parents. Over 50 photos, 344 footnotes, timeline of Campbell's life, and complete index.

HARRY POTTER

The Order of Harry Potter: The Literary Skill of the Hogwarts Epic
Colin Manlove

Colin Manlove, a popular conference speaker and author of over a dozen books, has earned an international reputation as an expert on fantasy and children's literature. His book, *From Alice to Harry Potter*, is a survey of 400 English fantasy books. In *The Order of Harry Potter*, he compares and contrasts *Harry Potter* with works by "Inklings" writers J.R.R. Tolkien, C. S. Lewis and Charles Williams; he also examines Rowling's treatment of the topic of imagination; her skill in organization and the use of language; and the book's underlying motifs and themes.

Harry Potter & Imagination: The Way Between Two Worlds
Travis Prinzi

Imaginative literature places a reader between two worlds: the story world and the world of daily life, and challenges the reader to imagine and to act for a better world. Starting with discussion of Harry Potter's more important themes, *Harry Potter & Imagination* takes readers on a journey through the transformative power of those themes for both the individual and for culture by placing Rowling's series in its literary, historical, and cultural contexts.

Hog's Head Conversations: Essays on Harry Potter
Travis Prinzi, Editor

Ten fascinating essays on Harry Potter by popular Potter writers and speakers including John Granger, James W. Thomas, Colin Manlove, and Travis Prinzi.

Repotting Harry Potter: A Professor's Guide for the Serious Re-Reader
Rowling Revisited: Return Trips to Harry, Fantastic Beasts, Quidditch, &
Beedle the Bard
Dr. James W. Thomas

In *Repotting Harry Potter* and his sequel book *Rowling Revisited*, Dr. James W. Thomas points out the humor, puns, foreshadowing and literary parallels in the Potter books. In *Rowling Revisted*, readers will especially find useful three extensive appendixes – "Fantastic Beasts and the Pages Where You'll Find Them," "Quidditch Through the Pages," and "The Books in the Potter Books." Dr. Thomas makes re-reading the Potter books even more rewarding and enjoyable.

Sociology and Harry Potter: 22 Enchanting Essays on the Wizarding World
Jenn Simms, Editor

Modeled on an Introduction to Sociology textbook, this book is not simply about the series, but also uses the series to facilitate the reader's understanding of the discipline of sociology and a develops a sociological approach to viewing social reality. It is a case of high quality academic scholarship written in a form and on a topic accessible to non-academics. As such, it is written to appeal to Harry Potter fans and the general reading public. Contributors include professional sociologists from eight countries.

Harry Potter, Still Recruiting: An Inner Look at Harry Potter Fandom
Valerie Frankel

The Harry Potter phenomenon has created a new world: one of Quidditch in the park, lightning earrings, endless parodies, a new genre of music, and fan conferences of epic proportions. This book attempts to document everything - exploring costuming, crafting, gaming, and more, with essays and interviews straight from the multitude of creators. From children to adults, fans are delighting the world with an explosion of captivating activities and experiences, all based on Rowling's delightful series.

POETS AND POETRY

In the Eye of the Beholder: How to See the World Like a Romantic Poet
Louis Markos

Born out of the French Revolution and its radical faith that a nation could be shaped and altered by the dreams and visions of its people, British Romantic Poetry was founded on a belief that the objects and realities of our world, whether natural or human, are not fixed in stone but can be molded and transformed by the visionary eye of the poet. A separate bibliographical essay is provided for readers listing accessible biographies of each poet and critical studies of their work.

The Cat on the Catamaran: A Christmas Tale
John Martin

Here is a modern-day parable of a modern-day cat with modern-day attitudes. Riverboat Dan is a "cool" cat on a perpetual vacation from responsibility. He's *The Cat on the Catamaran* – sailing down the river of life. Dan keeps his guilty conscience from interfering with his fun until he runs into trouble. But will he have the courage to believe that it's never too late to change course? (For ages 10 to adult)